IMAGES of America

LUNENBURG

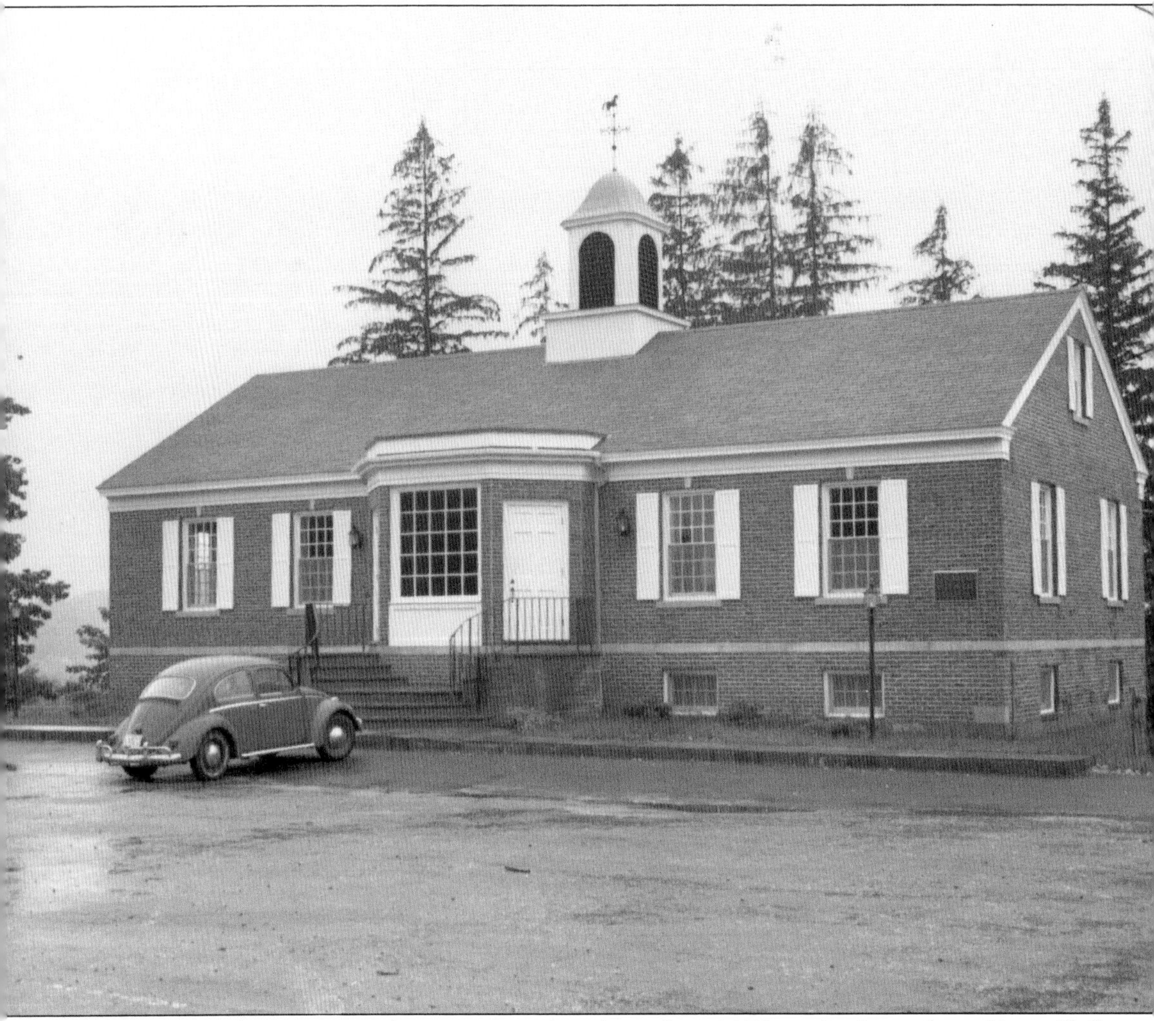

The Lunenburg Historical Society was first formed in 1897 in the Lunenburg Town Hall by a meeting of residents. The purpose of the society was to preserve and collect historical information and artifacts. It was hoped by doing so, the town would learn about our history. Dues were 50¢ and society meetings were limited to the residents in town and their descendants. In 1910, the Ritter Memorial Library offered the society a room in which to store their materials and artifacts.

The society was inactive between 1910 and 1937. It was then reorganized. John Duncan Brown willed the majority of his estate to the society for a building of its own. The site of the Old Center School was given by the town to build the society building. It was dedicated in 1966 and remains standing at 10 School Street.

IMAGES
of America

LUNENBURG

Lunenburg Historical Society
Inge H. Hunter and G. Barry Whitcomb

ARCADIA
PUBLISHING

ISBN 978-0-7385-0953-2

Published by Arcadia Publishing
Charleston, South Carolina

Printed in the United States of America

Library of Congress Catalog Card Number: 2001092560

For all general information contact Arcadia Publishing at:
Telephone 843-853-2070
Fax 843-853-0044
E-Mail sales@arcadiapublishing.com
For customer service and orders:
Toll-Free 1-888-313-2665

Visit us on the Internet at www.arcadiapublishing.com

Contents

ACKNOWLEDGMENTS

A project this size is more than one person could manage to complete alone. No one person has the expertise to function on so many different levels. The help of many people, combining their knowledge in different areas, put together this book with the sole purpose of preserving some of our history, making Lunenburg what it is today.

My coauthor, curator, and friend, G. Barry Whitcomb, has been a student of history over the years, following in the footsteps of his father, who was once president of the Lunenburg Historical Society. Barry's background in Lunenburg covers nine generations. Without Barry's help, this book would not have been possible.

William R. Bingham has been an enormous help, providing information from his many years of researching deeds. He provided information that we were unable to find in the town's early records.

Nancy L. Bigelow's knowledge of the town combines eight generations of family in Lunenburg and was a valuable asset. Her skill at finding information throughout the society building is unique.

Credit for a vital portion of our book goes to the three ladies who assisted with captions for our photographs: Mary E. Bingham, Elizabeth H. Burnap, and Helen K. Brockelman.

Pictures were loaned to us by Elizabeth H. Burnap, Nancy L. Bigelow, Mary E. Bingham, Dianne DelliCarpini, Barbara and Leo Lahti, Dennis Rinki, Martha S. Bradshaw, and Peter Lincoln (who climbed on a chair for the snapshots of the Civil War memorial tablets).

To the best of our present knowledge, information in the book is as accurate as possible. Research is an ongoing process.

INTRODUCTION

The Great and General Court of His Majesty's Providence of Massachusetts Bay at Boston on Monday, December 7, 1719, voted that two new townships be granted: North Town, now Townsend, and South Town, known as Turkey Hills.

The soil was excellent for vegetable crops and pastureland. Our three ponds were originally known as Unkechewhalom, Massapoag, and Catacoonamug. Mulpus Brook had the greatest flow of water and 8 to 10 mills located along its banks.

Historians know this area to be sparsely populated by Native Americans. Prior to the Pilgrims landing, nine tenths of the Native Americans died of a great pestilence. No documented accounts show any permanent residences in this area.

During the 1720 survey of the grant, the family of Samuel Page was found occupying a log cabin on Clark's Hill, where they had previously settled. By May 1721, all the land had been granted. There is no sure record of the sequence of the first houses. We know a letter sent to the Massachusetts General Court in March 1726 stated that 26 houses had been raised and 10 were inhabited. The best source we have suggests the Houghton House, so called, is one of the original houses built c. 1726 by Samuel Bennett. It is a saltbox style with a chimney base of 10 feet across and may have had five fireplaces. The names of other early house builders may have been Edward Hartwell, Philip Goodredge, Jonas Gillson, Joseph Page, Walter Beeth, Nathaniel Harris, Phineas Richardson, and Hilkiah and Benoni Boynton.

Lunenburg was officially granted a township on August 1, 1728. The name Lunenburg was a title that King George of England derived from a German dominion he owned. The first town meeting was called on August 19, 1728. The elected town residents assumed management of the town's affairs.

Highways in the early settlements in the wilderness were rough bridle paths through the woods. Travel was only by horseback until trees were cut, allowing an oxcart through. Trees on the edge were "barked" (cut into by an ax) to prevent people from getting lost.

In 1756, settlers in the western part of town decided they were sufficient in knowledge to run their affairs. They felt a ride of 5 to 10 miles to attend church or do business was an unnecessary burden. They filed petitions to be set off as a separate township. It was granted on February 3, 1764, and called Fitchburg. There were 44 families and about 250 people at this date.

In the years 1763, 1764, and 1765, the English Parliament claimed the "right to bind the colonies in all cases whatever." This was the point on which dispute turned.

With greater oppression and taxation by the acts of Parliament, the fateful day of April 19, 1775, came. At 9 a.m., the alarm was fired in Lunenburg to alert the two companies of minutemen. They had been organized in October 1774. Twenty-seven men under a command of Capt. John Fuller appeared in arms at the parade field on the lower common. Before leaving, Fuller planted a buttonwood tree, which became known as the Liberty Tree. They then took up the march to Concord and arrived in the evening. All action was over, and there was no need for their services. All returned home. State records show that 194 Lunenburg men saw service during the Revolution.

When the Civil War was declared, 102 Lunenburg residents enlisted. Two memorial tablets in memory of those who died in service were procured and may be seen on the wall of the upper room of the Lunenburg Town Hall.

The first church was built in 1728 at the location of the present Congregational church. The second church was built on the lower common in 1752 and torn down in 1830. The third church, built in 1830 on the upper common, was used as such until 1867, when the town bought the building, moved it 200 feet north, and remodeled it as the Lunenburg Town Hall we have today.

The first schoolhouse was built on the lower common in 1740. Schooling was also carried on at private homes. In 1738, the town voted to build five schoolhouses at $100 each. At later dates, they added four more schoolhouses. The last district school, known as the West School, closed in 1956. In 1892, the new No. 1 schoolhouse was built. It became a 12-year school in 1894.

Industrial activities were many and varied. First under way was a sawmill as early as 1726. Mills were built on all brooks in town. The last closed in 1926.

Printing and binding of books was active from 1820 until 1843. In 1837, 16,000 books were shipped. Blacksmith shops were many and busy from 1754 to 1932. Baskets of oak bands were made in a shop at the corner of Leominster Road and West Street. Straw hat making was a very big cottage industry. Ninety thousand hats were made in Lunenburg. By 1850, agriculture and farming predominated. Poultry, vegetables, and fruit farms were plentiful.

At the end of World War II, Lunenburg became a bedroom town for industries in the surrounding towns.

—G. Barry Whitcomb
Curator

One

Our Town

Early-18th-century houses in Lunenburg were generally copies of English-type houses, modified by the local ingenuity to meet the conditions of this new country. Three styles used during the period of time of our earliest development (1719–1760) were Colonial, saltbox, and Cape Cod.

"Our Town" introduces the reader to Lunenburg. In this chapter, we have included pictures of churches, schools, and municipal buildings. Also featured are "K" houses—a house or portion of an original house identified on the 1833 Cyrus Kilburn map of Lunenberg. These are the earlier houses still standing today, exhibiting some architectural integrity of the original house. Sometimes only one room remains. The remainder has been changed or remodeled over time. Other houses were built during later years.

Churches of different faiths are included, as the photographs will illustrate. Some have lasted long enough to have a photograph in our collection, while others survive only in a painting.

Buildings, in many cases, were once used for a specific purpose and, when no longer needed, were picked up and moved elsewhere. Schools were a prime example of moved buildings. As districts grew and demanded more space, the old buildings were sold, moved, and served in different capacities.

In our forefathers' days, it was quite common to move buildings from one place to another without giving it much thought. During that time, town folk did not have to cope with electricity, water, sewers, and the like. Life was simpler!

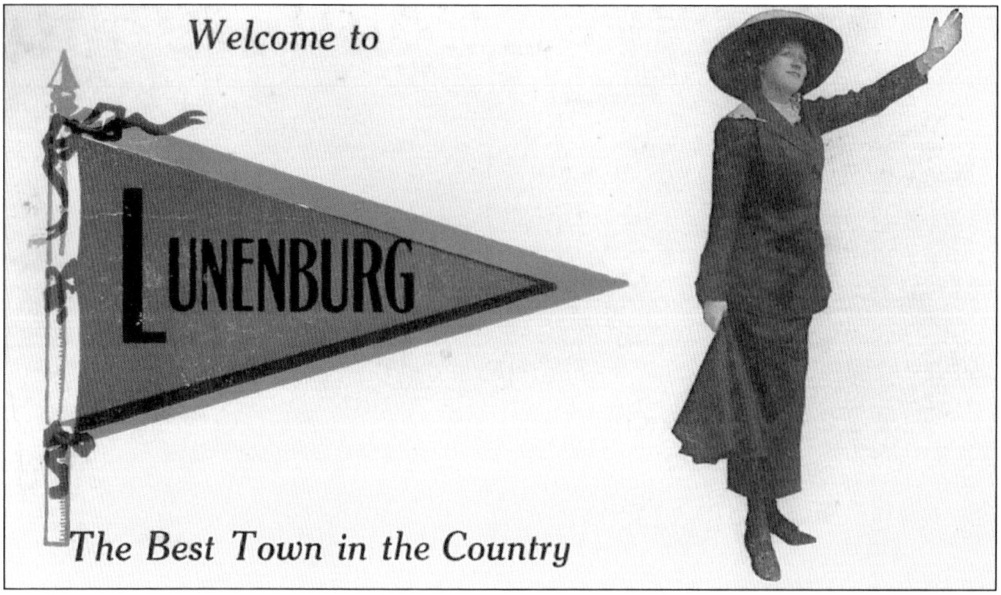

This welcoming postcard from the very early 1900s features one of our residents. It is especially effective in its simplicity, as it proclaims Lunenburg's place in history. Copies of this card have often been used by the Lunenburg Historical Society's curator, G. Barry Whitcomb, to introduce slide shows about the town's history. One hundred years later, many still insist that Lunenburg is "the best town in the country."

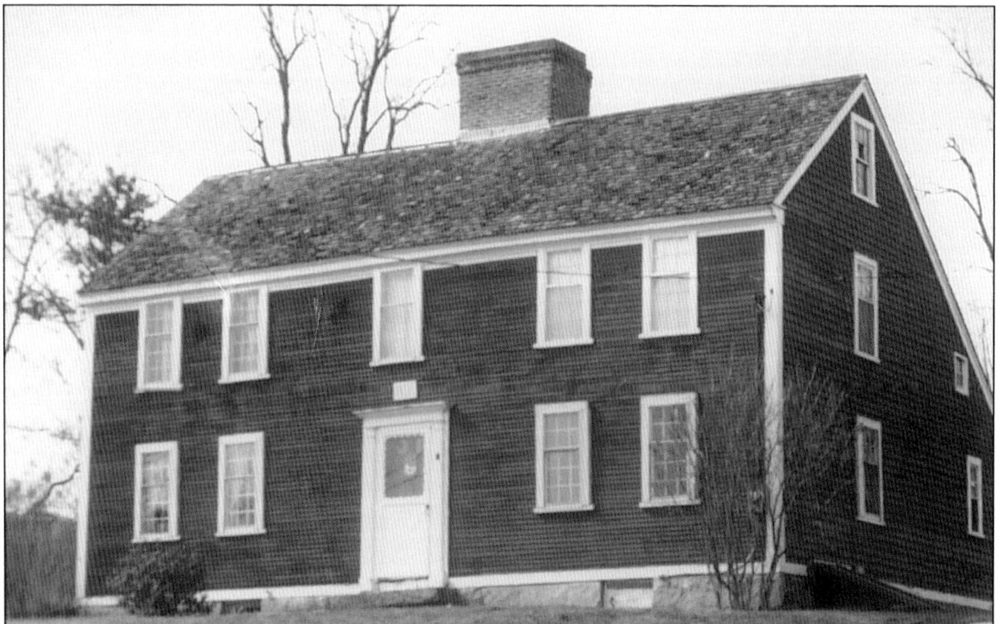

The Stephen Houghton House (K-189), located at 758 Lancaster Avenue, is important to Lunenburg for two reasons. First, the house was purchased by Eleazer Houghton from Samuel Bennett on March 20, 1726. It is the earliest signed deed found to date in Lunenburg. Second, Capt. Josiah Willard's sawmill, mentioned in the proprietor's records, established the ability of early settlers in Lunenburg to build with sawed beams and timbers evident in this house.

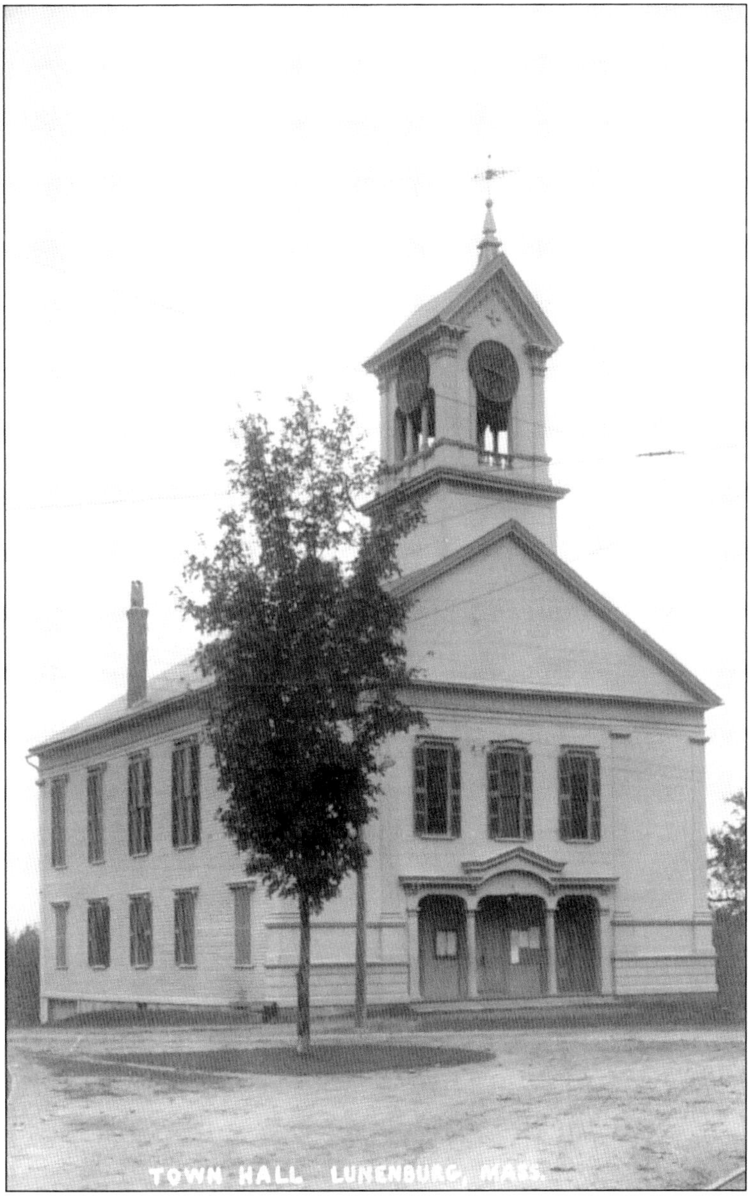

The present town hall is pictured here in 1909. This building was originally a church built by the Congregational Society in 1830. Located on the town's upper common, it was moved to its present site in 1867, jacked up, and another floor added beneath. This provided office space. The cellar still contains the original tree trunks supporting both floors. In the attic, one can see the original post-and-beam construction. Over the years, this building has served many different organizations and causes: temperance meetings (1878), Grange meetings, a banquet for the opening of the Fitchburg and Leominster Street Railway (August 7, 1901), dances, the first Lunenburg Catholic Mass (July 9, 1950), basketball games, school lunch programs and classes, celebrations, and a post office. It also garaged the town hearse, served as a jail, and stored guns and tear gas for our Home Guard in both world wars. Additions to the building include a town clock donated by Jacob H. Fairbanks (1894), the town vault (1939), a fire escape, and a ticket booth (1887).

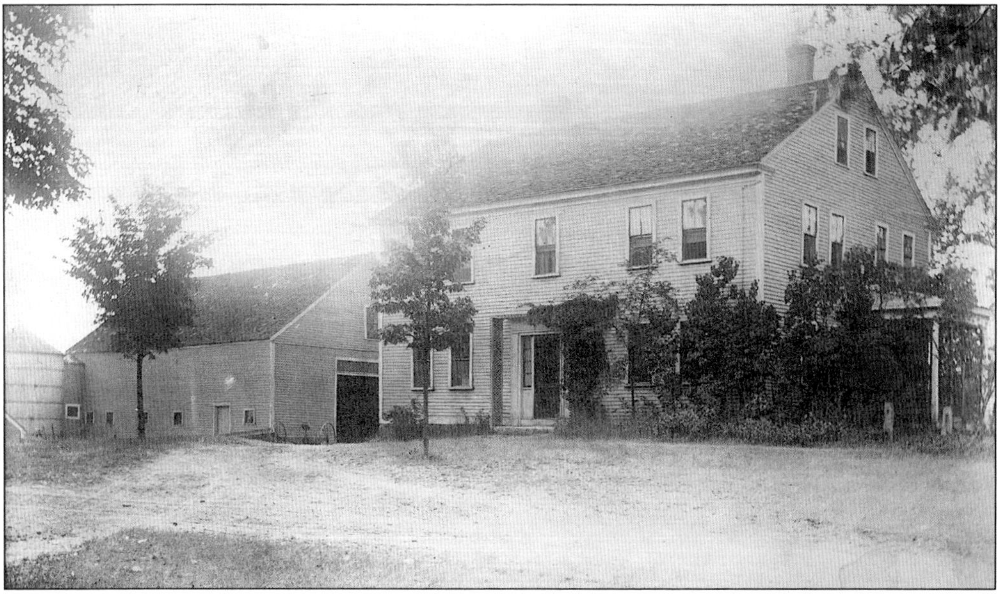

The Cyrus Kilburn house (K-127) was built on Lancaster Avenue and Kilburn Street early in the town's development. Kilburn was a teacher, surveyor, and botanist. In 1830, he was employed to do a survey of the town and made an extremely accurate map, which showed every road and house. The house was destroyed by fire in 1914, and another one now stands on the same spot.

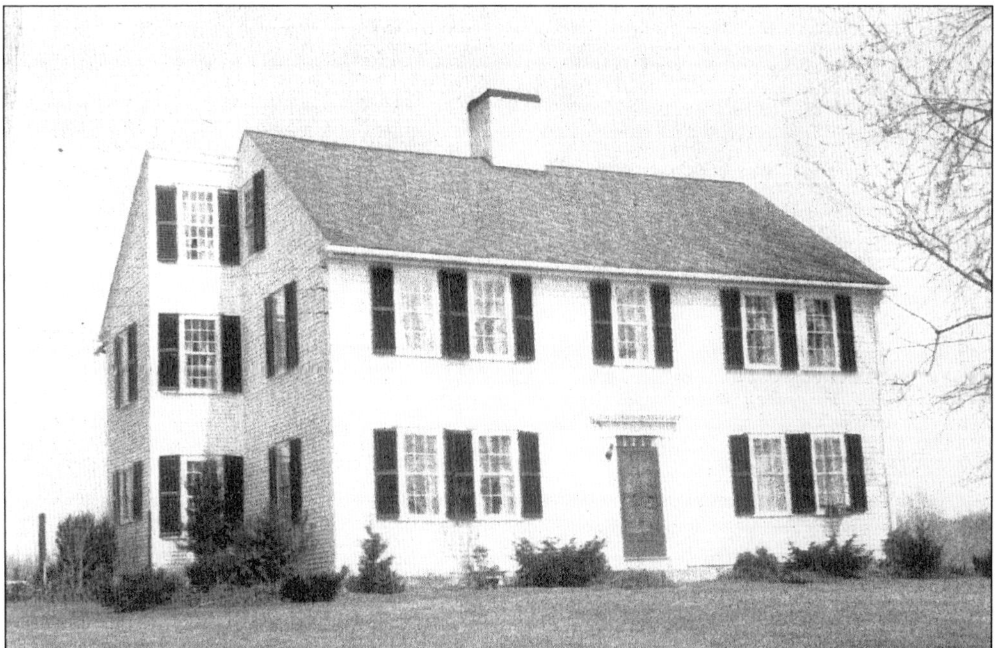

The original chimney in this house at 64 Beal Street ends about three feet above the present attic floor. This has led to the conclusion that it was built in the Cape Cod style, with another floor added later. Built in 1734, it is called the Stickney House (K-71) after Stephen Stickney. The house remained in the Stickney family until 1907.

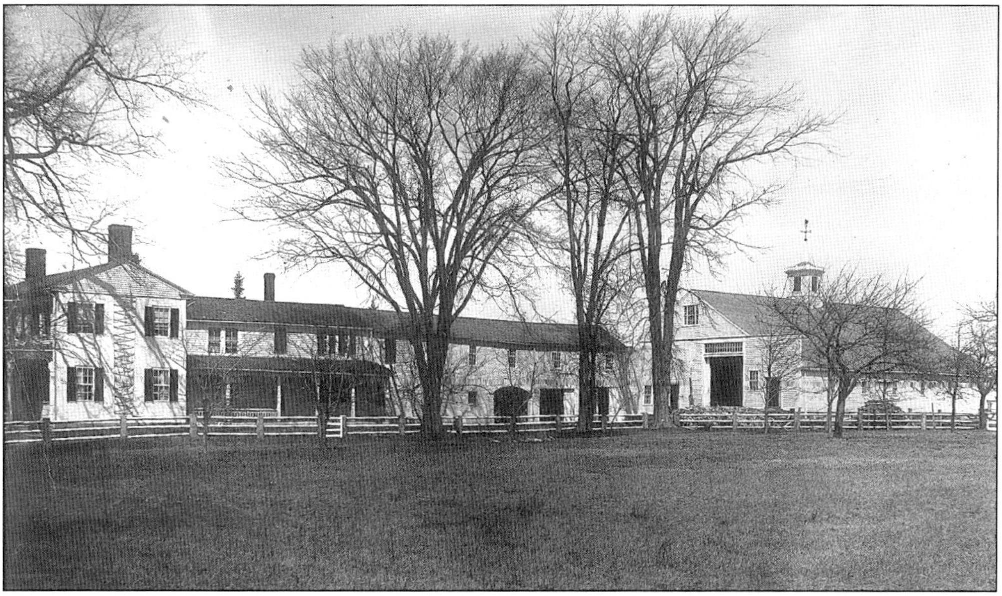

Elmdale (K-117), built *c.* 1769 at 125 Lancaster Avenue, was home to Rev. Zabdiel Adam's family for 25 years. William Greenough & Son printed Bibles here. Samuel Emerson's wife and daughter operated it as a convalescent home. In 1937, the barn and most of the land was sold to Roger Bigelow for a dairy farm. Present homeowners are Dr. John and Elaine Murphy.

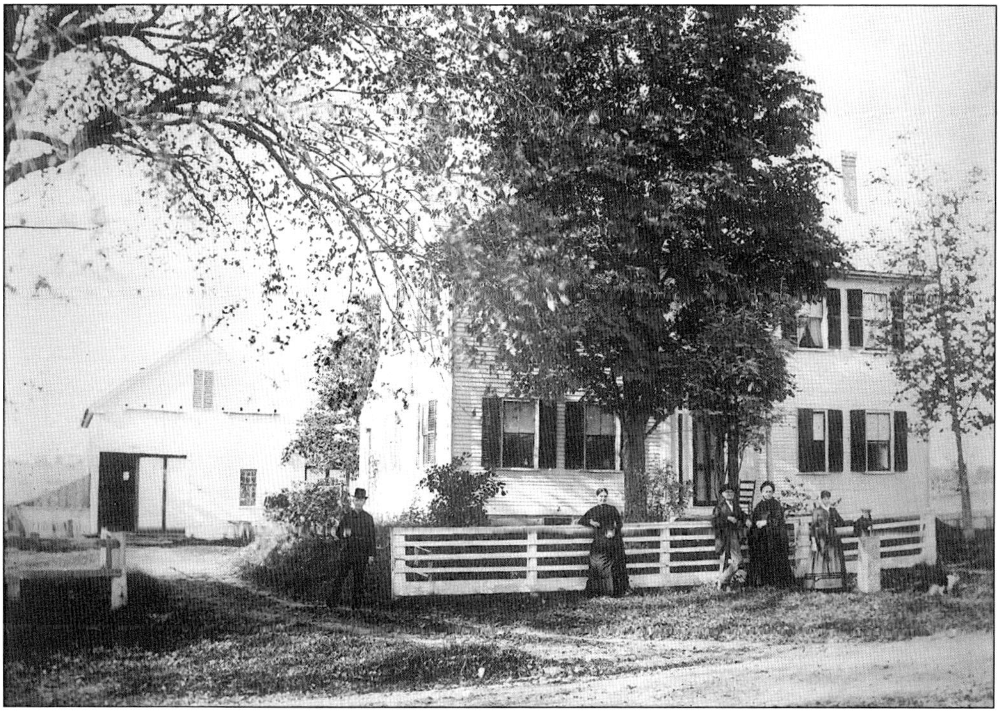

This building was known as the Cunningham House (K-10), later the Gilchrest House. Built *c.* 1815 by Nathaniel Fellows Cunningham, it was moved from nearer the center of town to its present site on 86 Lancaster Avenue in 1843. Its owner, Mrs. G. Whittemore, bordered some scholars who attended the nearby Lunenburg Academy.

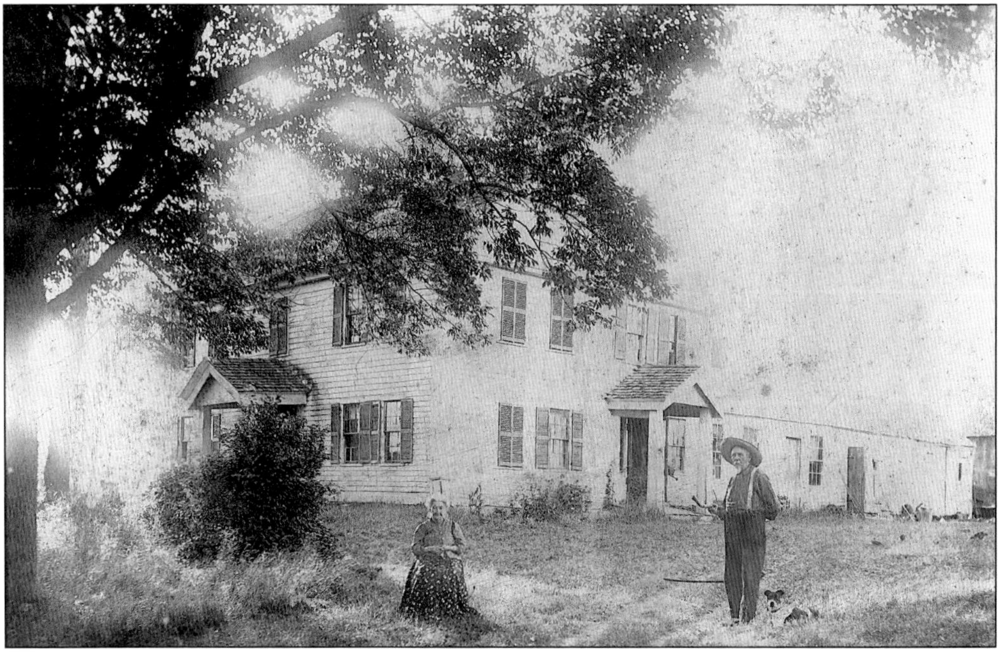

In this 1911 photograph, Mr. and Mrs. Danforth stand in the front yard of the Foster Beal residence (K-70) at 106 Beal Street. The Danforths maintained the property for the nationally known ornithologist, naturalist, and mathematician, whose work took him all over the country. The Beals owned this property for 37 years. Beal always considered himself a citizen of Lunenburg and wanted his family to grow up here.

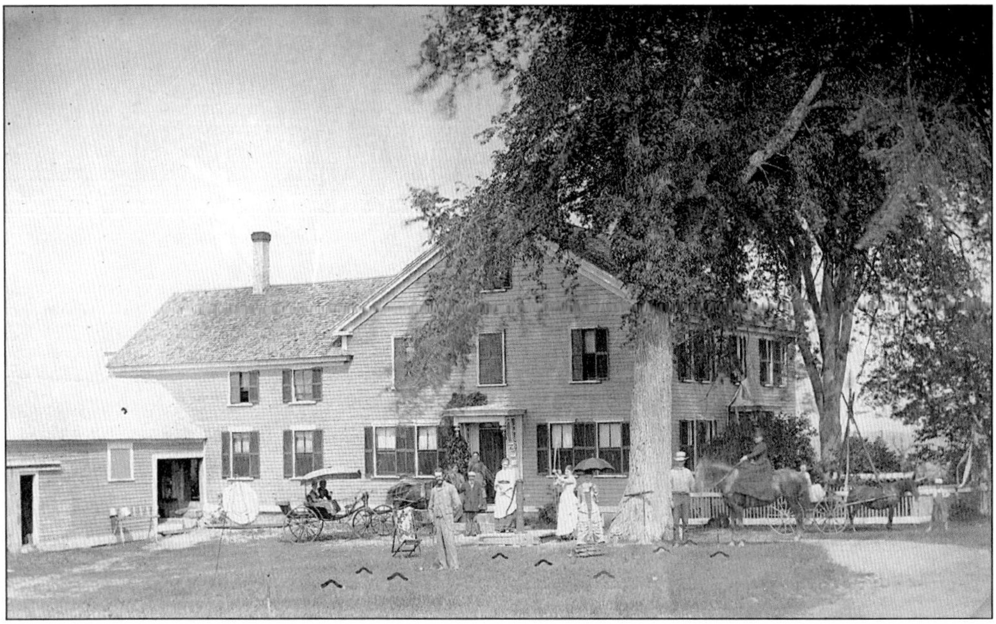

This house was purchased in 1783 by Peter Brown and was on the site of 321 Elmwood Road. The road was the Old County Road, which was the main thoroughfare to Groton and ended up coming in by the Bull Run Restaurant. This is a typical scene showing summer enjoyment with friends and family. (Courtesy of Mary E. Bingham.)

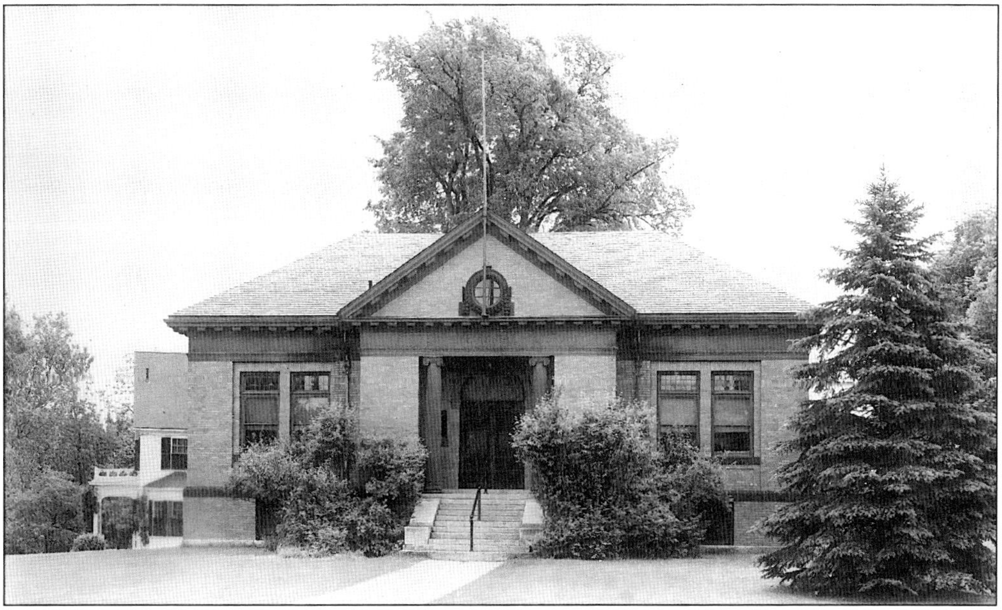

The Ritter Memorial Library is shown here after its dedication in August 1910. The library was a gift to the town from Catherine Ritter Watson, wife of Boston physician Abraham Watson. It was given in memory of her mother, Elizabeth Ritter and grandmother Catherine Ritter. The town hired Alpheus K. Francis to build the library. When he died, his son Sidney H. Francis completed the structure.

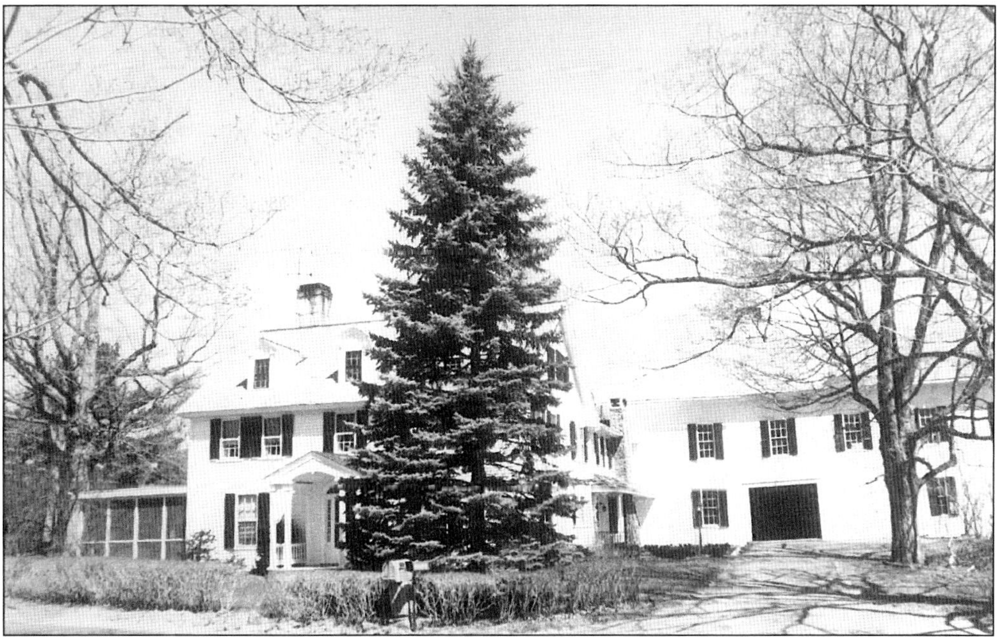

Lunenburg has always had its share of resident physicians. One of the town's earliest was Dr. John Dunsmoor, whose house was on this site at 322 Northfield Road. Dunsmoor built the house (K-42) in 1762, and it remained in the Dunsmoor family for over a century. The farm was sold in 1864 to the Joseph Cushing family, who, over the next 91 years, changed it to its present grandeur.

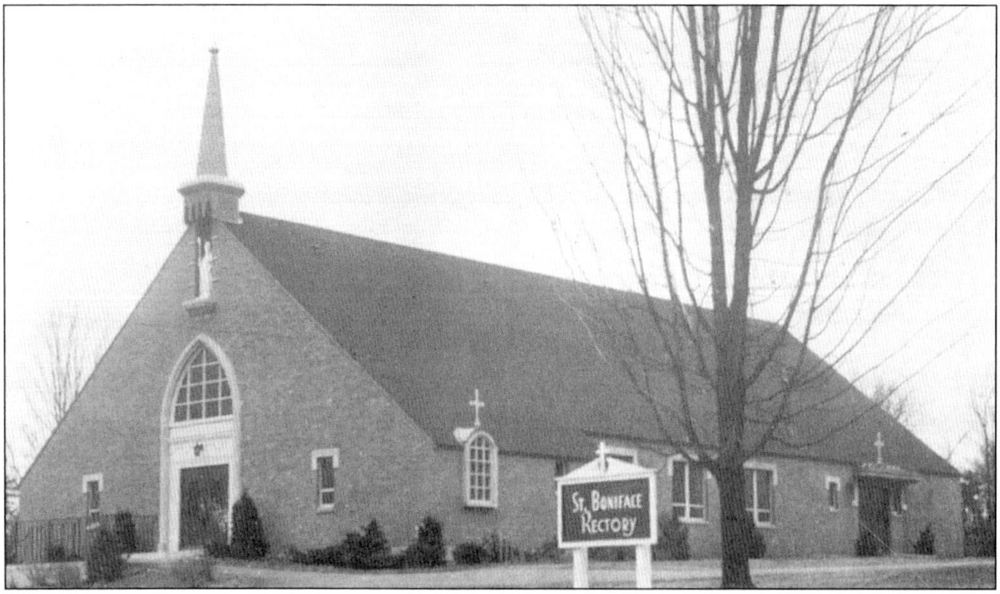

In 1950, Bishop Wright of Worcester established the first Catholic parish in Lunenburg, to be known as St. Boniface. At first, Masses were said at the Whalom Ballroom, the Lunenburg Town Hall, and the roller-skating rink. In 1952, the church bought a rectory with adjacent land on Massachusetts Avenue. Construction of the church began in 1952, and it was formally dedicated in 1954.

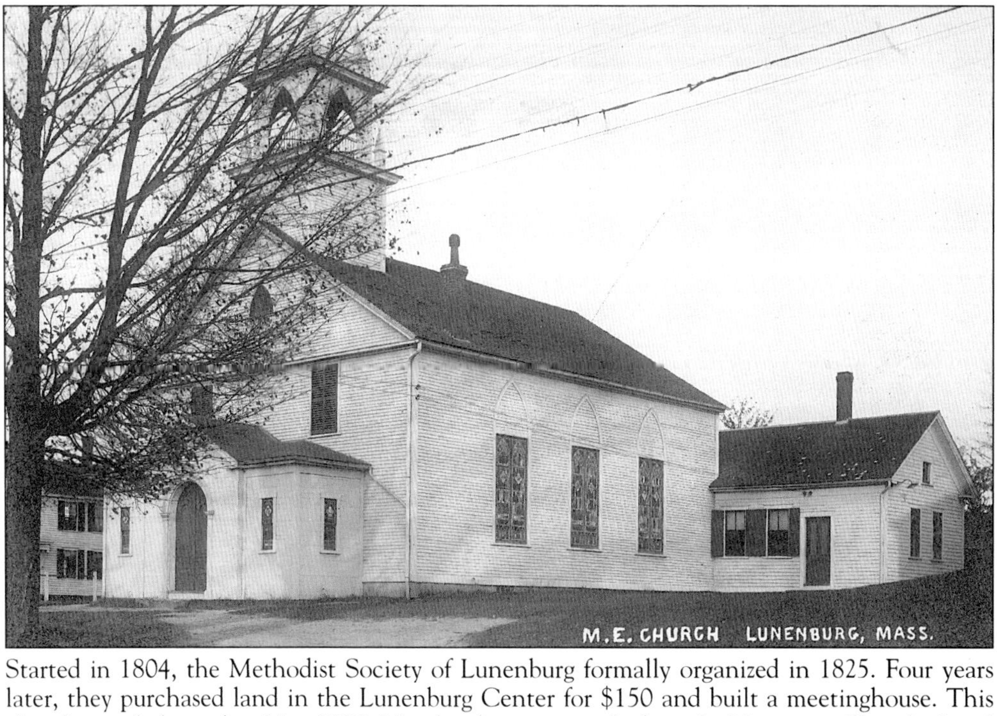

Started in 1804, the Methodist Society of Lunenburg formally organized in 1825. Four years later, they purchased land in the Lunenburg Center for $150 and built a meetinghouse. This church was dedicated in May 1830. Membership increased when the Unitarian Church closed its doors in 1865. In March 1975, the Methodists and Congregationalists joined to worship in their church, becoming the United Parish of Lunenburg.

In 1835, the First Evangelical Congregational Society was formed. It was not until the society had weathered a variety of religious and political storms that it was able, in October 1844, to occupy its own church in Lunenburg Center. This is the same building on the same site pictured here. Generous gifts over the years provided the church with a bell (1859), an organ (1923), and a new parsonage (1930s).

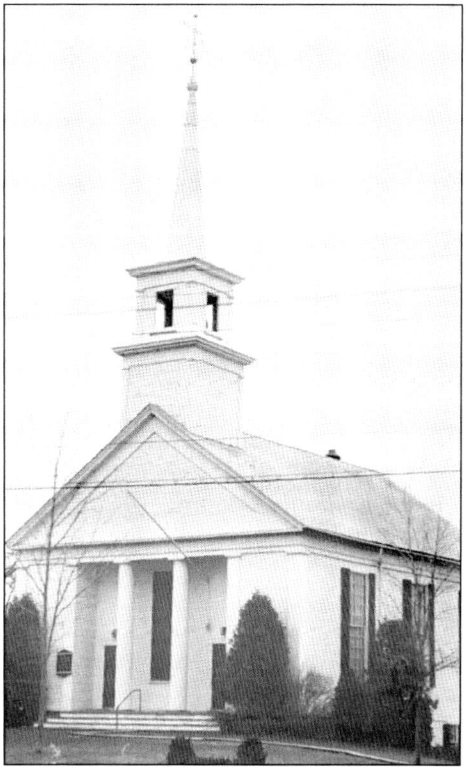

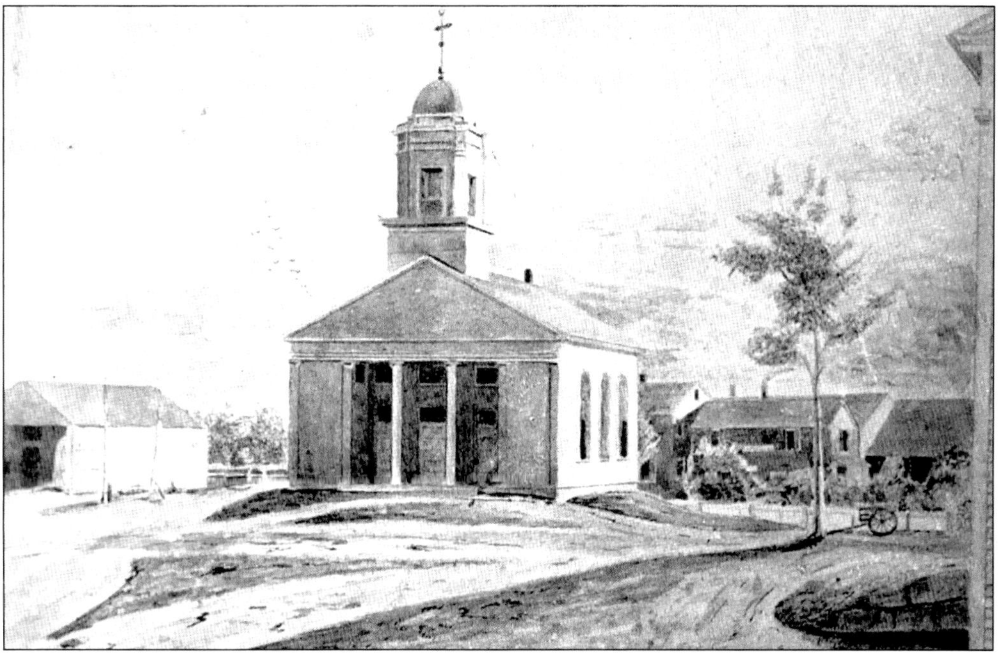

The building shown in this old painting is a church erected in 1830 by Congregationalists. The site on which it stood is today the upper common. It later became a Unitarian church. In 1867, it was purchased by the town, moved 200 feet north to its present location, and used from that time to the present as our town hall.

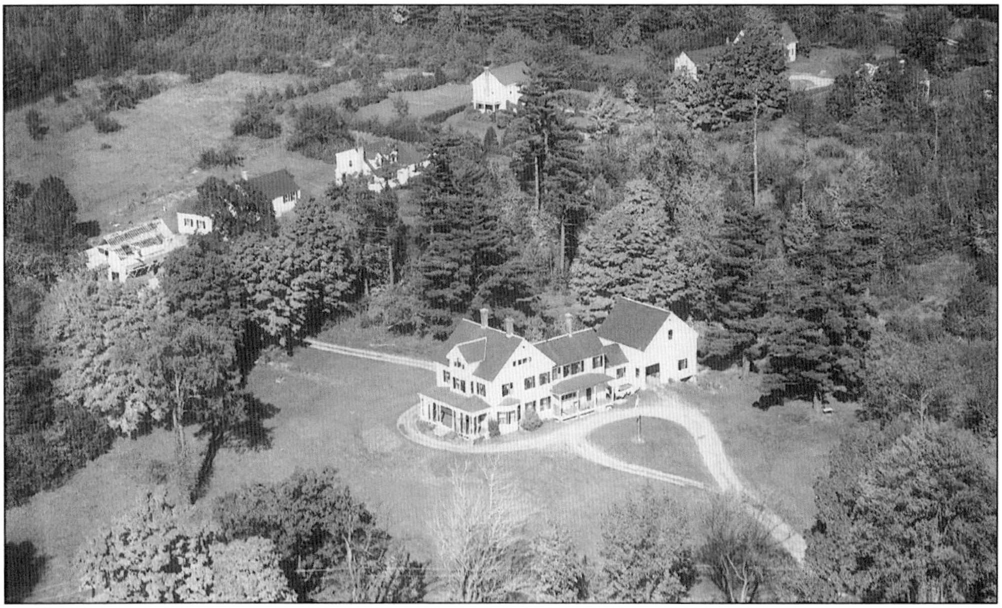

The house in this aerial view is now the Miller-Sawyer-Masciarelli Funeral Home, at the junction of Chestnut Street with Massachusetts Avenue. A house was built on this lot *c.* 1868 by James A. Litchfield, Civil War veteran and state representative. This house was moved, and Litchfield built the existing one in 1895. It was later owned by his grandson Rodney Brown and sold to Howard Miller.

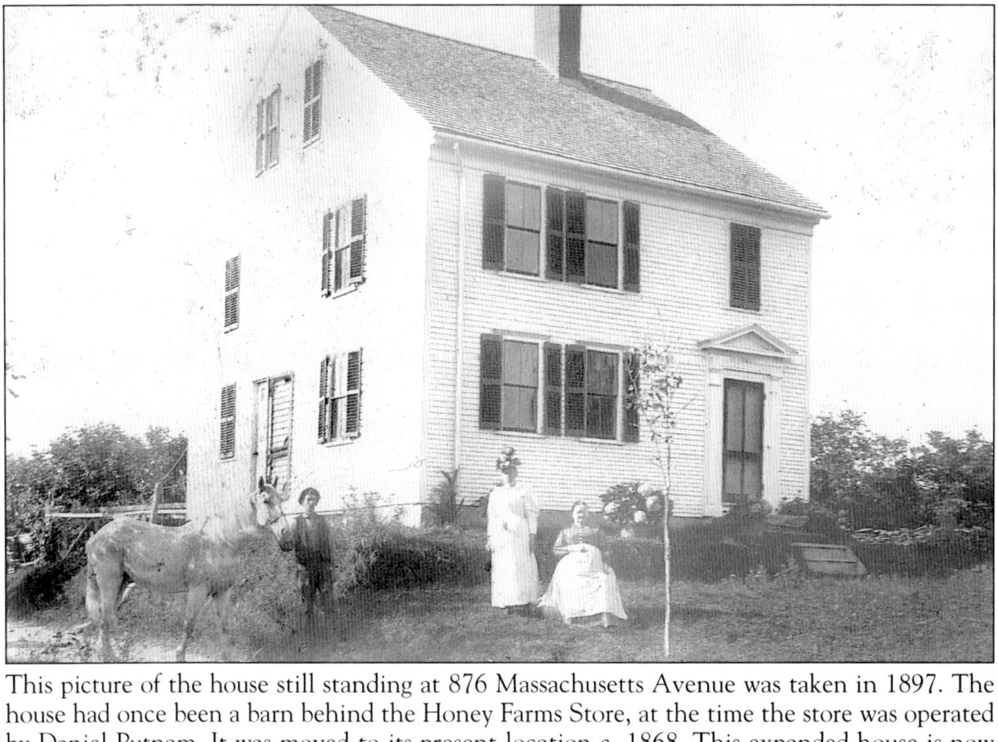

This picture of the house still standing at 876 Massachusetts Avenue was taken in 1897. The house had once been a barn behind the Honey Farms Store, at the time the store was operated by Daniel Putnam. It was moved to its present location *c.* 1868. This expanded house is now the property of Charles and Sally Dyer.

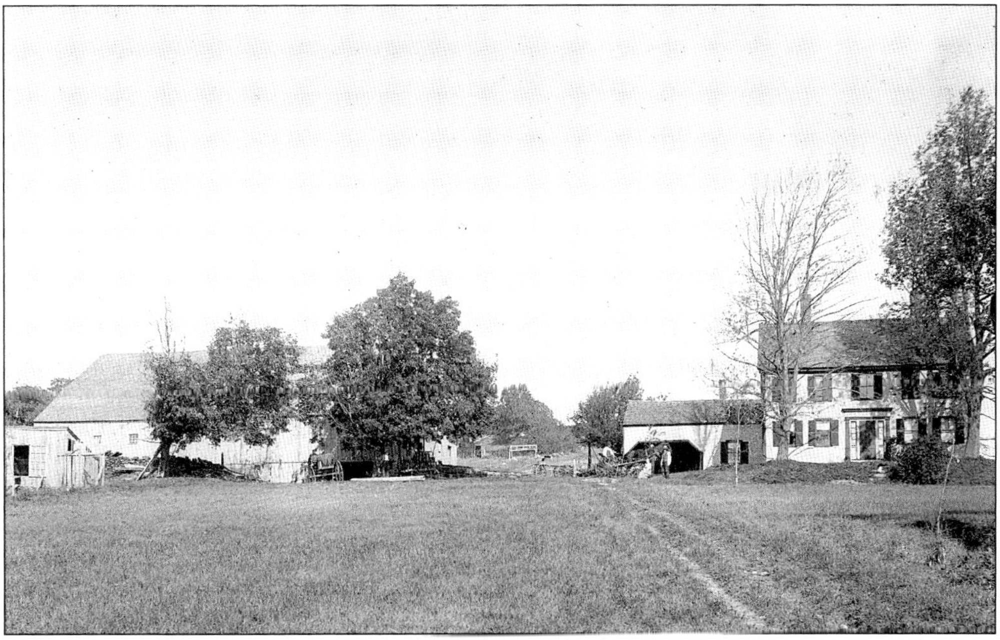

The Jedediah Bailey house is situated on the northerly side of Page Street, easterly from Lancaster Avenue. Samuel Page, the first settler, lived here in a house, no longer standing, as early as 1719. The Baileys acquired the property in 1761 and kept it until 1863. Its site is unusual, being 1,000 feet from the road unlike most early houses.

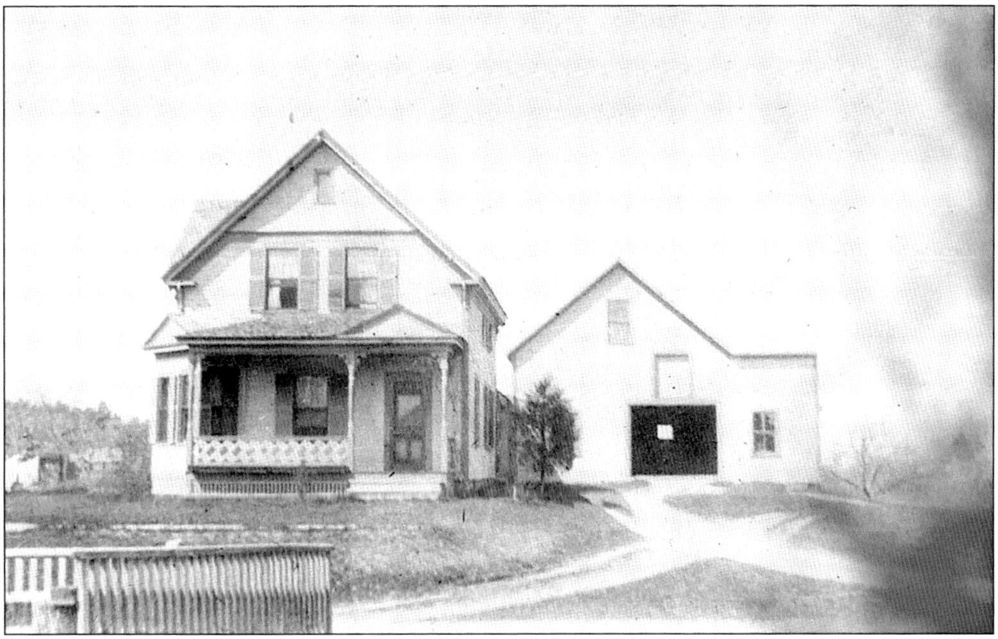

William Harley built this house at 919 Massachusetts Avenue in 1901. It was the lifelong home of his daughter Willa J. Harley, a second-grade teacher for more than one generation of Lunenburg students and a Girl Scout leader for many years. She was a dedicated gardener, and it seems appropriate that her former home is now the Flower Barn, operated by Donna Proctor Cameron and Lois Cameron Filiau.

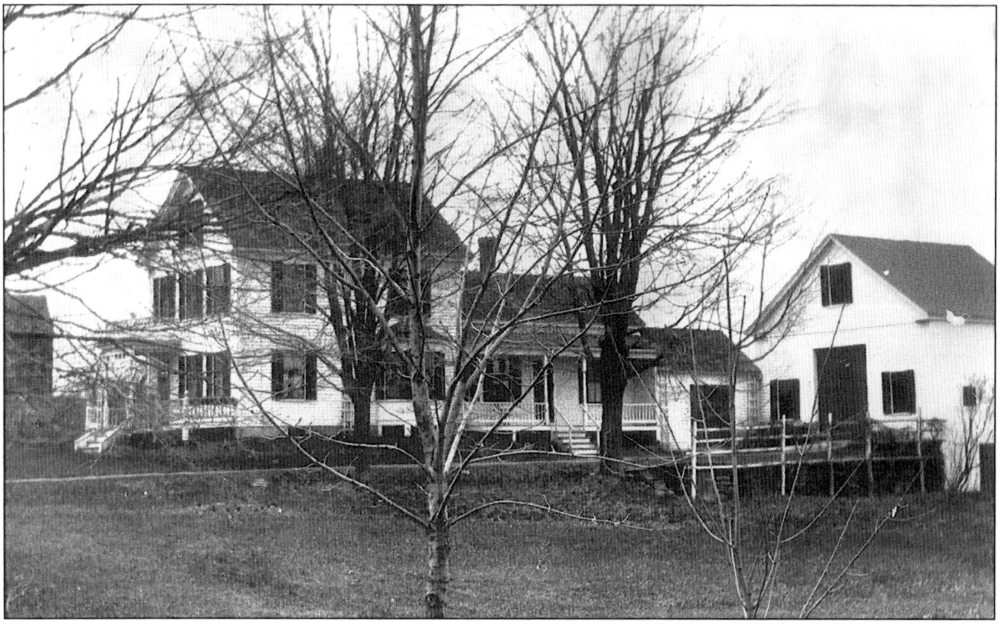

Another of Lunenburg's noble homes was located at 42 Highland Street. After the house built by Montaque burned, Charles E. Goodrich purchased the land in 1890 and built a house on the site of the original. The house remained in the family until the death of his daughter Ruth in 1973. Thereafter, the property was owned by Ed and Barbara Field and later by David and Joanne Demers.

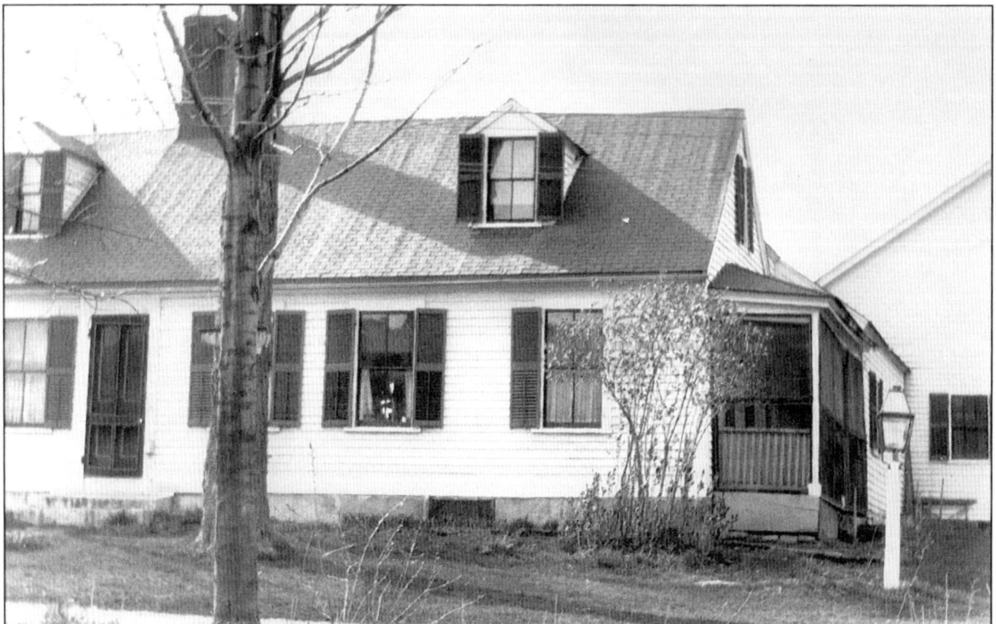

This is the Jimmy Clifton house, part of which was constructed of lumber from a discontinued schoolhouse on the lower common. It was one of only two houses on Whiting Street, known as Two Rod Road due to its width. Jimmy Clifton was a town character best known for his habit of exaggerating and telling tall stories.

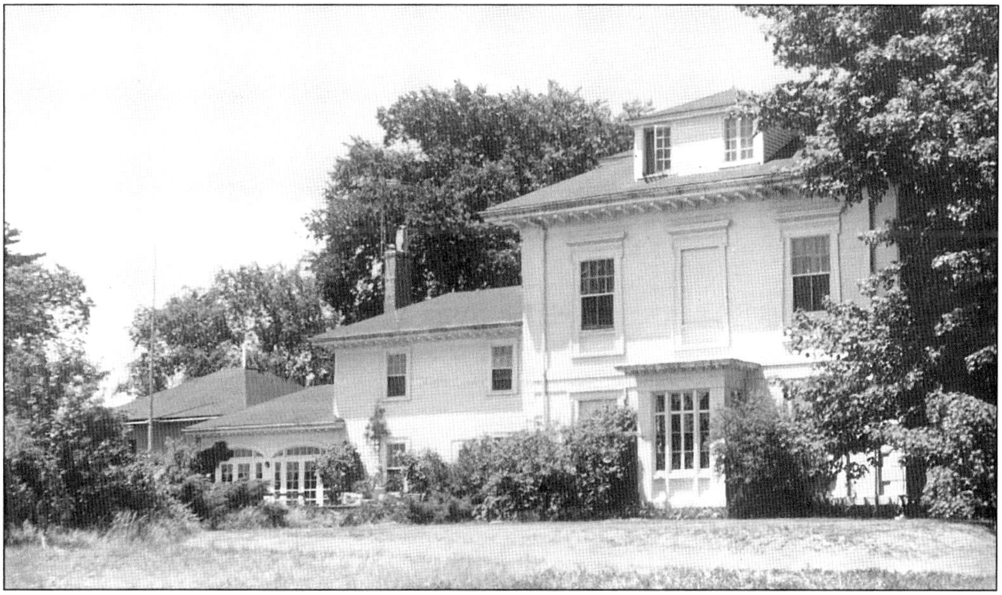

In 1845, James Savage (nationally known Boston lawyer and originator of the first savings bank in America) came to Lunenburg and established a summerhouse on Sunnyhill Road. This *c.* 1940 photograph shows the south side of the house. The Savage family continued to spend its summers here until his death in 1873. The house was destroyed by a spectacular fire in 1958 and another built on the site.

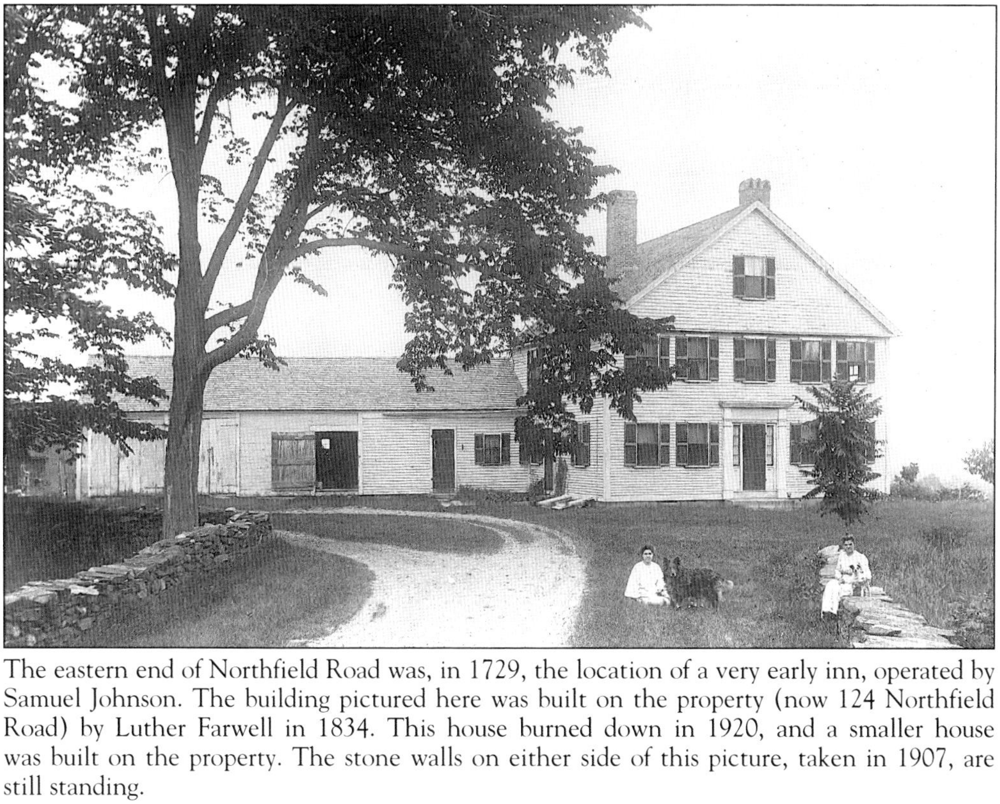

The eastern end of Northfield Road was, in 1729, the location of a very early inn, operated by Samuel Johnson. The building pictured here was built on the property (now 124 Northfield Road) by Luther Farwell in 1834. This house burned down in 1920, and a smaller house was built on the property. The stone walls on either side of this picture, taken in 1907, are still standing.

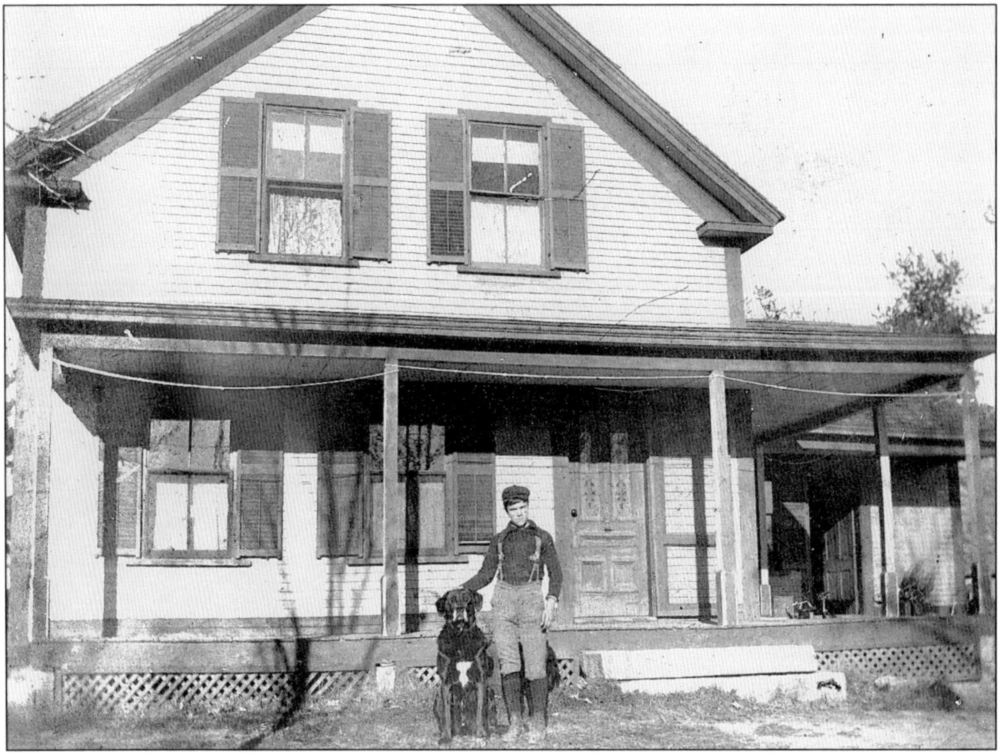

In this 1898 photograph from the Lancey family album, the morning sun shines on the home of Gilbert Cook at 1801 Massachusetts Avenue. The dog sits attentively beside his happy friend, young Chester Alden Lancey, who was the little brother of Leroy Lancey. Although the boy, his dog, and the neighboring school exist only in the pages of history, the house still stands on the same site.

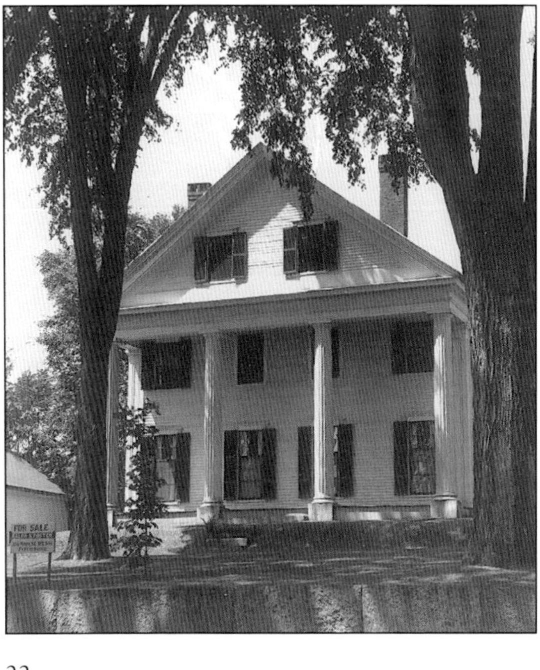

This imposing Greek Revival house was built by Nathaniel Cunningham Jr. at 42 Leominster Road in 1843. It remained in the Cunningham family until 1928. Designed by Cunningham's wife, the house had 13 to 14 high-ceilinged rooms and 10 fireplaces. Although the facade retains its original appearance, the remainder has been altered over time.

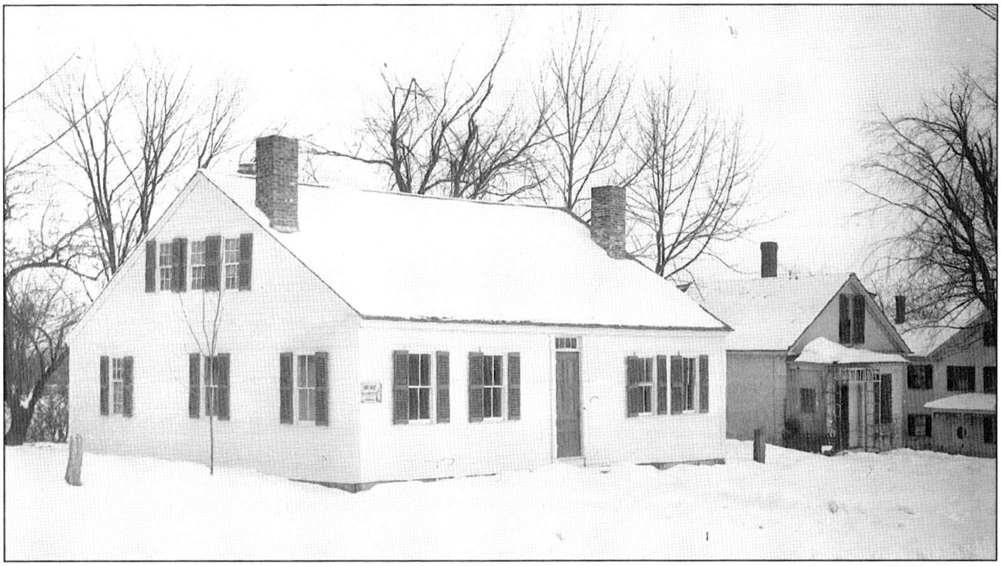

The Richardson House was built at 19 Lancaster Avenue *c.* 1771. Joseph Bellows acquired the land as part of a 650-acre parcel and was probably the builder. The brick building visible on the right side (built in 1835 and now a private home) was once schoolhouse No. 1. Water for the school was carried by the students from a well in the Richardson House.

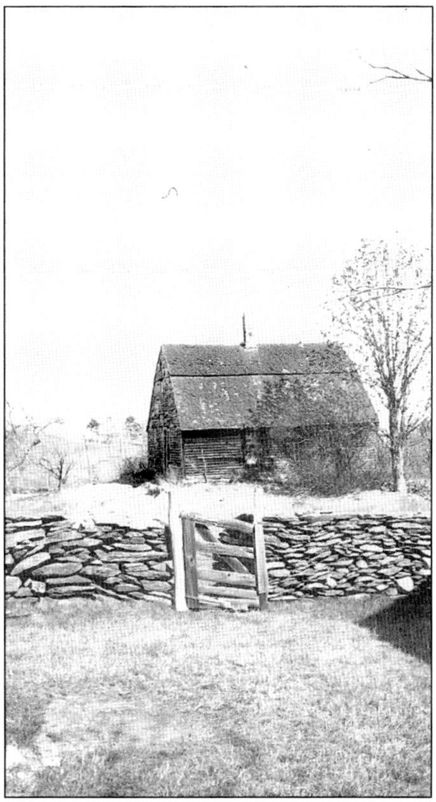

Capt. John Fuller's homestead, located at the corner of West Street and Electric Avenue, is shown in this *c.* 1920 photograph. Fuller planted a buttonwood tree at his house the same date he planted our famous Liberty Tree on the lower common in 1775. This tree still stands at the site of the Fuller homestead. Captain Fuller became a delegate to the convention, ratifying the Constitution of the United States in 1778.

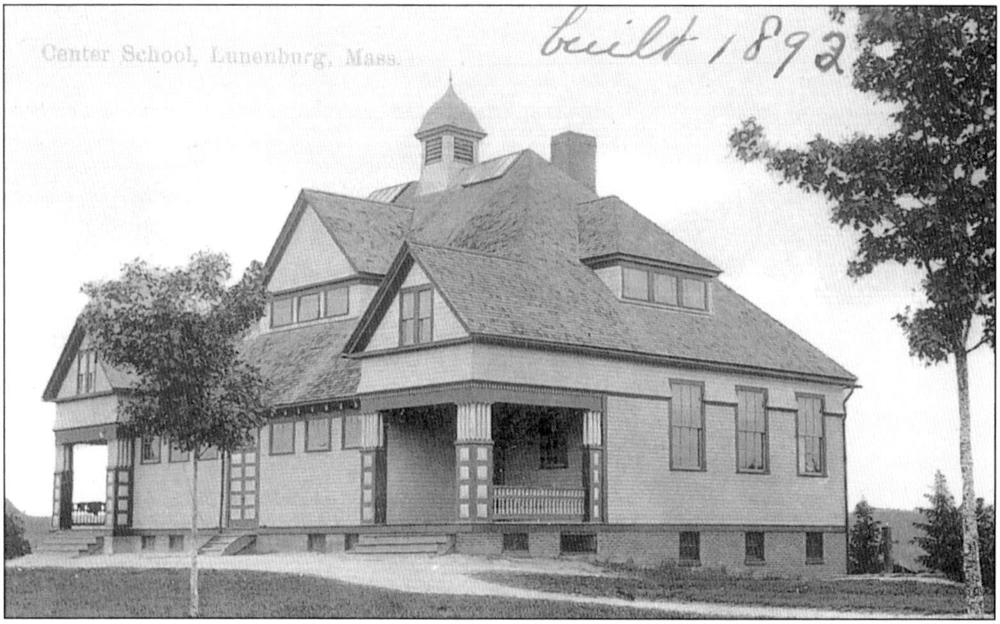

The Center School, built in 1892, was designed by architect Henry Francis. Initially, it offered instruction for grades 1 through 8. In 1895, however, high school classes were organized under principal Clifton Putney, who earned the handsome sum of $12.50 per week. Leroy Lancey was its first graduate having gone through all 12 years. Overcrowding in this school necessitated the building of a second story (pictured below) in 1910. This larger building served the scholars in grades 1 through 12 until 1924, when it became necessary to build a junior-senior high school to accommodate the town's growing population. The building was torn down in 1964. The town made this site available for a new building. A year later, the present Lunenburg Historical Society at 10 School Street was dedicated.

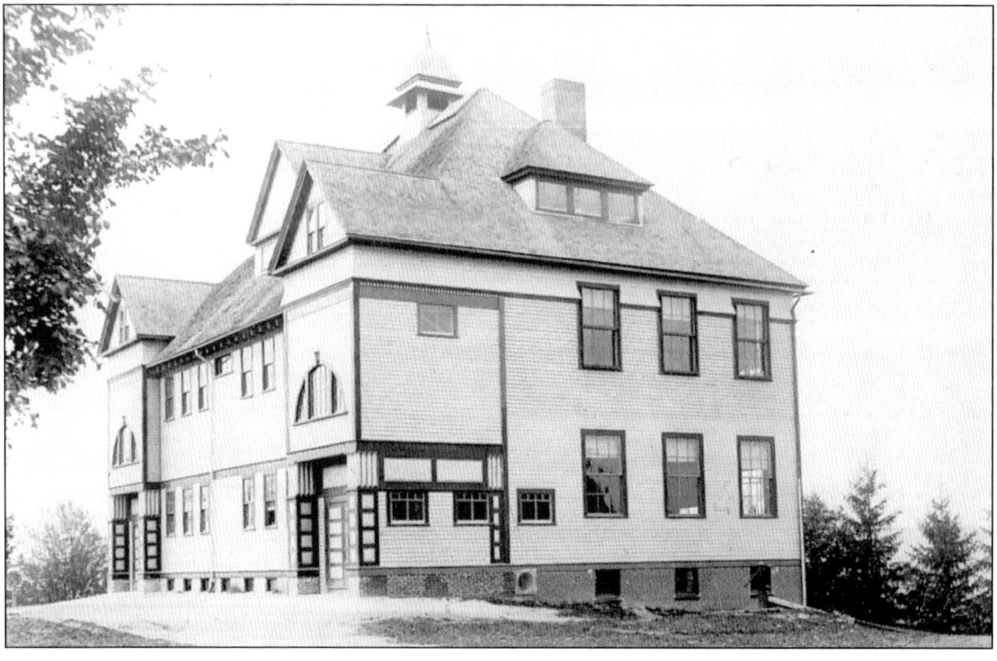

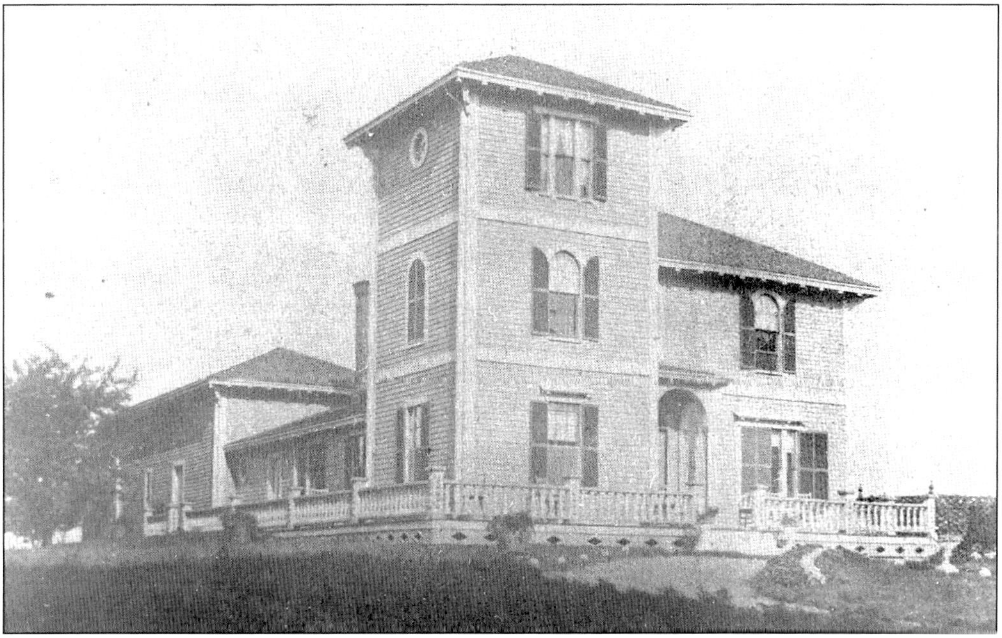

The house at 94 Main Street was built in the Italianate style by Daniel Farwell Snow in 1849. It is called the Locke place after later owners. Its distinctive features include a fireplace in every room, a brick oven in the kitchen, and handmade screws. The elegant wooden fence bordering the corner of Main Street and Oak Avenue follows the edge of the property.

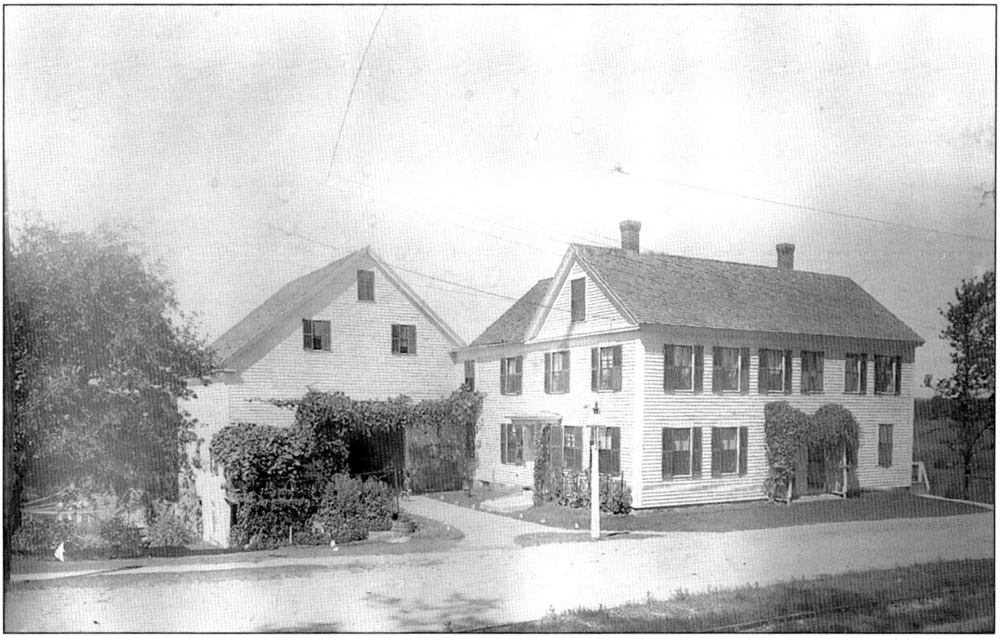

The left portion of this house is thought to have been a store built by Dr. John Taylor, the first physician in town. It was purchased by Ruben Walker Snow (*c.* 1870), who moved it farther north on Main Street to the right of the present Décor & More Shop. An equal-size addition was built onto its right side, making it a duplex. The attached Snow barn burned in 1948, and the house was torn down in 1981.

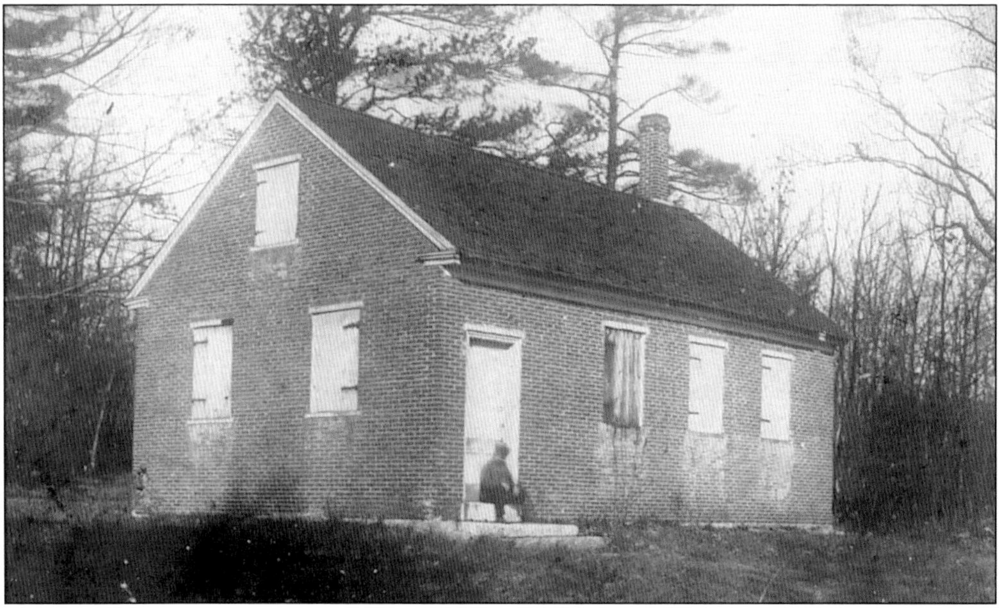

In District No. 3-West, the first school building of which there is any record, was a wooden structure located, in 1834, on West Street, close to the intersection of Electric Avenue. The second building at this site in this photograph, *c.* 1880, was a two-room brick building. When the town purchased the schoolhouses from the districts in 1869, many of the old buildings were sold to individuals in town.

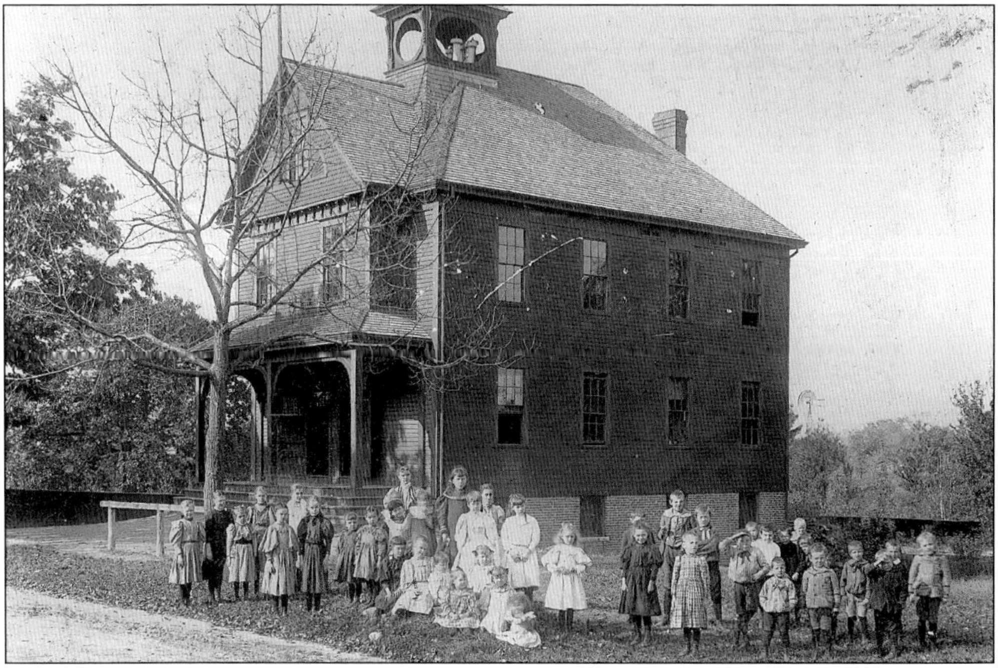

Known as the West School, this building was the third structure to serve District No. 3. It was built in 1889 on the corner of Whalom Road and Youngs Road and has the distinction of being the longest in-use, outlying school in town. It ended its use as a school in 1956 and was then used by the Veterans of Foreign Wars until fire damaged the structure in 1975.

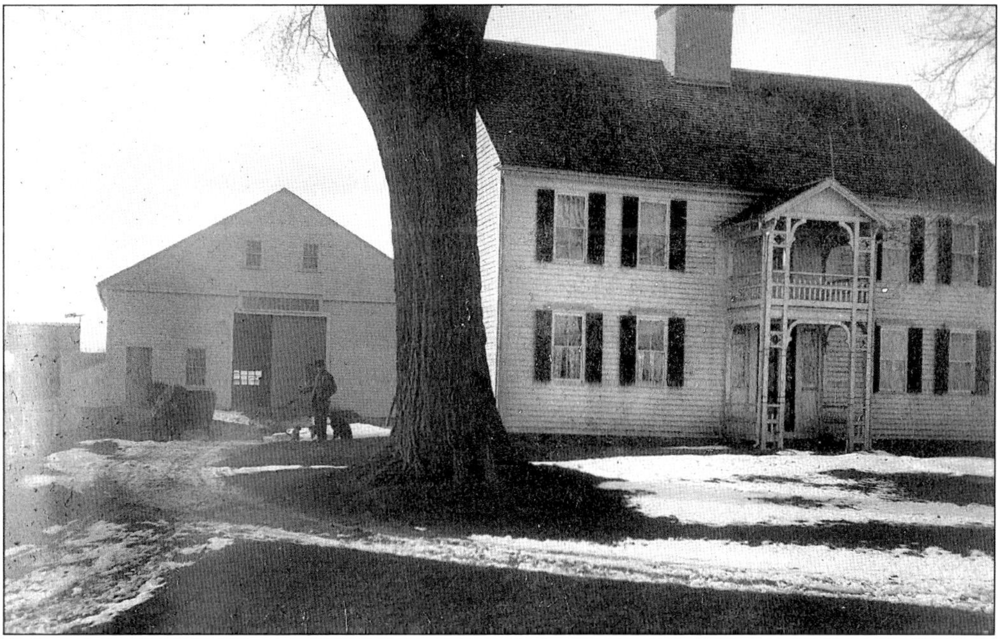

This beautiful old house was known as the T.L. Willis House (K-118), located at about 156 Lancaster Avenue. It may have been built *c.* 1770 by Josiah Goldsmith. It survived for 150 years, when a fire of undetermined origin destroyed it on May 14, 1934. A 250-year-old elm was also destroyed when the heat from the fire caused its sap to boil beneath the bark.

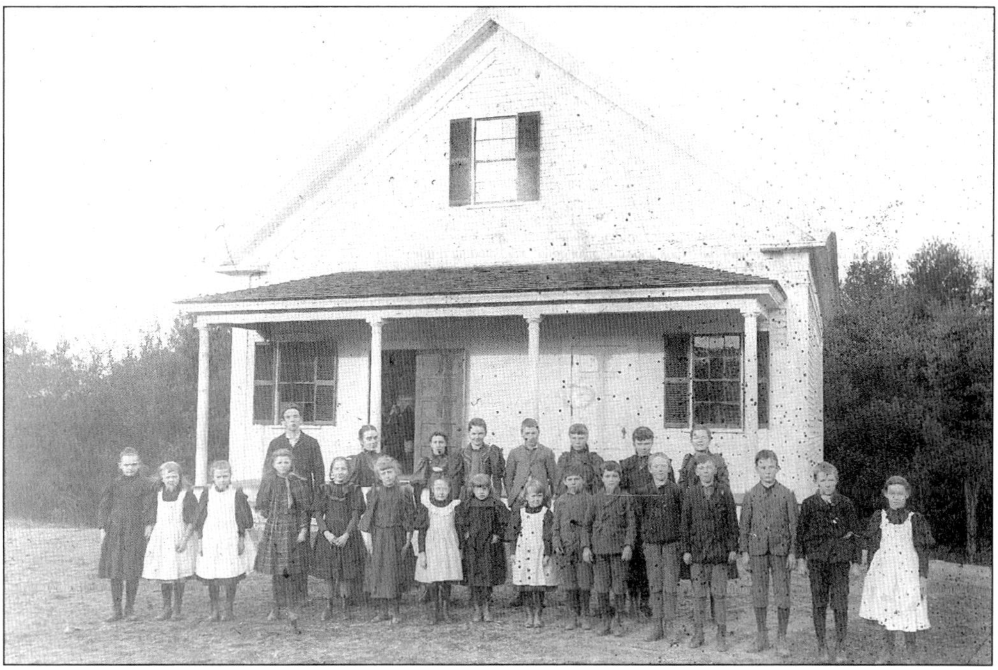

The Mulpus School on Massachusetts Avenue, adjacent to the Cowdry Lot, opened its doors to the pupils in the eastern section of town in 1895. Among its special features were a beautiful playground and proximity to Mulpus Brook. In warm weather, the brook became a natural swimming pool during recess. This was the first school in town to raise a flag on its grounds.

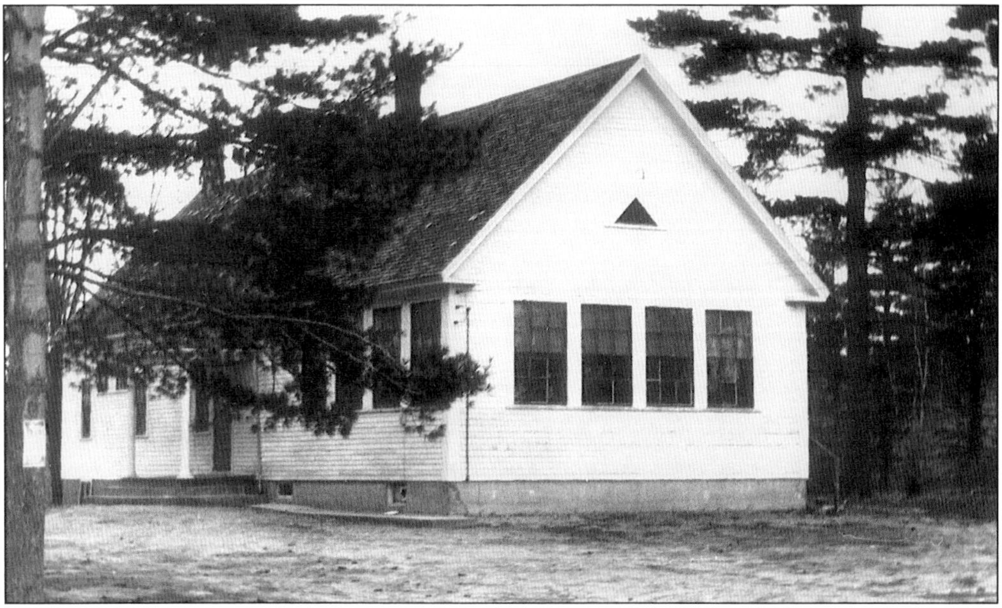

This North School was the last of several that served the north end of Lunenburg. It was designed to accommodate the pupils of two schools, No. 4 and No. 6. It was located at 463 Chase Road, just south of West Townsend Road. In 1928, the pupils who attended this school were transported to the Center School. This building was sold and became a café and dance hall until it burned in 1936.

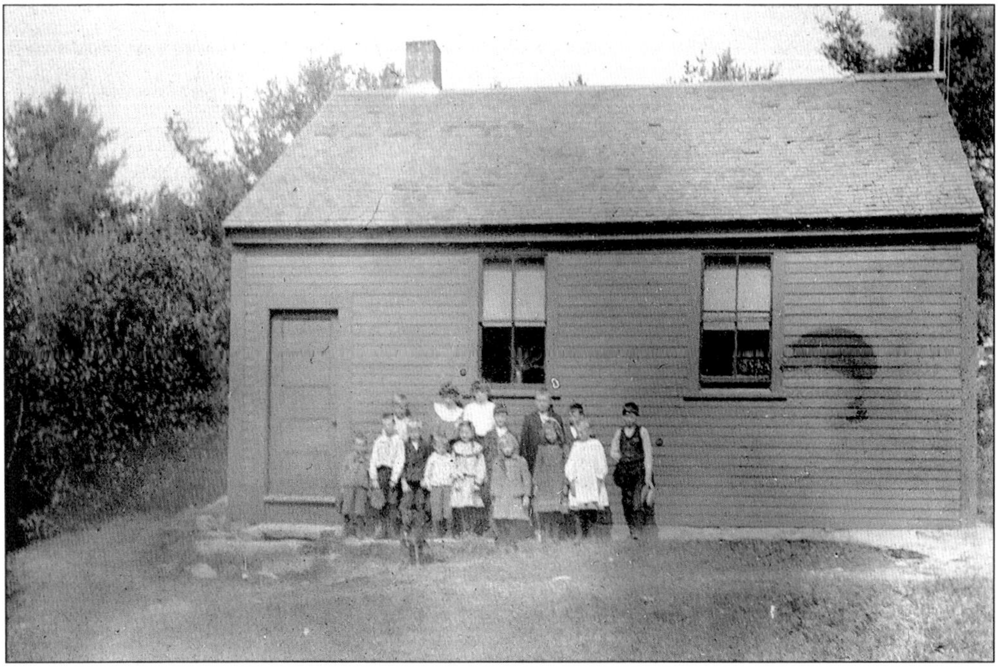

This photograph shows the second school building in District No. 5. It was located on Flat Hill and served students in that area from 1848 to 1895. After its demise as a school, the building was sold in 1896 to E.L. Fairbanks for $62 and became an addition to his home on Flat Hill Road.

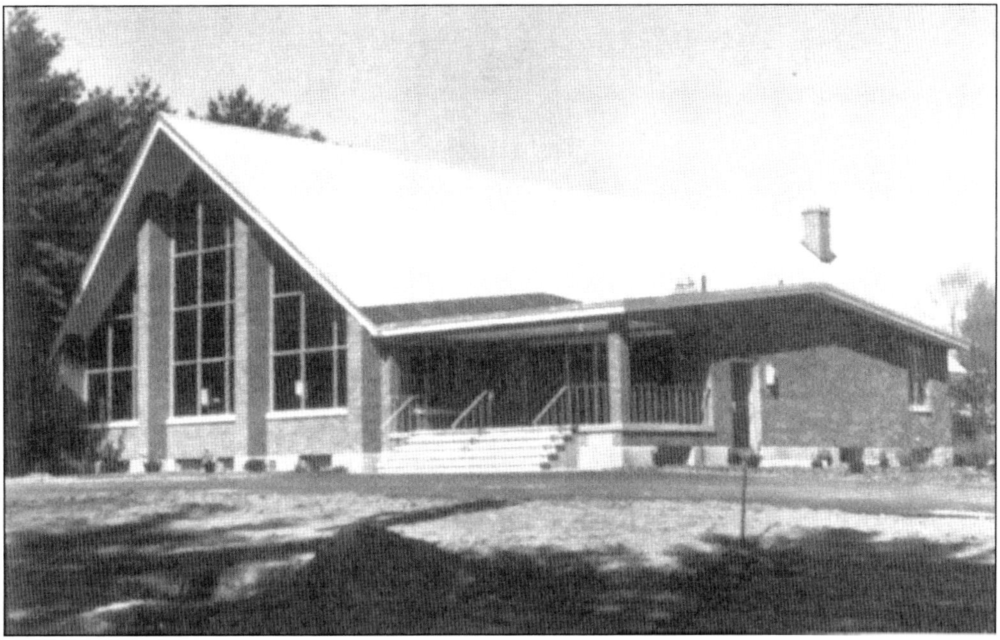

The Pilgrim Covenant Church was originally a church in Fitchburg. They relocated to Lunenburg. The congregation purchased 4.7 acres on the corner of Beal Street and Chase Road for the total of $87,000 on June 16, 1960. They built a new edifice on this lot in 1965. The cornerstone was laid on November 1, 1964, and the building dedicated on Palm Sunday in 1965.

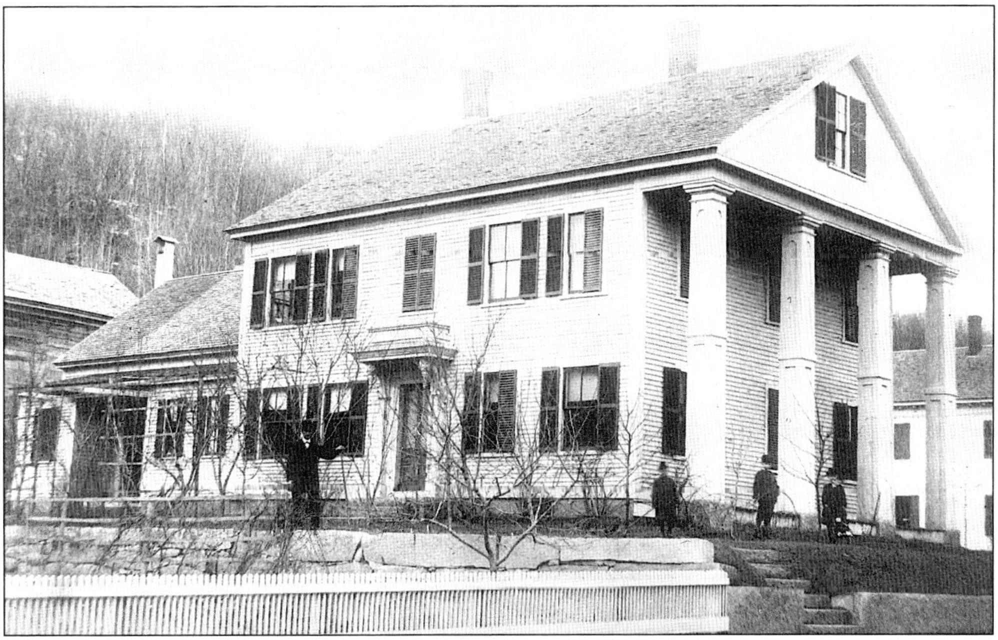

Old Lunenburg Academy was built in 1841 near 100 Lancaster Avenue. Its primary purpose was to prepare young men for admission to college and to prepare young women for an appropriate role in society. In 1841, it had 51 females and 51 males. Among its students was Luther Burbank, who later became world famous. In 1867, it was moved to Fitchburg near Rollstone and Kimball Streets.

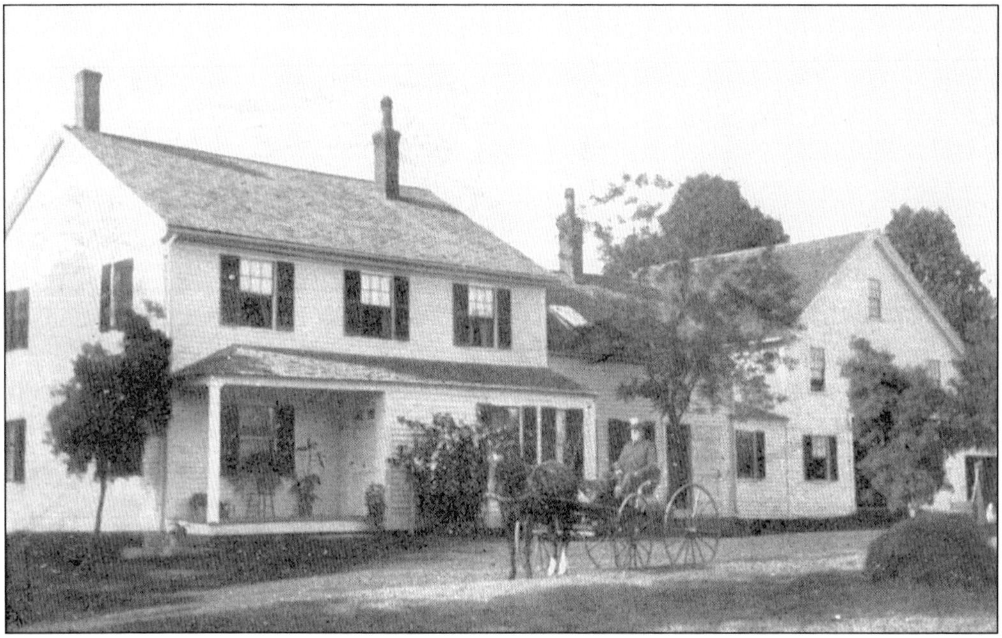

This house standing at 42 Main Street is called the Jones House. The house was built in 1835 from the lumber of a discontinued schoolhouse on the lower common. The barn portion of the house was lumber from the first town hall in 1839 and became part of the Jones House.

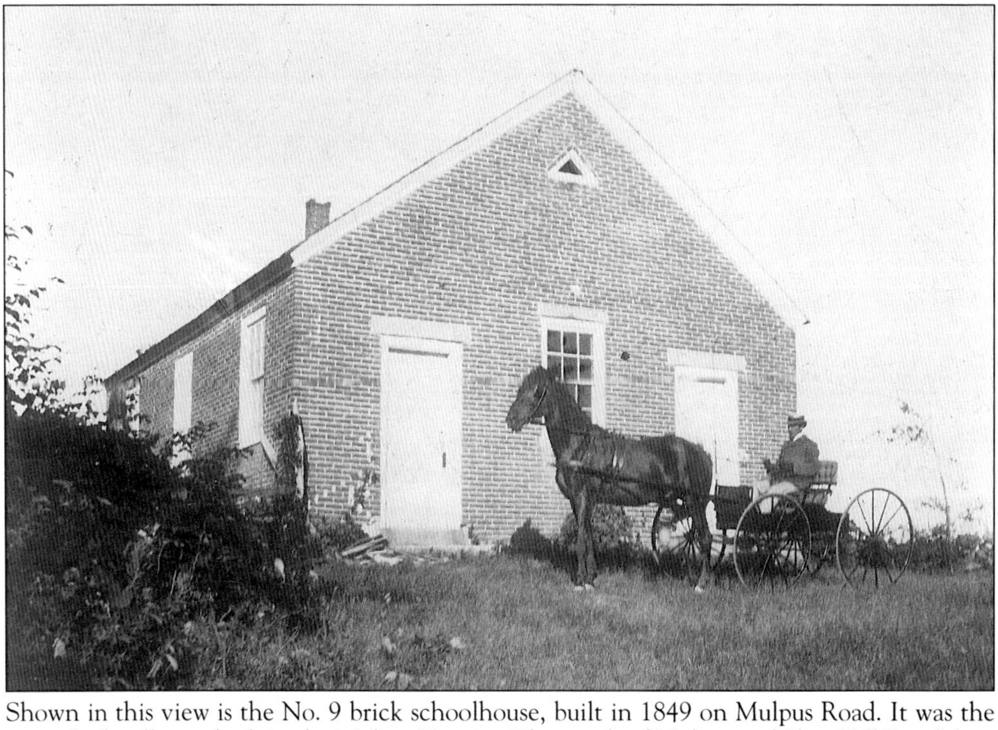

Shown in this view is the No. 9 brick schoolhouse, built in 1849 on Mulpus Road. It was the second schoolhouse built in the Mulpus District. The pupils of Mulpus and Flatt Hill Road then went to a building off Massachusetts Avenue called new No. 7 until the Center School was built in 1892. This school building was sold to Luther E. Lane for $45.

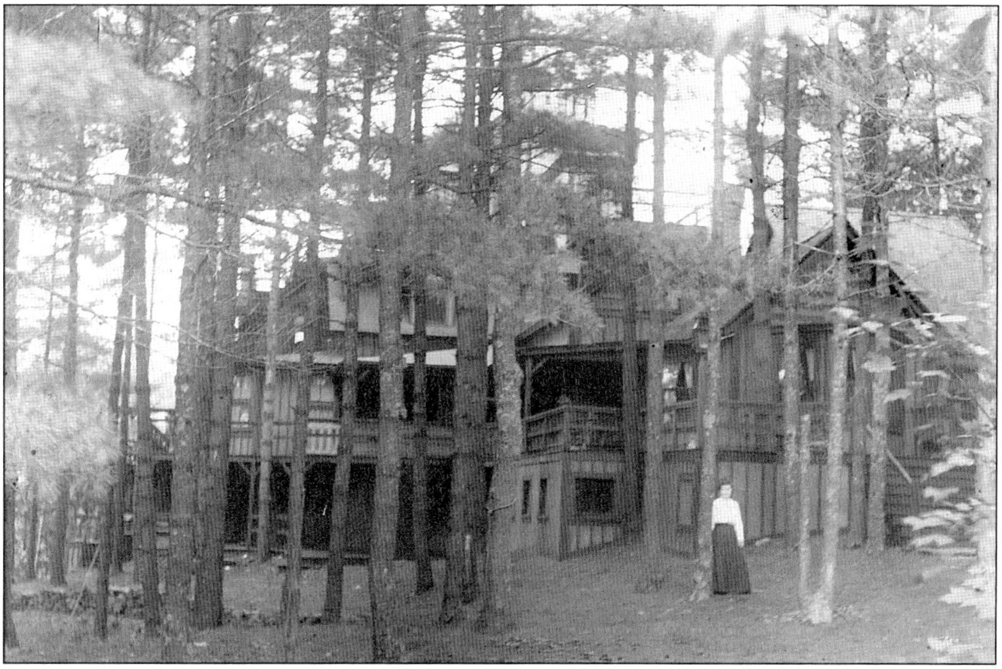

Benjamin S. Pray had a three-room cottage on Page Street. As he became more and more wealthy, he designed and built it into a "castle" that eventually had 14 rooms with tower and turrets and a room built around a tree. The house, named "Castle Kitt," burned and was totally destroyed in the spring of 1908, when a kerosene lamp was carelessly dropped.

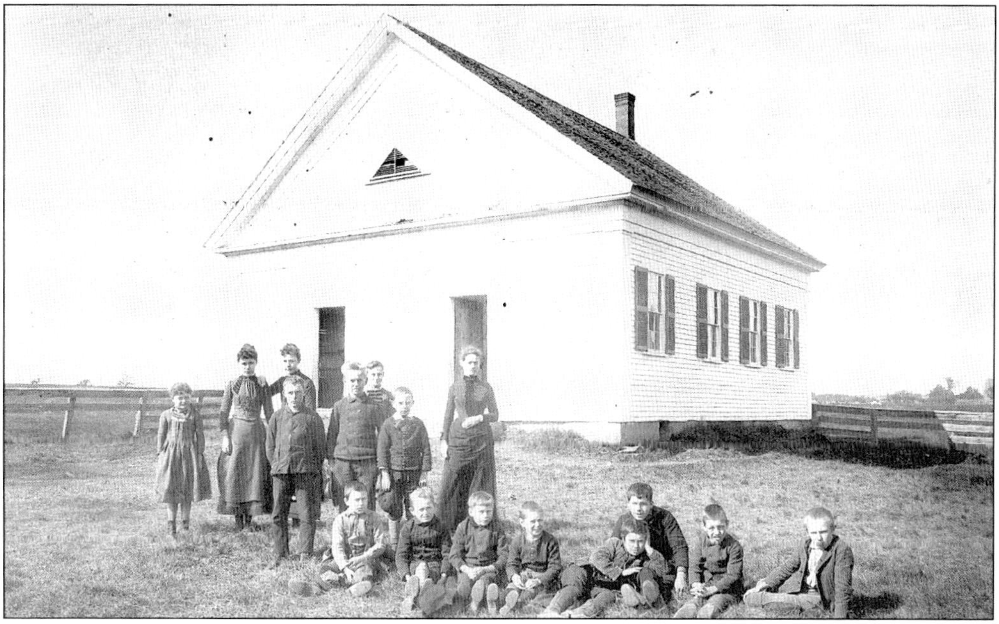

This is the Farwell School in District No. 7, located on the corner of Oak Avenue and Northfield Road. This building, the second to occupy the site, was built in 1852. It was the first school in town furnished with modern seats and desks and properly supplied with blackboards. It was moved in 1895 to Massachusetts Avenue.

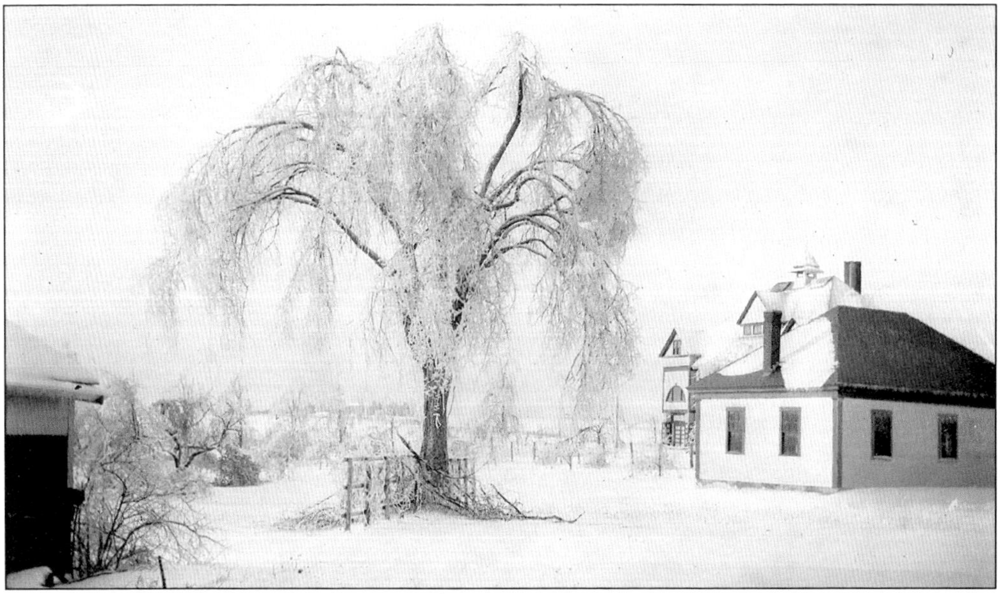

The town voted in 1783 to appropriate $500 to build five different schools. As far as can be determined, the No. 2 school was one of the five. No. 2 was built at the corner of Goodrich Street and Lancaster Avenue. The upper photograph shows the third No. 2 school. In 1869, this school was purchased by the town for $750.95. The school was then moved to the center of town and remodeled as our first fire station. In the bottom photograph, we see how garage doors were installed. In years following, it was raised up and additions were added in front and below. In the back portion of our present station is the portion of the original school.

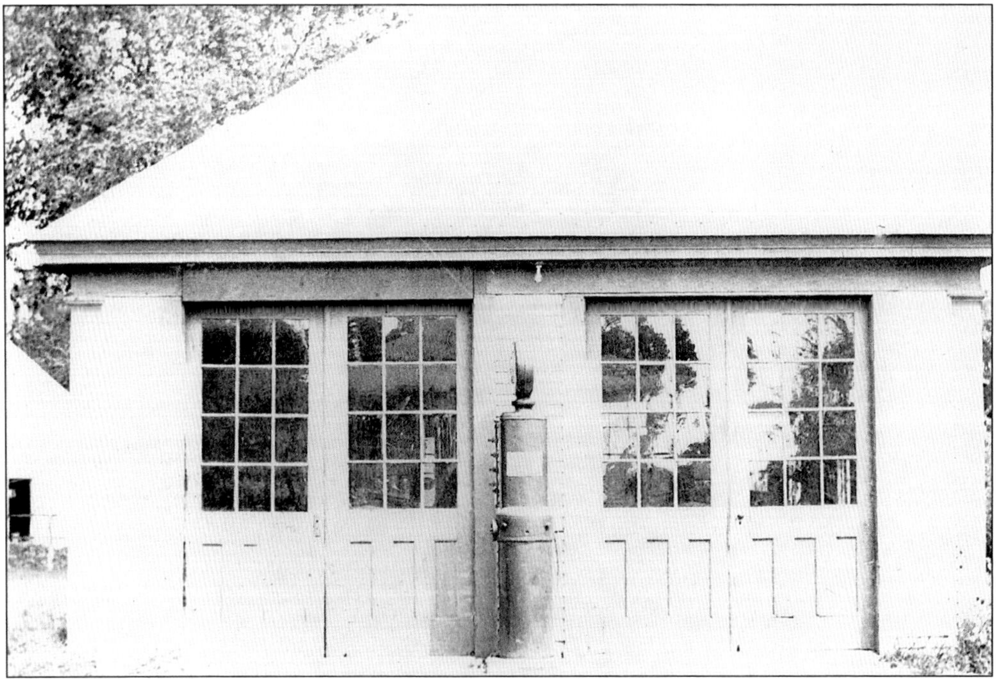

Two

OUR CITIZENS

Lunenburg has been home to many interesting and notable residents over the years. Some were born, raised, and died here, while others shared their lives with us for a short period. All have, in some way or another, made important contributions to our history.

Samuel Page (1672–1747), known as "Governor," was our first settler. He was in the party for the original survey of Lunenburg and was one of the town's first selectmen. Benjamin Bellows II (1712–1777) held many offices in town: constable, school committee member, and town clerk. He rose through the ranks in the Revolutionary War and became brigadier general. Cyrus Kilburn (1800–1882) was a teacher for 20 years and the surveyor famous for the 1833 map of Lunenburg. Col. Edmund Cushing (1774–1851) held positions of treasurer, clerk, selectman, first postmaster of our town, state representative, presidential elector, state senator, and lieutenant colonel. Judge Luther Stearns Cushing (1803–1856) authored *Cushing's Manual of Parliamentary Rules* (used in Lunenburg's town meetings) and several other law books. He served in Boston on the Court of Common Pleas and reported Massachusetts Supreme Court decisions. Luther Burbank developed his famous white rose potato off Main Street. George S. Boutwell served as governor of Massachusetts. George Treat Paine signed the Declaration of Independence. This is only a limited list of notable citizens to whom Lunenburg owes its debt of gratitude.

"Our Citizens" also recognizes bands, church groups, clubs, sports groups, prominent portraits, school classes, and veterans of different wars.

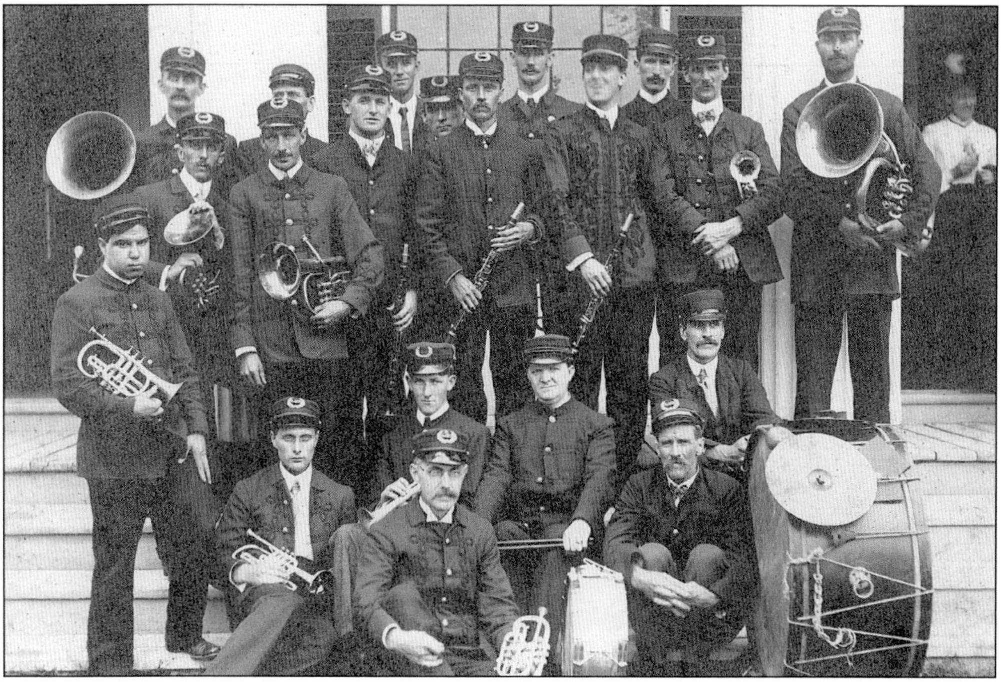

The Lunenburg Military Band, consisting of 17 men (including their leader, George Riley), was formed on January 6, 1900. In 1905, the band was part of the dedication ceremonies for a new bandstand on the upper common. They also gave a supper and concert in the town hall. Supper was 25¢, and admission was 15¢ for adults and 15¢ for children.

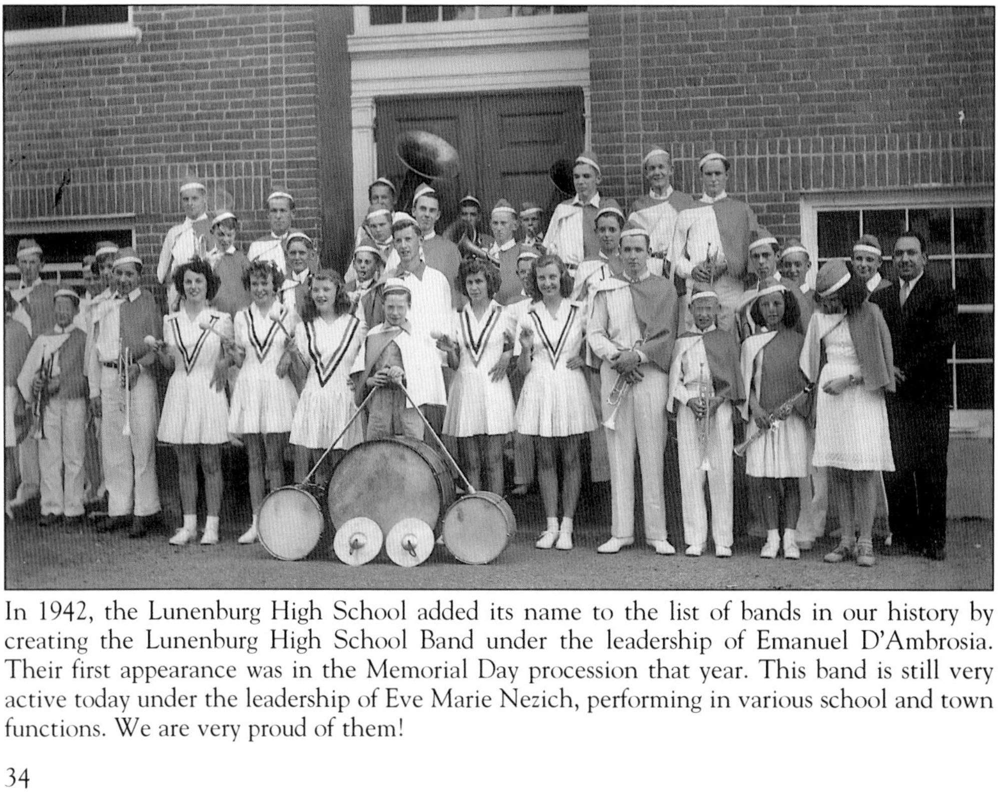

In 1942, the Lunenburg High School added its name to the list of bands in our history by creating the Lunenburg High School Band under the leadership of Emanuel D'Ambrosia. Their first appearance was in the Memorial Day procession that year. This band is still very active today under the leadership of Eve Marie Nezich, performing in various school and town functions. We are very proud of them!

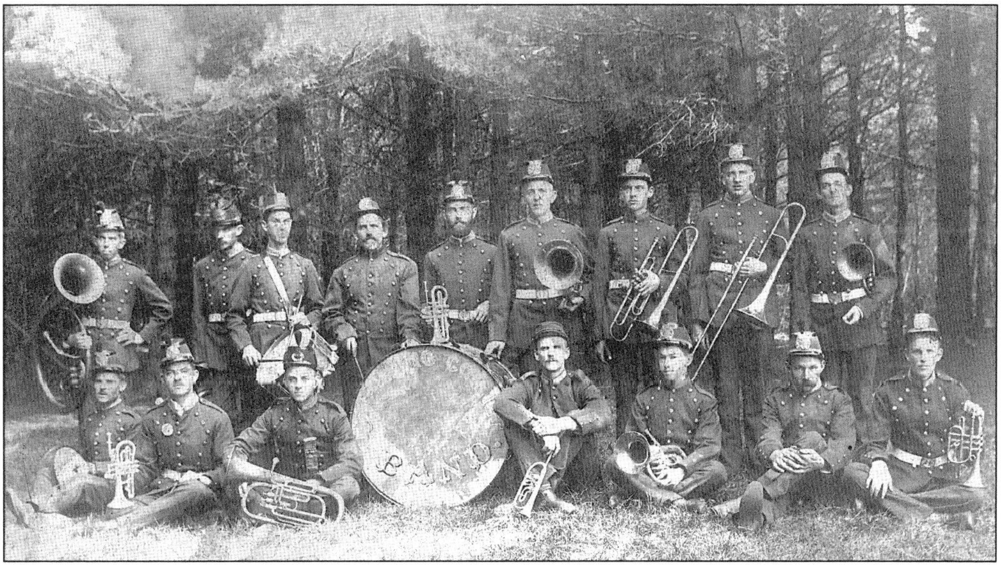

Everyone loves a band, and Lunenburg is no exception. Our first band was formed in 1884 and called the Lunenburg Cornet Band. It was organized by Alden Wilbur Lancey and even had its own bandstand near the intersection of Flat Hill Road, the "Lane," and Elmwood Road. It was composed of the best musicians in the surrounding towns. Their first new uniforms were worn in 1889 at the Memorial Day procession.

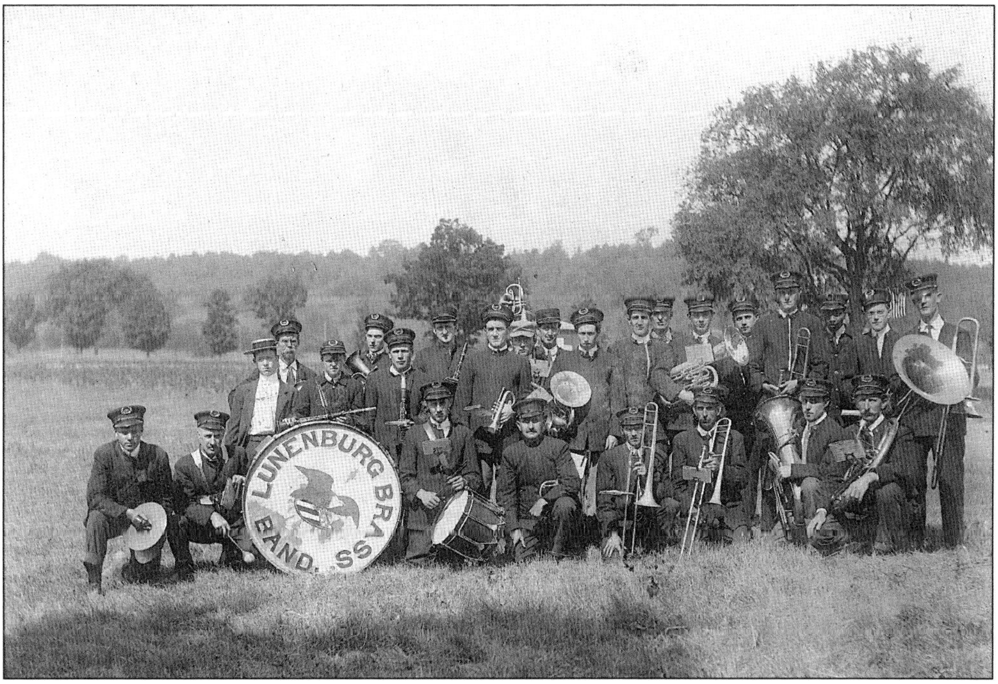

For a short period of time, Lunenburg had two bands. The second band, named the Lunenburg Brass Band, was organized in 1897 with G.E. Clark as its leader. The band's first performance was at the town hall, featuring jigs and reels. This band was known for its distinctive bright-red uniforms with brass buttons. When James Gilchrest was its leader, the band practiced in his sawmill on Highland Street.

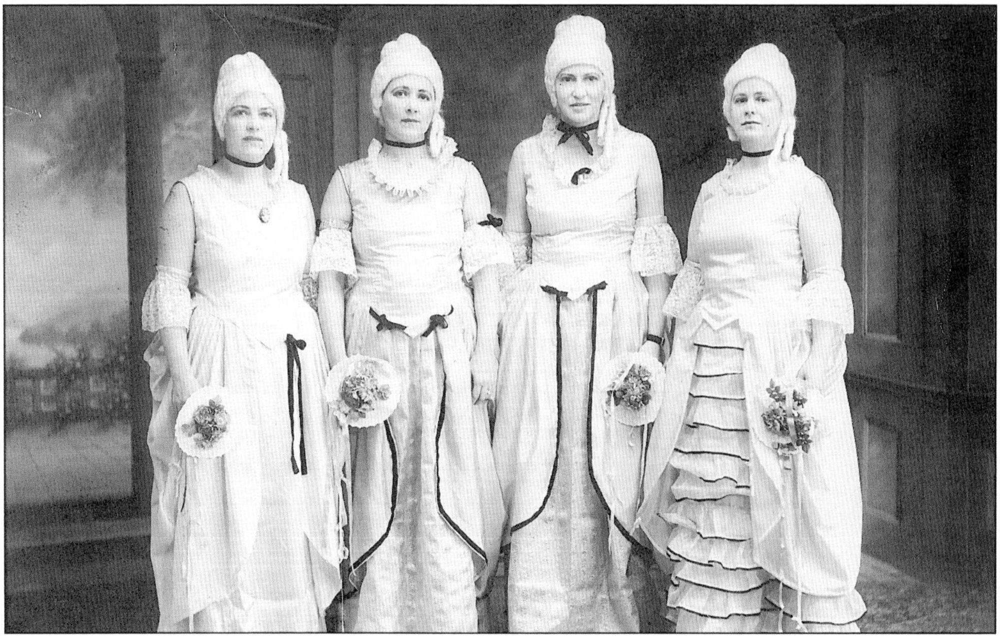

The Woman's Club of Lunenburg presented the Martha Washington Quartet. This February 20, 1932 photograph shows the quartet appropriately dressed for the period of history they represent. The Colonial ladies, from left to right, are Capitola Willard, Hazel Hadd, Dorothy Churchill, and Eleanor Murchie. The Woman's Club of Lunenburg has provided many great services to our town over the years.

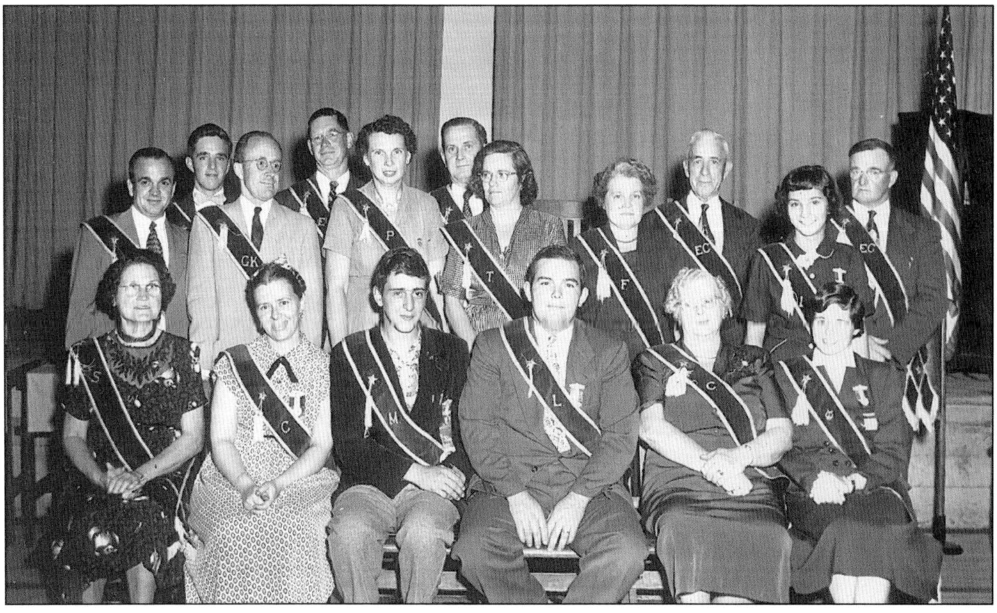

Many Lunenburg residents were active in the Grange. Individual Granges are part of the National Fraternal Organization, whose purpose is to aid and assist the rural farmer. Annual Grange fairs, and a variety of entertaining and social programs, were sponsored by Lunenburg's Grange No. 169. These programs were always well attended. This photograph shows the officers of the Lunenburg Grange in 1953.

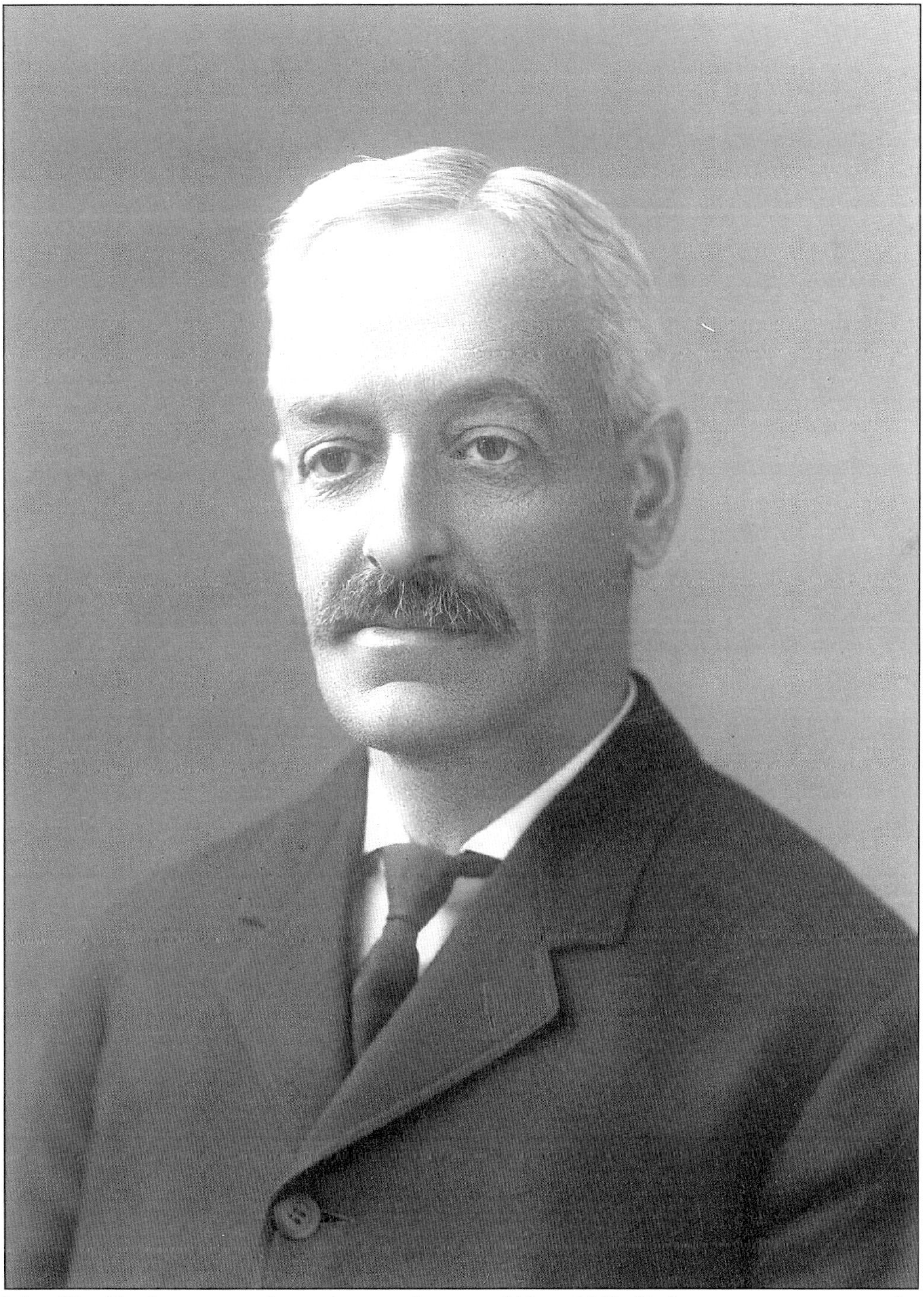

John Wooldredge came to Lunenburg at the age of 19 in 1869. He became prominent in the social, political, and official life in Lunenburg. He lived to celebrate his 95th birthday. He was a trustee of the town library for 43 years, selectman for 17 years, assessor, overseer of the poor, member of the Lunenburg Board of Health, and town auditor. He became an authority of Lunenburg's history. He died in 1945.

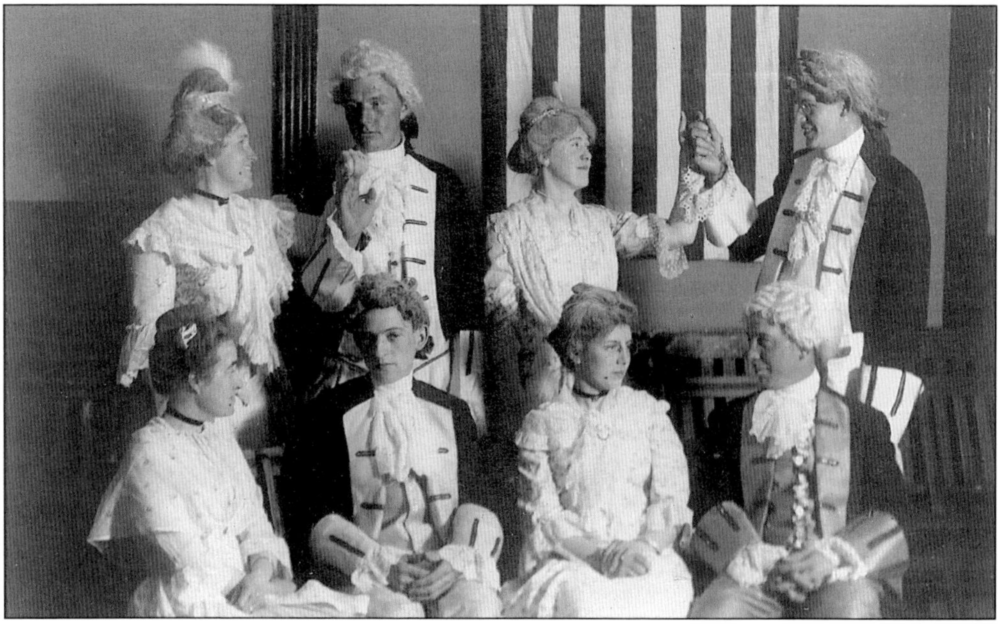

The Lunenburg Grange was, in the mid-20th century, an active organization and sponsored many colorful and entertaining social events. Here, on February 24, 1915, are some talented members of the Grange costumed as minuet dancers at a Colonial party. The dancers are, from left to right, as follows: (front row) Mrs. E.C. Smith, H. Carr, P. Cass, and H. Whitcomb; (back row) Mrs. F. Francis, R. Hoisington, Ms. B. Lancey, and E.C. Smith.

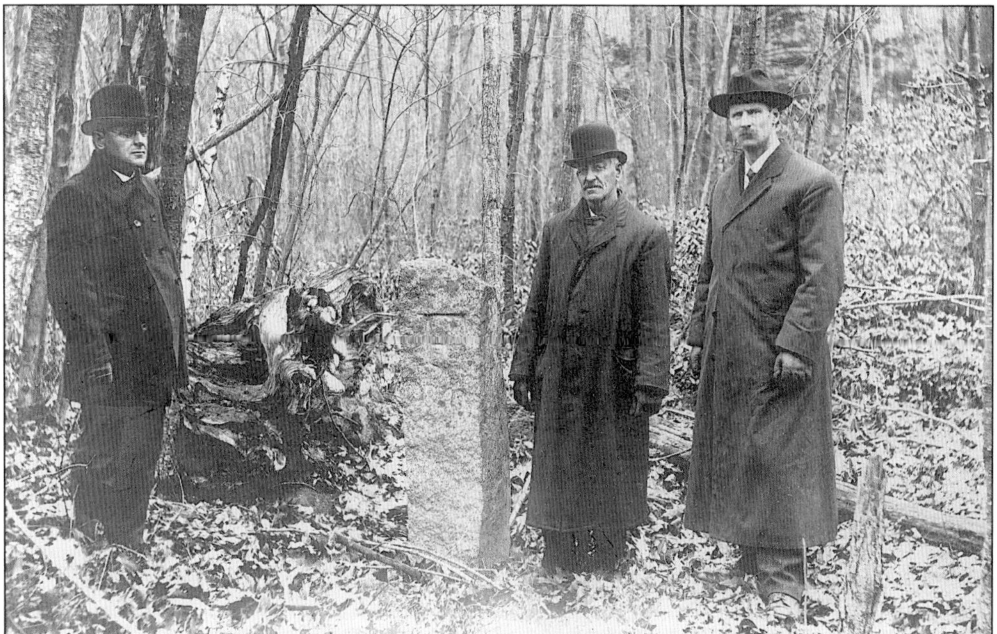

In this c. 1913 photograph, the Lunenburg Board of Selectmen is fulfilling its role of fence viewing, one of the board's duties at that time. They are "inspecting the bound between Lunenburg and Fitchburg on the West Townsend Road." Their attire suggests the time of the season. From left to right are George Williams, John Wooldredge, and Ernest K. Proctor.

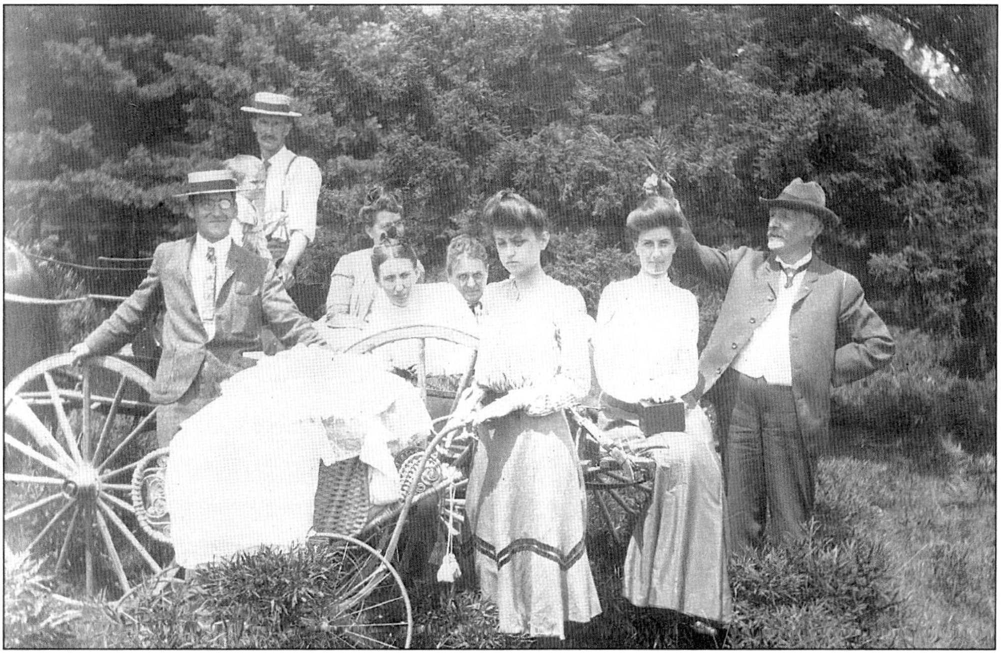

Thanks to the Rodney Brown family, we are able to witness the Brown and Litchfield families enjoying a picnic in 1905. The summer gathering joined three generations of the Litchfields and Browns, including the newest member of the family, seen with his wicker baby carriage. This picnic took place on the side yard of the Litchfield property, located at the intersection of Massachusetts Avenue and Chestnut Street.

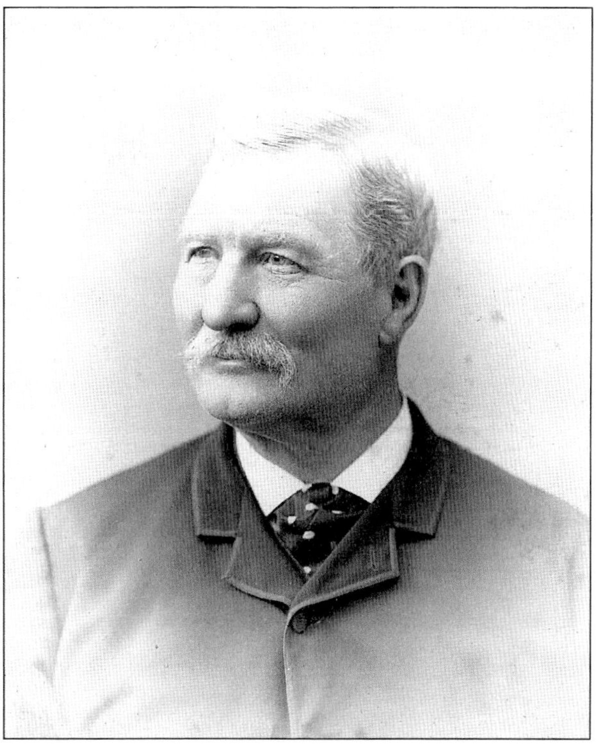

Charles Artemus Goodrich was the great-grandson of one of our early proprietors, Philip Goodrich. Charles attended the Lunenburg Academy and, at 17, became a teacher allied with the educational interests of our town. He also served as selectman, assessor, justice of the peace, notary public, and overseer of the poor. He lived in a section of town known as "Goodrichville" with four other Goodrich families.

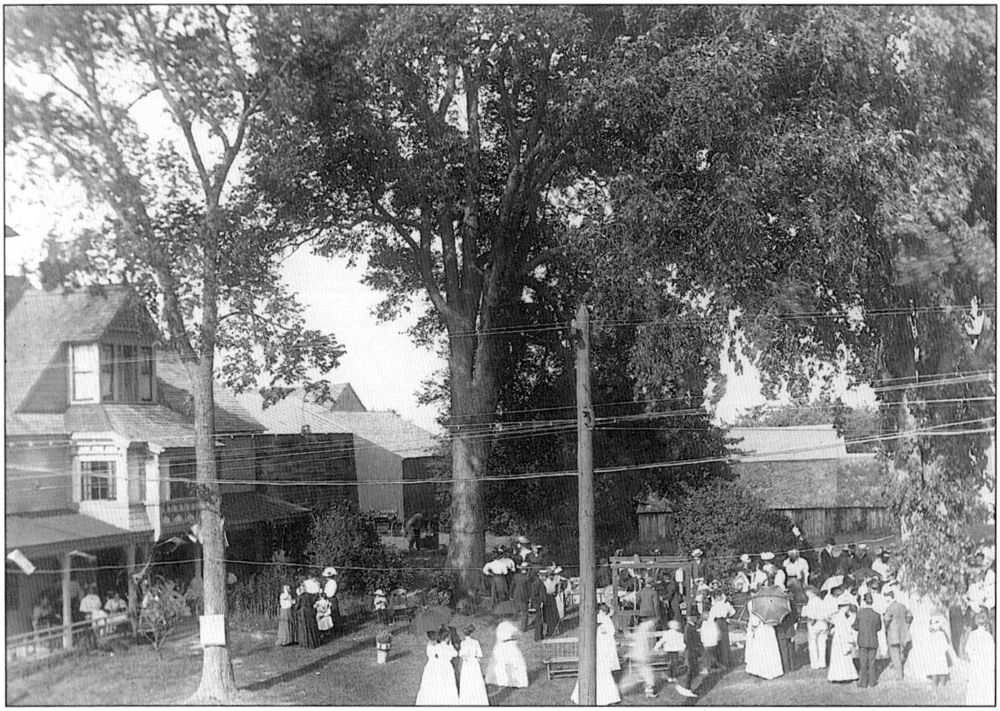

The Lunenburg Farmer's Club was gathered here on a lawn between the Eagle House and the Congregational church, now the corner of Main Street and Memorial Drive. Formed in 1848, the group was the first town organization in the country with the purpose of promoting agriculture. The club ceased activity sometime during or after the Civil War. In 1895, all club property was donated to the Lunenburg Grange No. 169. The photograph below was taken on the same day but slightly to the right, so the entire view would be available for the club.

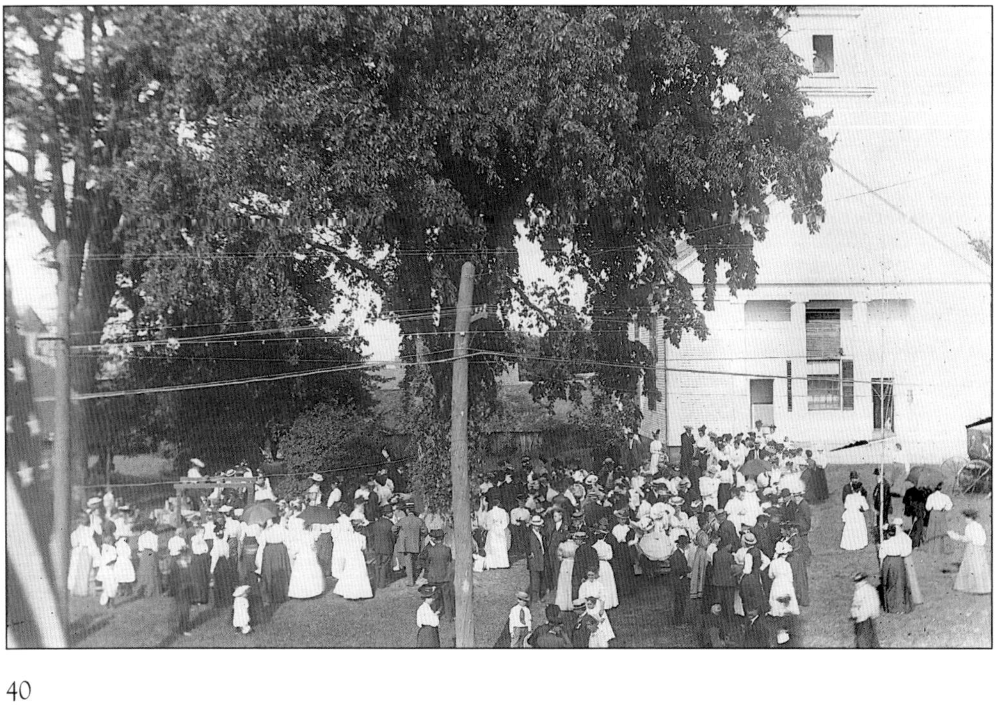

In 1920, next to his home at 906 Massachusetts Avenue, dapper Carl E. Brown poses in his fashionable raccoon coat. This gentleman always greeted Lunenburg folks with a smile in "his" post office. He served as postmaster for 30 years. First appointed by President Wilson in 1915, reappointed by Presidents Harding, Coolidge, Hoover, and Roosevelt, until the civil service system changed this requirement in 1939.

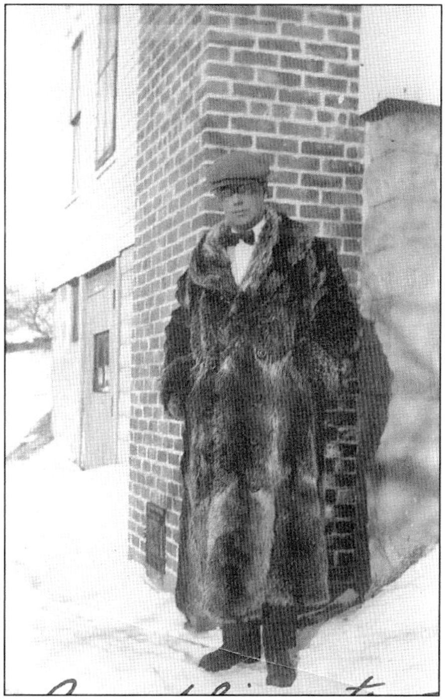

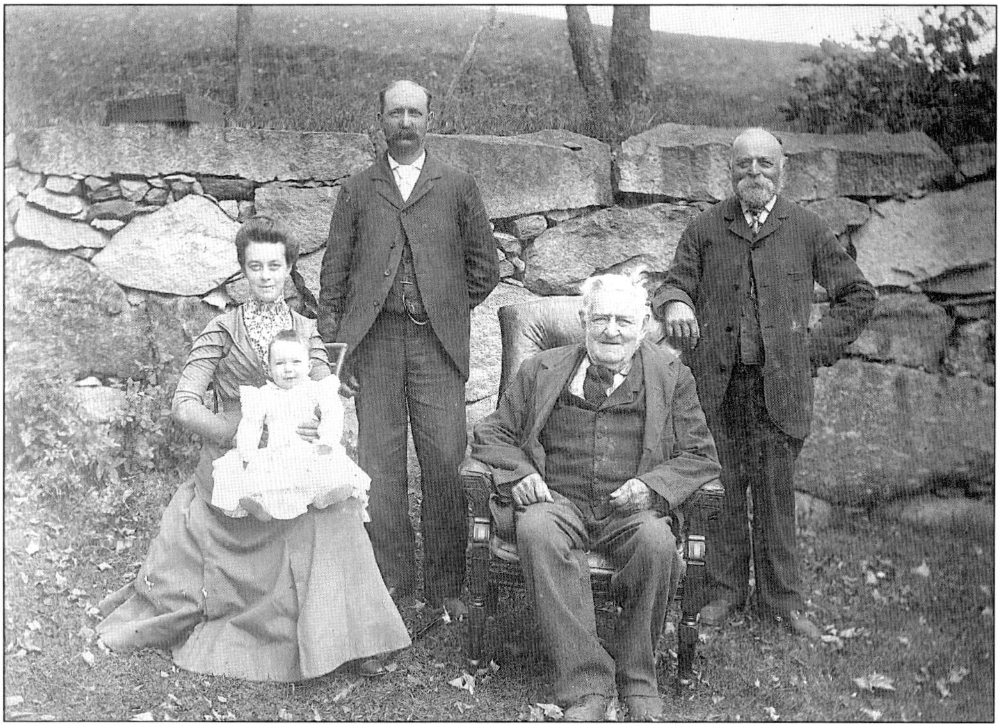

This picture, taken on October 3, 1901, shows five generations of the Cook family. From left to right are the following: (front row) Lena (Cook) True, Dorothy Cook True (five months old), and Abel Cook (94 years old); (back row) Henry Albert Cook and George Albert Cook. The Cook name is a familiar one throughout the history of Lunenburg.

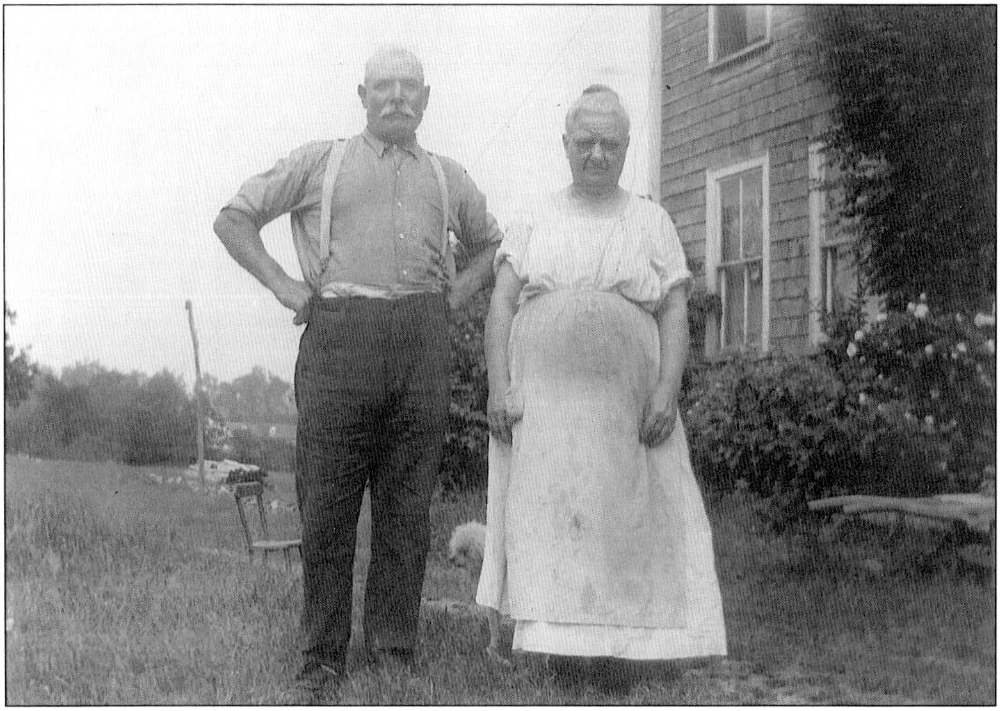

This photograph shows Frank Wornham and wife Hester Brown Wornham, who lived in one section of a Dickinson family house located on Holman Street. Both worked for Arnold Dickinson on Northfield Road for several years. On November 2, 1912, they bought this property from the Dickinsons. On November 4, 1912, the Wornhams transferred the property to Susan Dickinson. (Courtesy of Martha S. Bradshaw.)

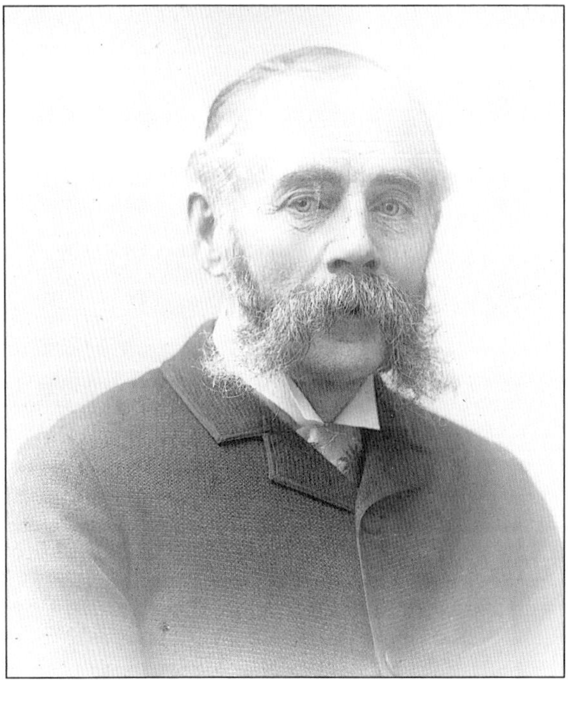

Charles Gates Bigelow was born in Paxton in 1839. He served in the Civil War for three years. Mary Jane Goodrich of Lunenburg became his wife and, in 1886, they moved into a farm at 991 Lancaster Avenue, now the Stillman Farm. Bigelow was made a deacon of the Congregational church for life and was highly regarded by the townspeople.

Most photographs of Margaret Proctor as a young woman are action shots, showing her involved in one of her many athletic endeavors. However, this photograph from one of the Proctor family albums given to the Lunenburg Historical Society shows a quiet side of the young athlete, who became a teacher, a legendary coach, historian, and wife of another well-known Lunenburg citizen, Harold Harley.

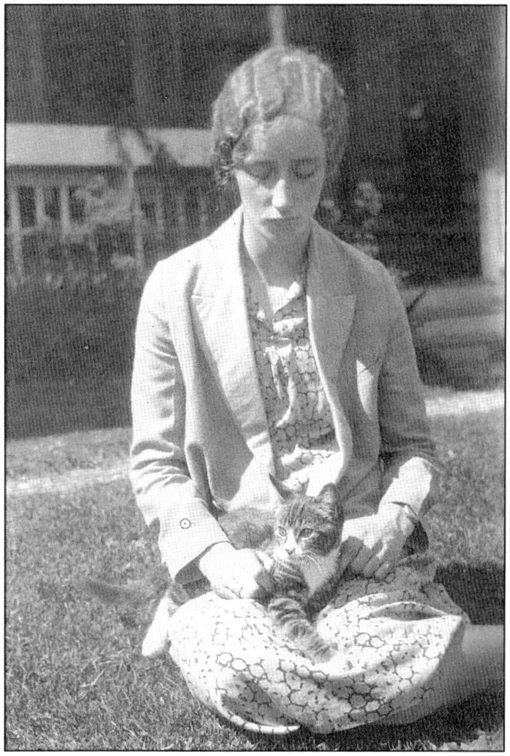

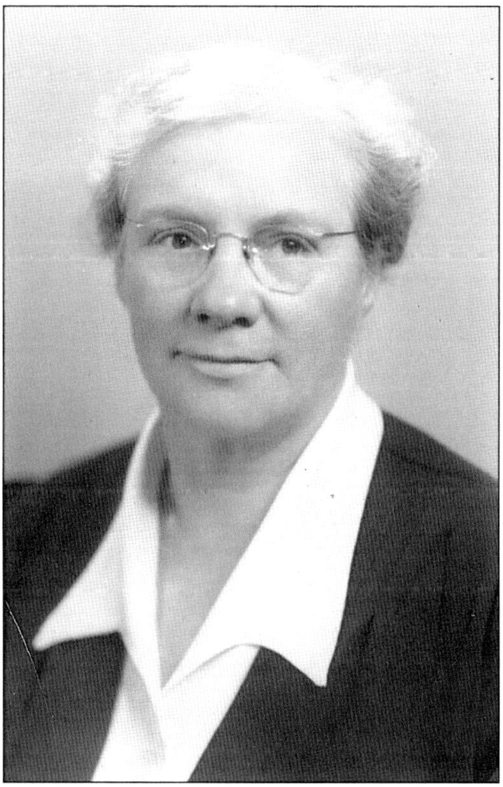

Margaret Allmanritter Fiske taught school for 50 years. Graduating from Boston University in 1908, she continued her studies in Mexico, France, and Canada. She came to Lunenburg's high school in 1935, becoming a highly respected teacher. After her death in 1968, an annual M.A. Fiske Award was established in her memory for the Lunenburg student showing the greatest improvement in English.

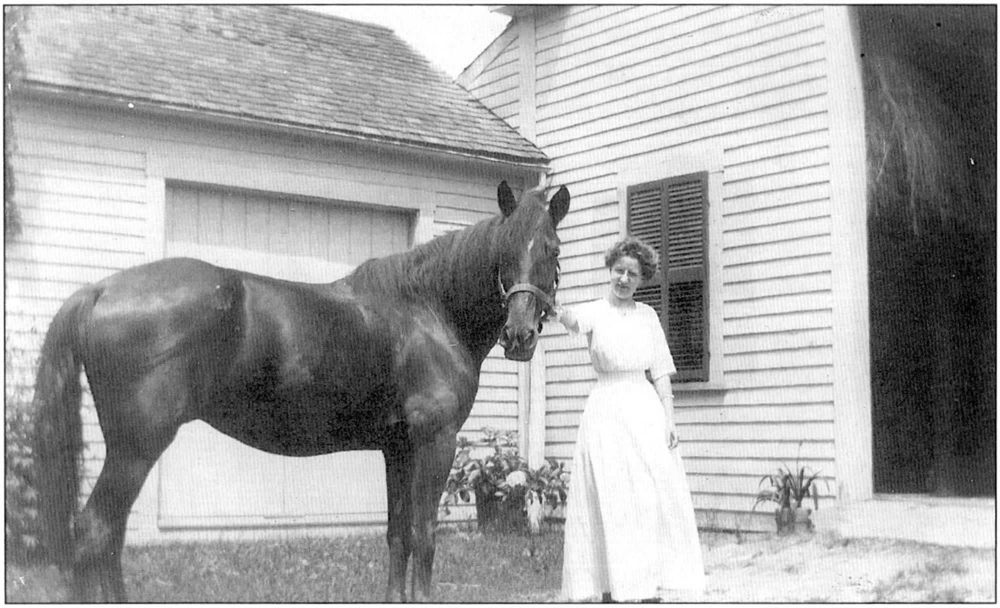

Ruth Evelyn Goodrich was born in Lunenburg in 1888 in the Bellows house. When she was two years old, her father built the house at 42 Highland Street, where she continued to live until her death in 1973. A 1905 graduate of Lunenburg High School, she went on to college and became a teacher. She taught for 17 years in various town districts. Ruth Goodrich is pictured here with her horse in 1910.

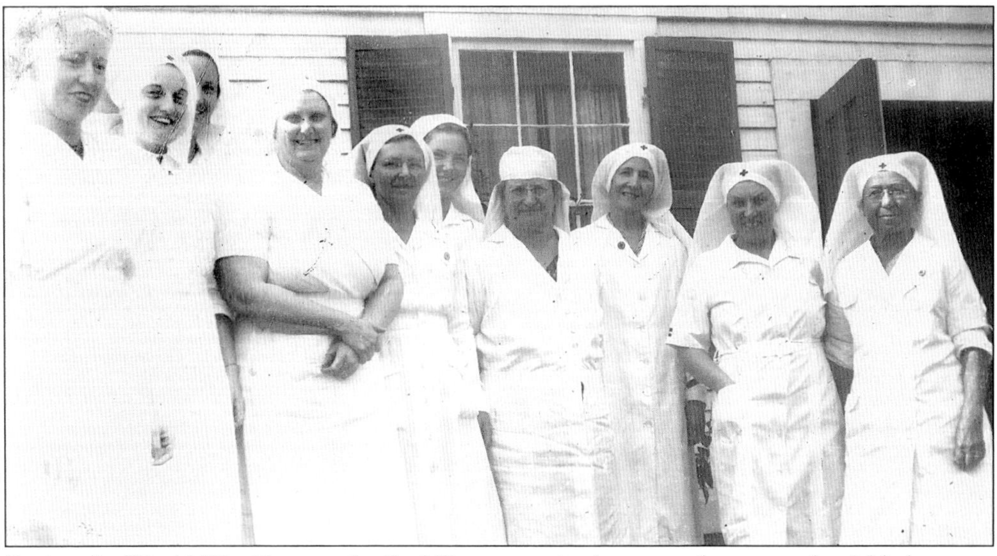

During the World War II years, the Red Cross organized groups of women who folded squares of gauze into surgical dressings for the armed forces. These Lunenburg women, along with a few Girl Scouts, worked weekly at the Center School, the Congregational church vestry, or in private homes. Pictured from left to right are unidentified, Ruth Jowders, unidentified, Mrs. Lawrence Gale, Mrs. Clifford Hague, Betty Hidden, Mrs. Donald Frazier, Mabel Eaton, Mrs. Val Huntington, and Ella Luke.

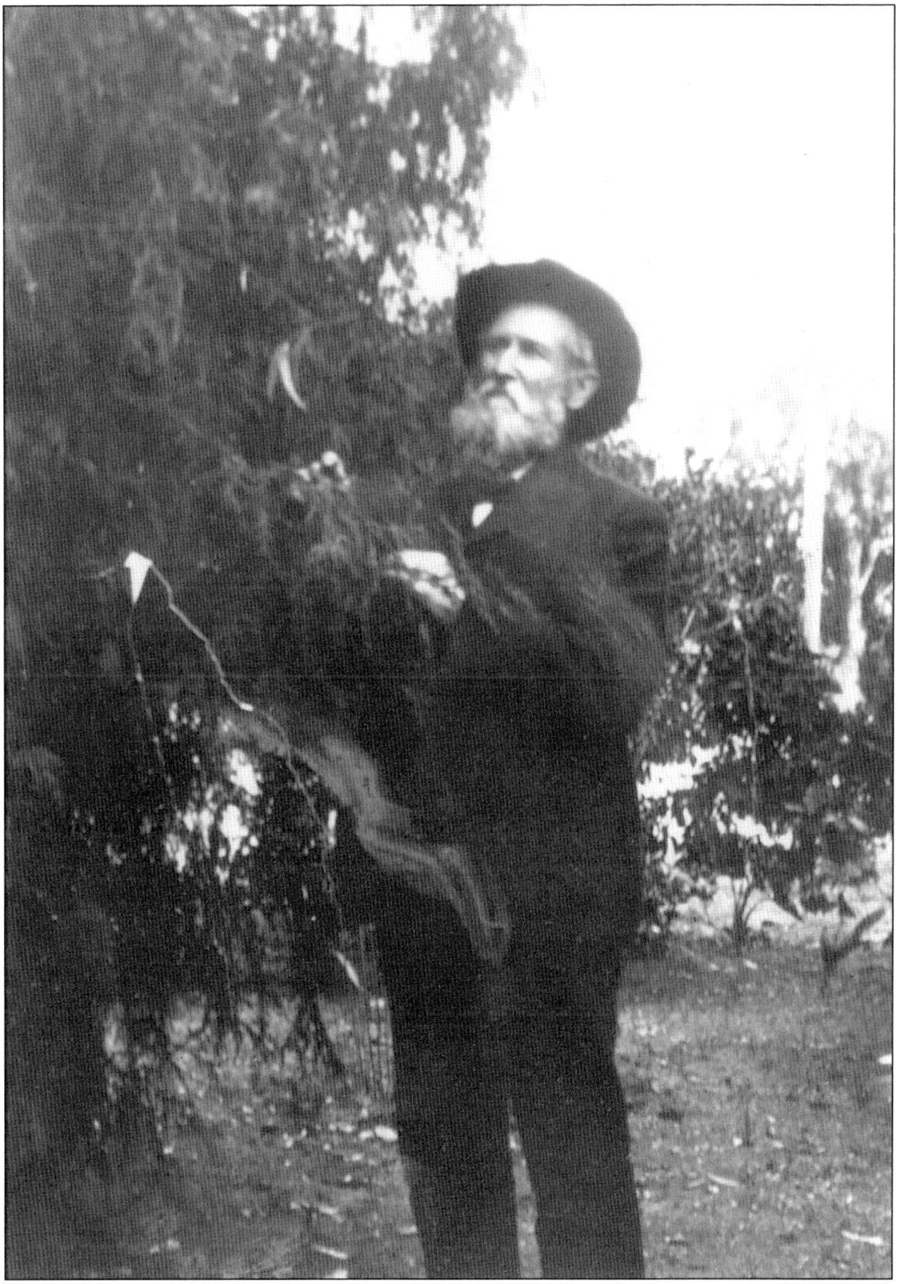

Foster Ellenborough Lascellas Beal always considered himself a resident of Lunenburg despite his travels and various positions held in other places. He maintained a home on Beal Street, where this photograph was taken. Beal Street still bears his name. He was a graduate of MIT and later instructed mathematics there. He was a veteran of the Civil War. His specialties included economics and ornithology. Several books on wildlife were written by him, proving the usefulness of birds and leading to state and federal laws to protect them. He was appointed to the Iowa Agricultural College as a professor of geology, civil engineering, and zoology. In 1891, he became associated with the Iowa Agricultural College Department of Agriculture. Beal passed away in 1916.

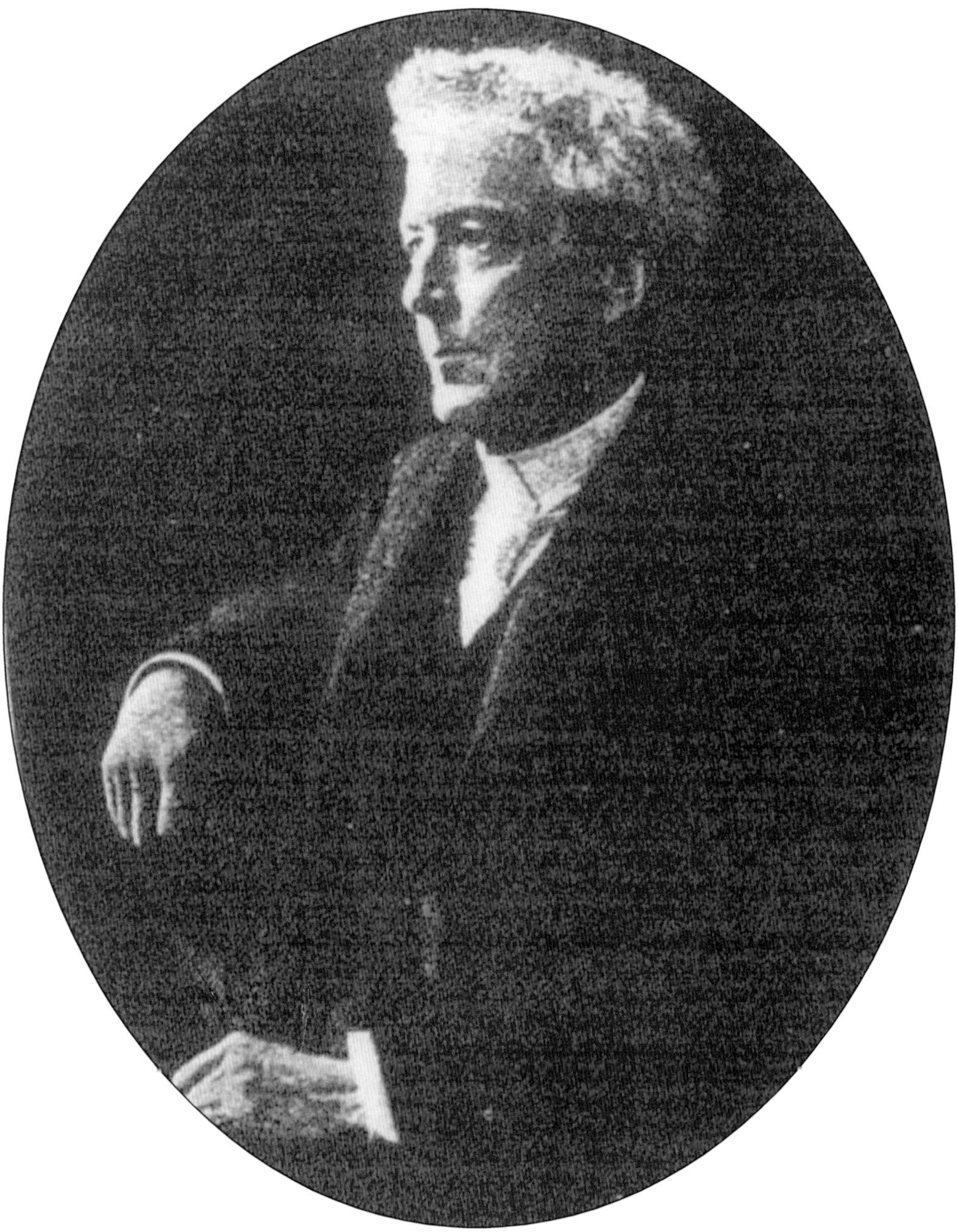

One former Lunenburg resident who made the Hall of Fame for Great Americans was Luther Burbank, shown here. He lived here from 1872 to 1875 in the Jones house at 42 Main Street. While attending the Lunenburg Academy, Burbank met the teacher who was most influential in starting him on his career—J.J.H. Gregory. While living in Lunenburg, Burbank developed his white rose potato in back of his house on Main Street. He later sold the seed potato to Gregory and obtained the money needed to go to California, where he later became a famous naturalist. Although Burbank resided in Lunenburg for a short time, we are still proud to acknowledge that his potato was developed here in our good soil and gave him the start he needed to become world famous in the field of horticulture.

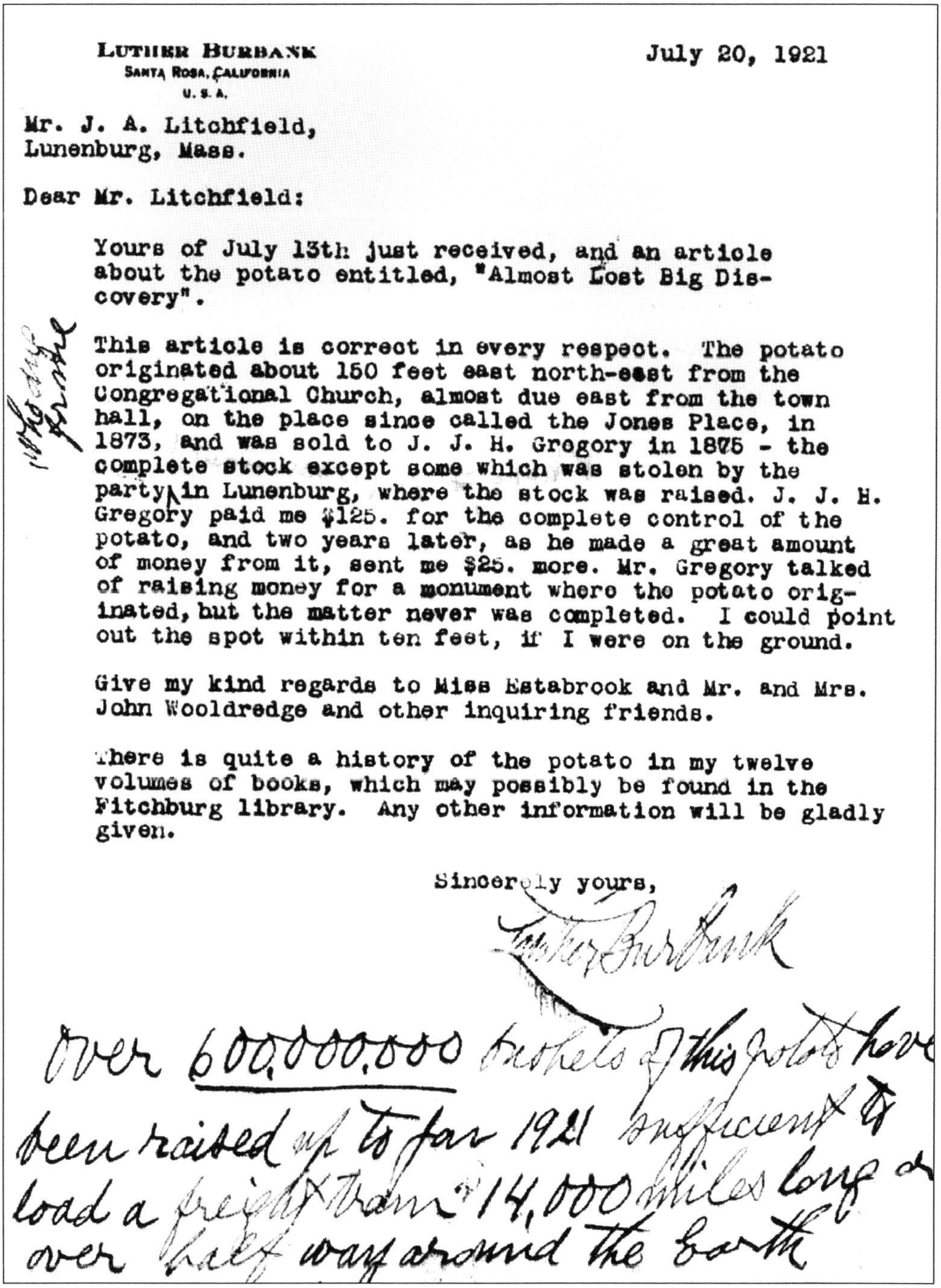

LUTHER BURBANK
SANTA ROSA, CALIFORNIA
U. S. A.

July 20, 1921

Mr. J. A. Litchfield,
Lunenburg, Mass.

Dear Mr. Litchfield:

Yours of July 13th just received, and an article about the potato entitled, "Almost Lost Big Discovery".

This article is correct in every respect. The potato originated about 150 feet east north-east from the Congregational Church, almost due east from the town hall, on the place since called the Jones Place, in 1873, and was sold to J. J. H. Gregory in 1875 - the complete stock except some which was stolen by the party in Lunenburg, where the stock was raised. J. J. H. Gregory paid me $125. for the complete control of the potato, and two years later, as he made a great amount of money from it, sent me $25. more. Mr. Gregory talked of raising money for a monument where the potato originated, but the matter never was completed. I could point out the spot within ten feet, if I were on the ground.

Give my kind regards to Miss Estabrook and Mr. and Mrs. John Wooldredge and other inquiring friends.

There is quite a history of the potato in my twelve volumes of books, which may possibly be found in the Fitchburg library. Any other information will be gladly given.

Sincerely yours,

Luther Burbank

Over 600,000,000 bushels of this potato have been raised up to far 1921 sufficient to load a freight train 14,000 miles long or over half way around the earth

This letter from Luther Burbank is a personal one to John A. Litchfield of Lunenburg from Burbank's home in California. Both gentlemen became good friends when Burbank was living in Lunenburg. This friendship continued over the years.

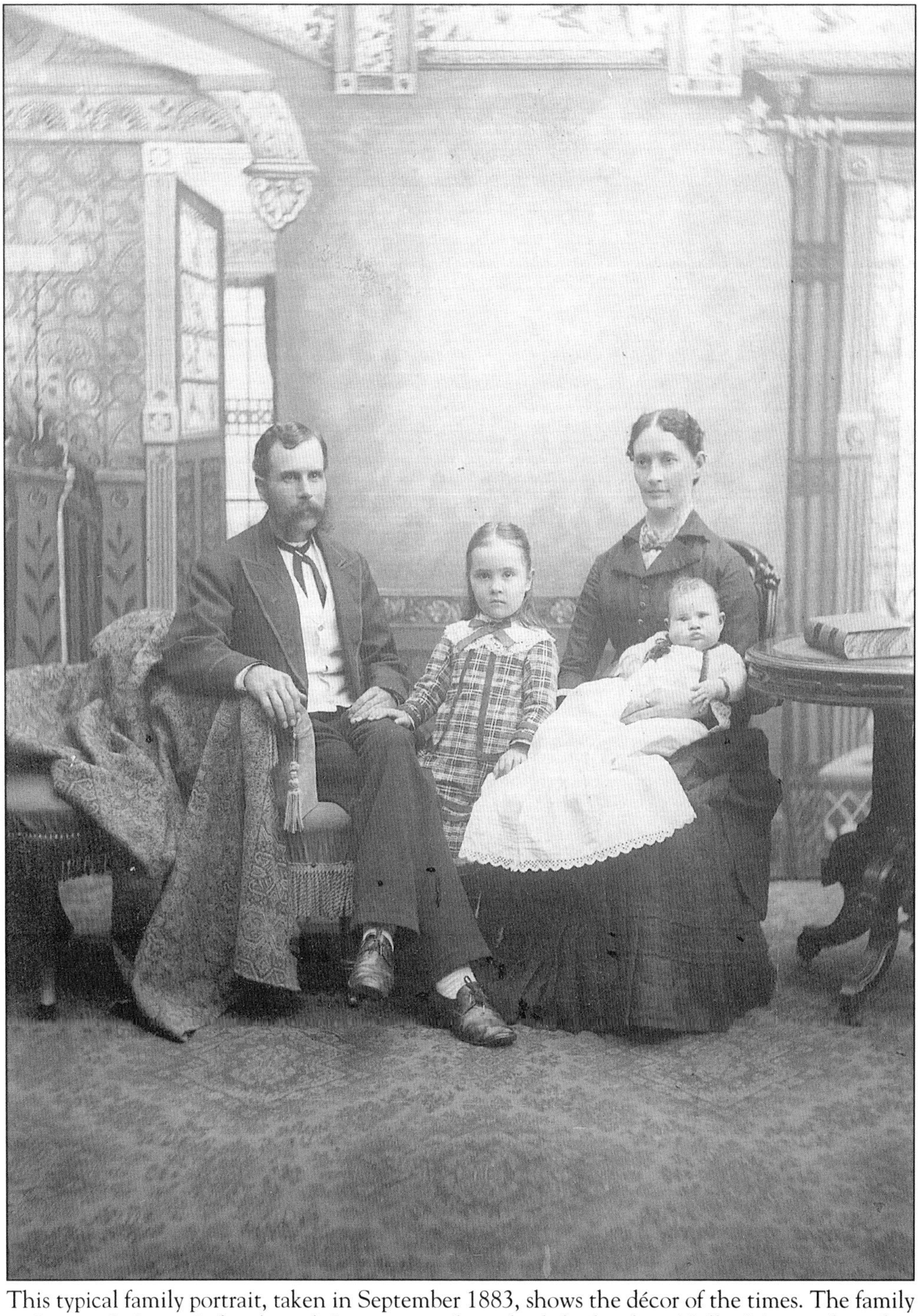

This typical family portrait, taken in September 1883, shows the décor of the times. The family is George C. Jewett's family with Jewett seated on the left, daughter Nellie May, and mother Julia Ann (Howard) Jewett holding baby Arthur. Jewett had served his time in the Civil War and was starting his family during the ensuing years of peace.

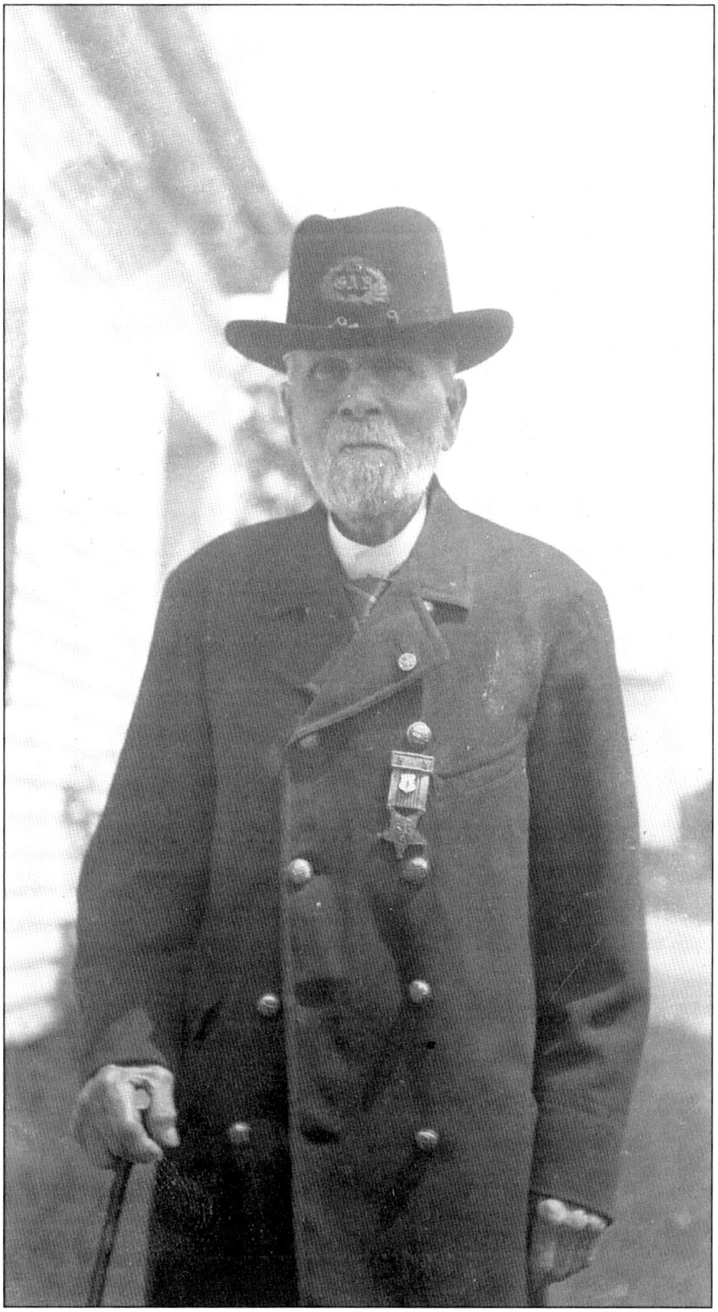

George C. Jewett was born in Lunenburg in 1846. He enlisted for one year in the Civil War. Jewett was the last surviving member in Lunenburg of the Grand Old Army of the Republic. He could be seen in uniform proudly marching in the Memorial Day and Fourth of July parades for many years. He also served as president of the Soldiers' Memorial Association for 44 years, beginning in 1893. Jewett, in 1925, designed a pattern for a tolling hammer for the Congregational church's bell. This addition made tolling the bell easier for those willing to take on the task. The hammer was cast by the Neely Bell Company of Troy, New York, at a cost of $15.75.

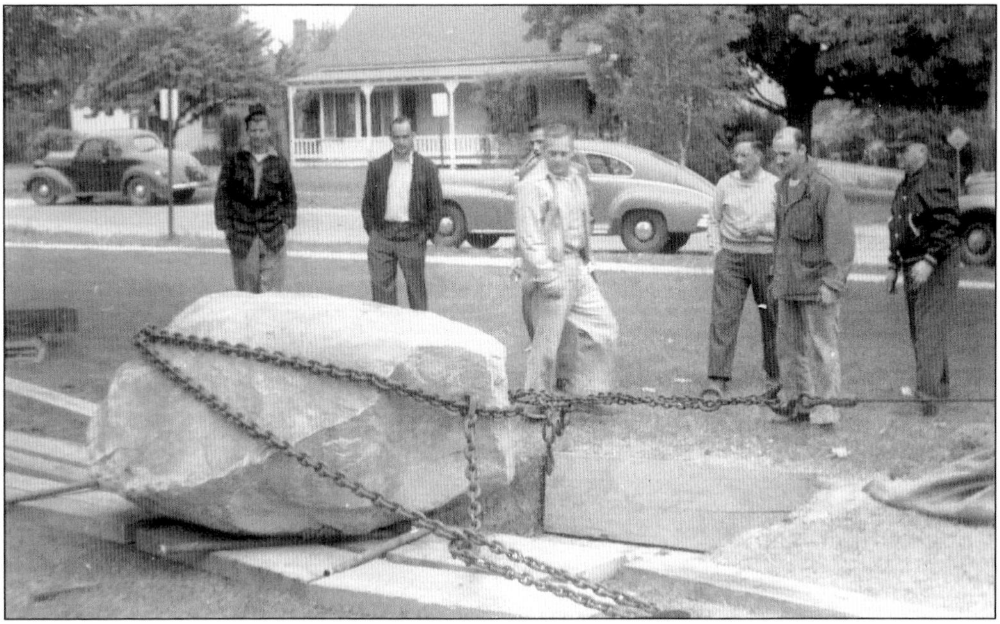

After World War II, Lunenburg dedicated a memorial to the men who gave their lives from 1941 to 1945. The above photograph shows some of the gentlemen present when the stone was dragged to its current site in front of the Ritter Memorial Library. The men in the picture are, from left to right, unidentified, Ray McIntyre, two unidentified, Ray Butterfield, Pat Latore, and Bill Deming. The memorial was dedicated on Memorial Day 1949. The bronze plaque in the lower photograph reads, "Lunenburg dedicated this tablet in memory of those who made the supreme sacrifice," and the 14 names are listed: Fredrick C. Cross Jr., Roderick S. Cross, Clarence A. Dyer, John W. Fortune Jr., Robert V. Gale, Kenneth C. Gove, Kauko K. Haapalainen, Alton Jones, Walter A. Monaghan, Jorma Palonen, Edwin Rill, Walter W. Rill, L. Fredrick Schultz, and Norman E. Tonseth.

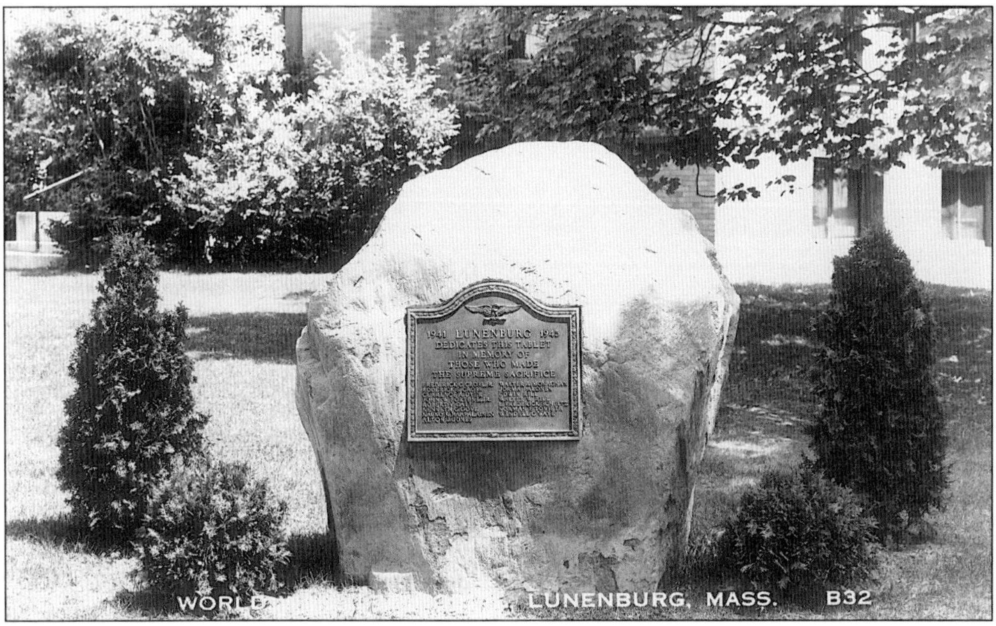

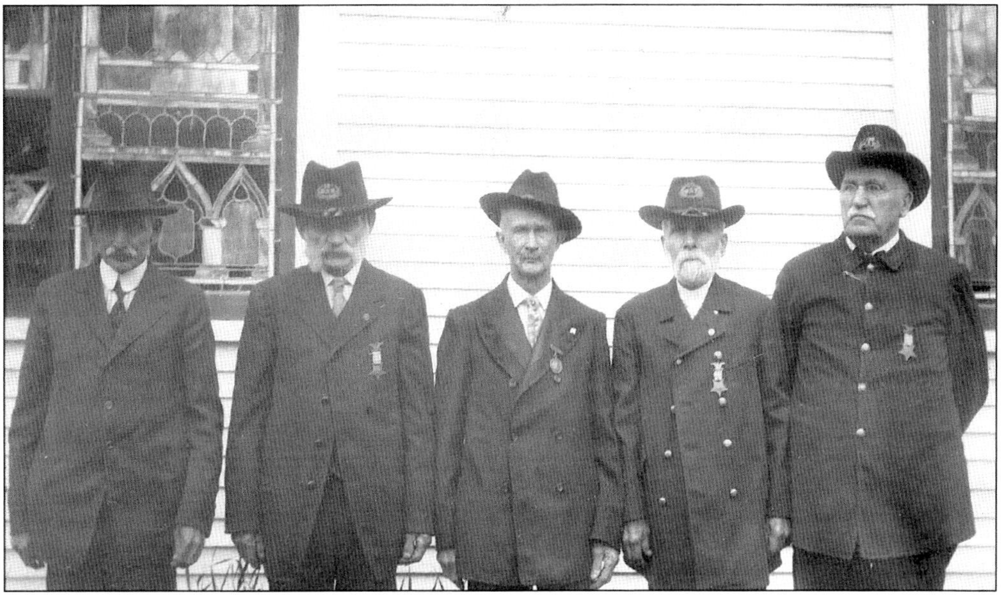

Some of Lunenburg's oldest surviving Civil War veterans, posing in front of the Methodist church, are, from left to right, Alfred Billings, Stillman Stone, John E. Lyons, George C. Jewett, and James A. Litchfield. The first man to enlist in the Civil War from Lunenburg was John E. Lyons. His patriotic fervor was so great he walked to Boston to sign up. Lunenburg has erected two marble memorial tablets (shown below) in the upper floor of the Lunenburg Town Hall. These tablets were carved by William F. York of Nashua, New Hampshire, and bear the names and regiments of those who enlisted in our country's defenses and gave their lives. These tablets remain in our Lunenburg Town Hall today in their honor and show our appreciation of their sacrifice. (Tablet photographs courtesy of Peter Lincoln.)

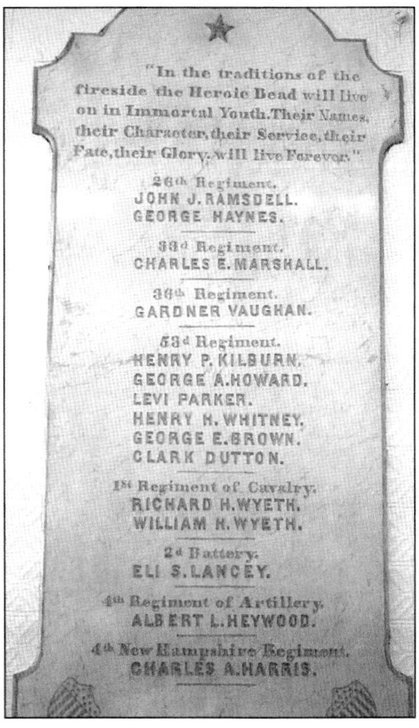

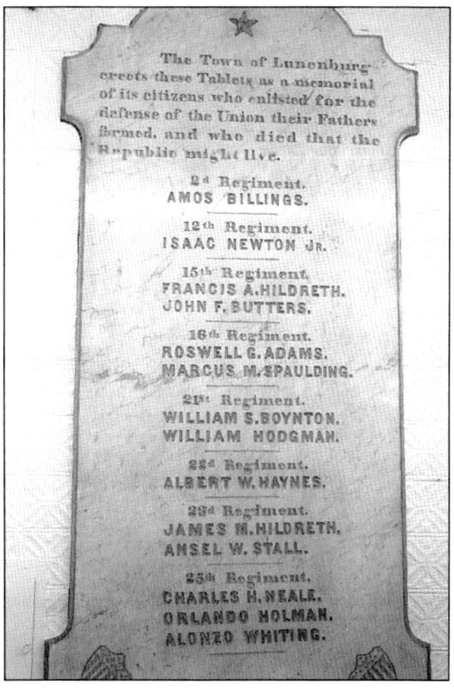

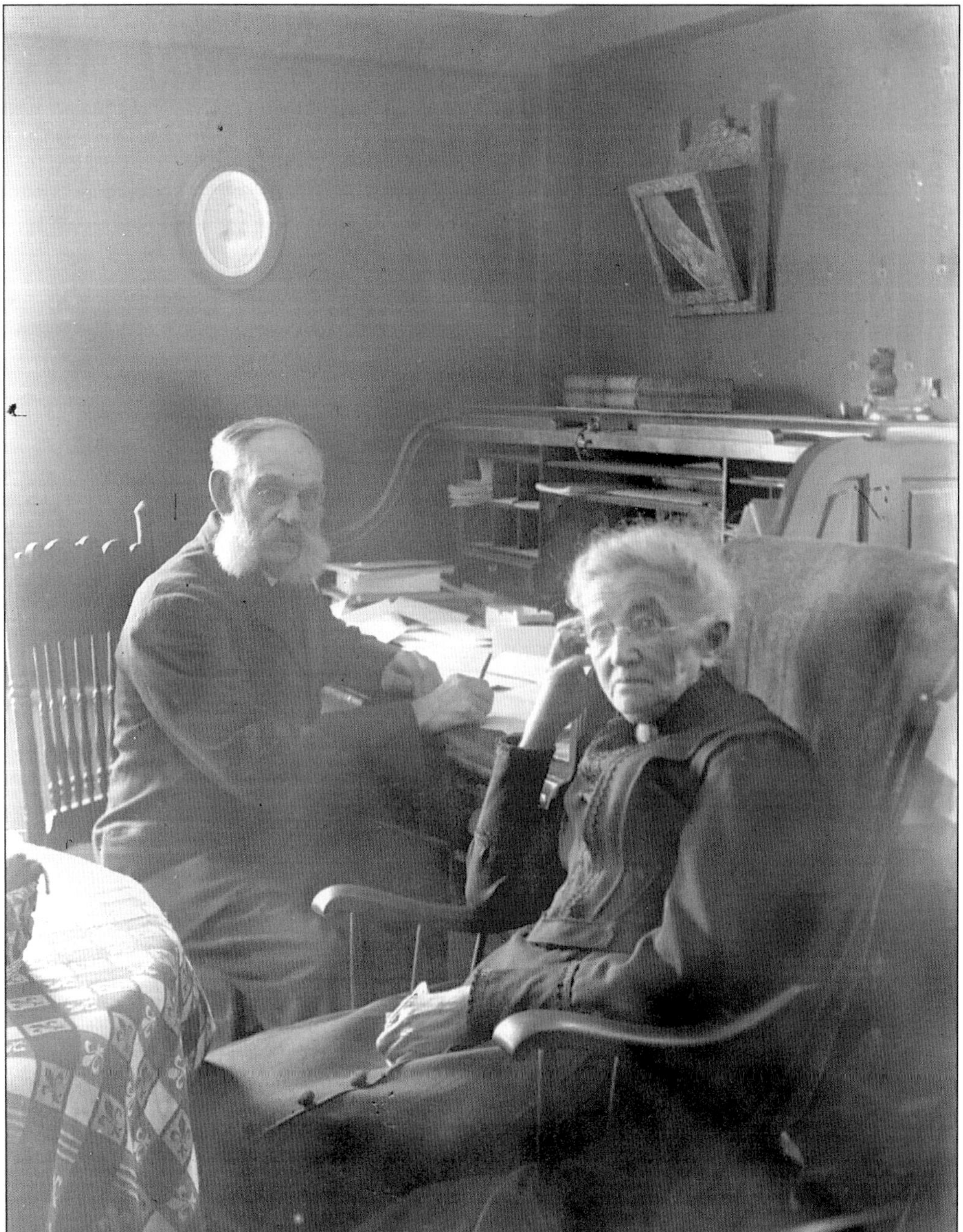

In 1914, Stillman and Cara Stone were photographed as they quietly observed their 50th wedding anniversary in the comfort of their home at 790 Massachusetts Avenue. After serving in the Civil War in the Vermont Militia, Stillman came to Lunenburg and purchased the buildings and farmland now referred to as the Stone Farm. He and his wife lived in the farmhouse and owned the land on both sides of Massachusetts Avenue, all the way to Sunny Hill Road. He served as town clerk for 23 years. He was also a selectman and assessor. Stillman Stone, having lived a full life, died at the age of 95 in 1931. His impressive desk (pictured here) is preserved in the Lunenburg Historical Society building.

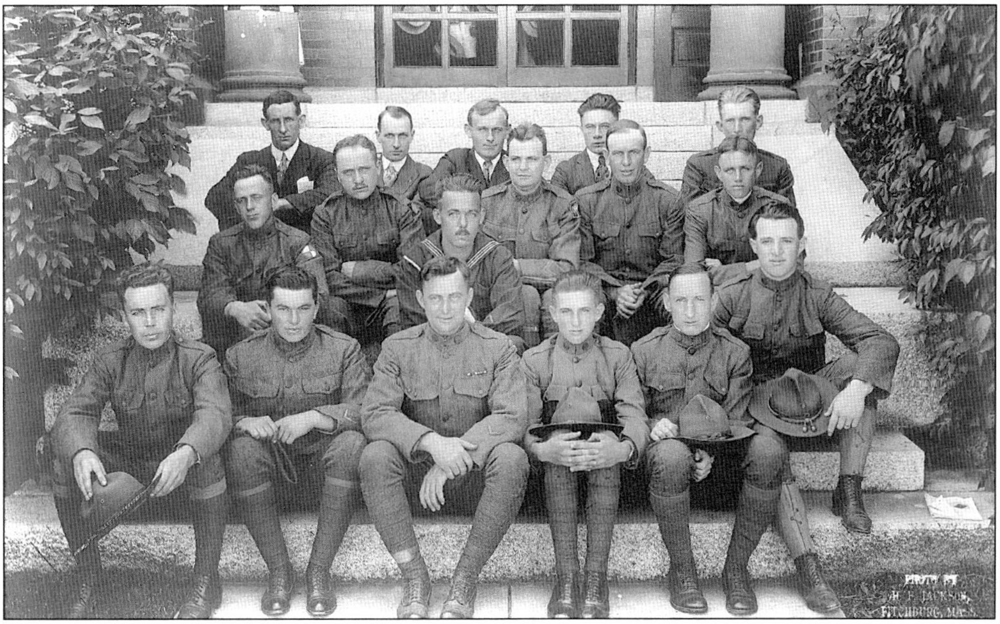

Seated on the granite steps of the Ritter Memorial Library, these World War I military men are, from left to right, as follows: (first row) Ralph Bickford, Clarence J. Chase, ? Graves, Maurice F. Carr, and William W. Warren; (second row) Orville D. Martin and Chester W. Page; (third row) Stacey Heath, unidentified, Winthrop F. Harley, George M. Stiles, and Harold L. Harrington; (fourth row) Clarence E. Brown, unidentified, Chester W. Mossman, Joseph Dupuis, and unidentified.

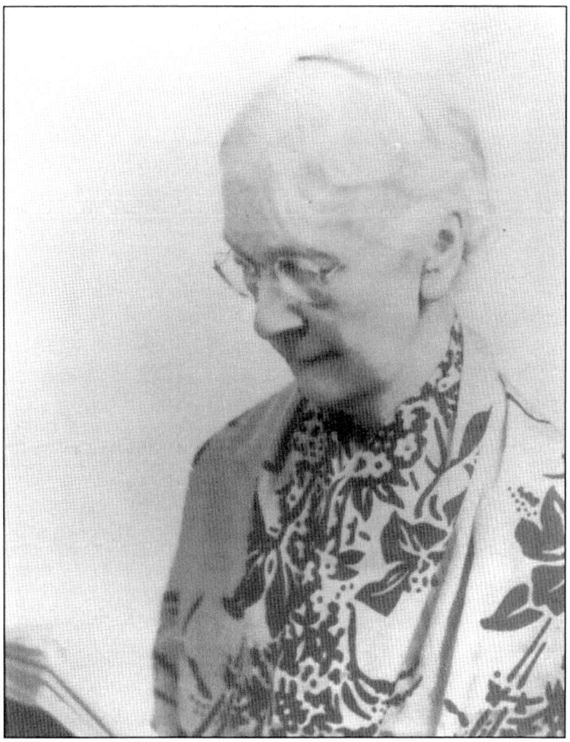

May V. Estabrook grew up in Lunenburg and became a teacher. Her first teaching position was in District No. 7. Later, she taught history, French, and English at Lunenburg High School from 1899 until her retirement in 1918. She served on the Lunenburg School Committee while teaching until the state prohibited this combination of service. She organized hot cocoa for 2¢ for children coming to school without breakfast. She died in 1947.

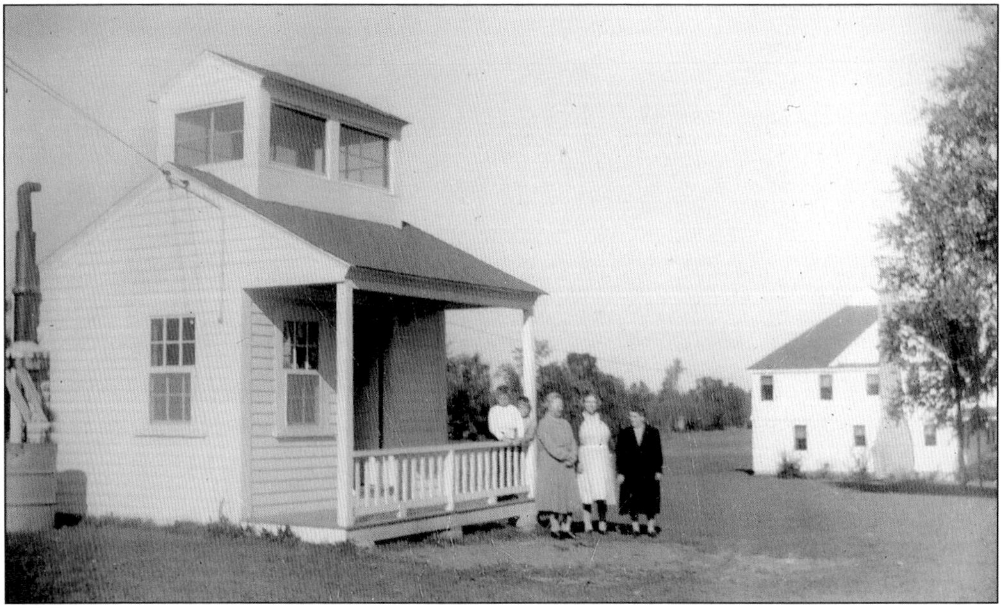

In the early 1940s, local residents served in the Lunenburg Observer Corps. They identified aircraft seen or heard flying over the center of town. These observations were reported by telephone to the U.S. Army First Fighter Command. This building on Memorial Drive served as the observation post and was manned 24 hours a day during World War II by volunteers from high school age to senior citizens.

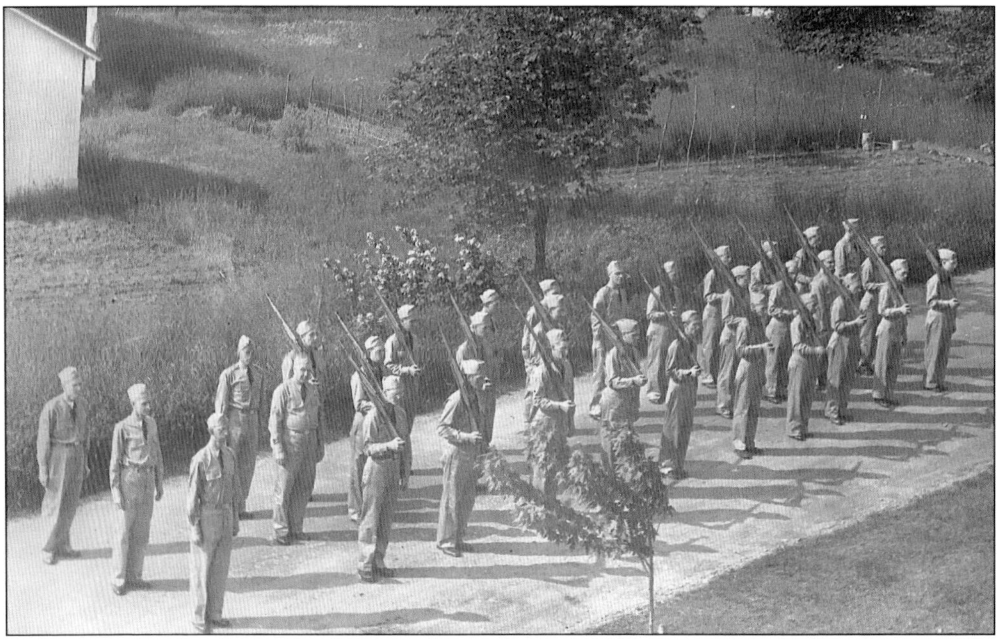

Many men, exempt from military service by reason of age, family responsibility, or physical disqualification, joined the state guard during World War II. The local unit drilled regularly under the leadership of Capt. Raymond Butterfield. They stand here on the lawn near the Eagle House. Several high school age boys who were members eventually entered the armed services when they were older.

Born in Durham, Maine, a graduate of Colby College, Andrew Karkos came to Lunenburg in 1940 to teach history and mathematics at the high school. The following year, he was appointed principal. For 17 years, he played many educational roles in the high school, from teacher, coach, guidance counselor, and principal until his retirement from the school system in 1958.

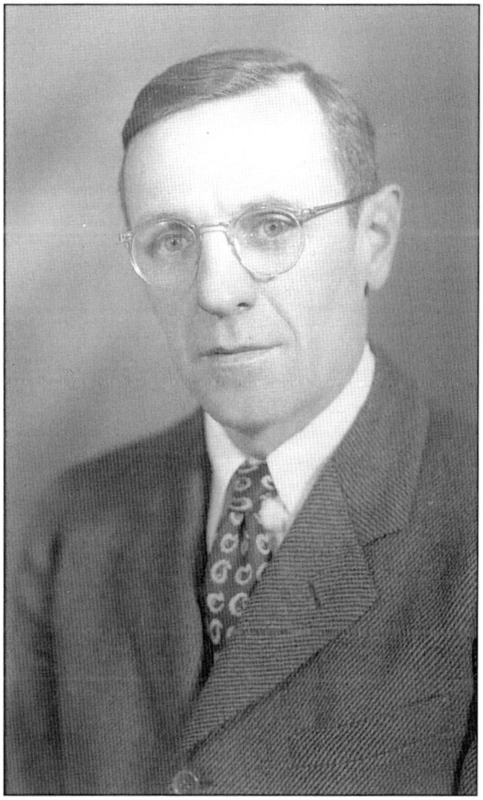

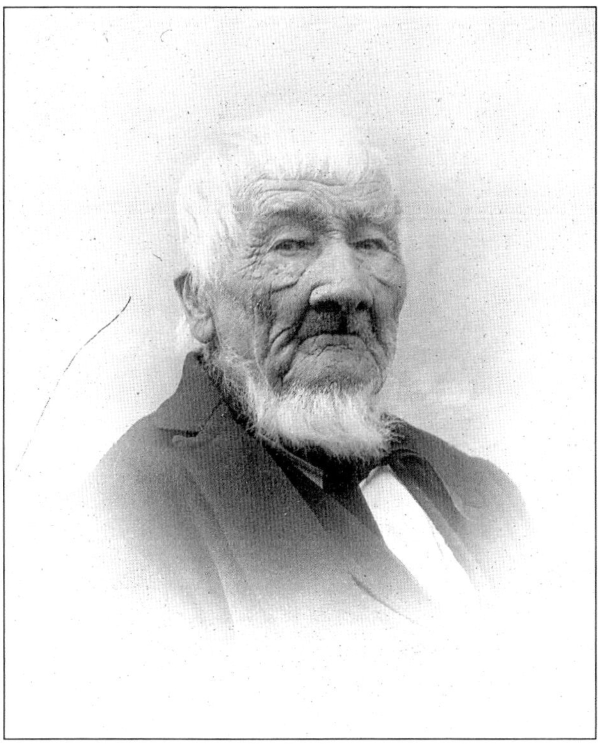

Benjamin G. Whiting was a successful cabinetmaker. He was born in 1804 in the house at 93 Lancaster Avenue, built by his father, Esek, in the late 1700s. Whiting and his sisters lived here their entire lives. Whiting amassed an impressive and valuable mineral collection, some of which were worthy of a museum. The complete collection and display cabinets were gifted to the Lunenburg High School.

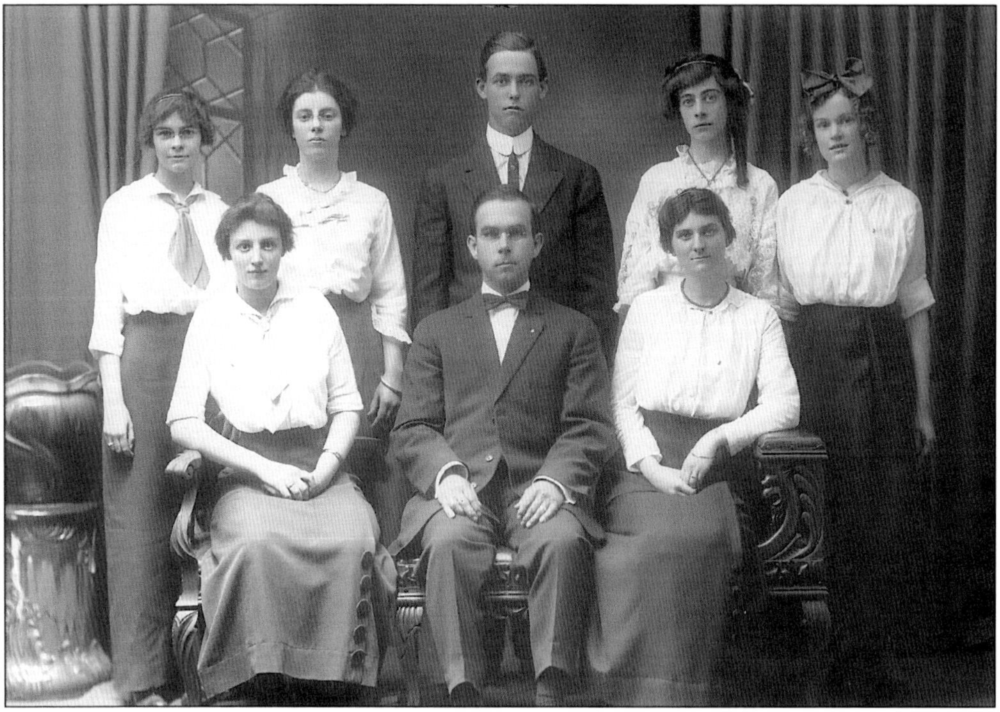

Looking suitably somber and dressed appropriately as they contemplated their future, these seven Lunenburg High School graduates (Class of 1914) pose primly with principal Claude A. Gray. From left to right are the following: (front row) Blanche Whitcomb, Claude A. Gray, and Doris Nickelson; (back row) Mary Keith, Pauline Case, Orville Martin, Lucy Proctor, and Eleanor Harley.

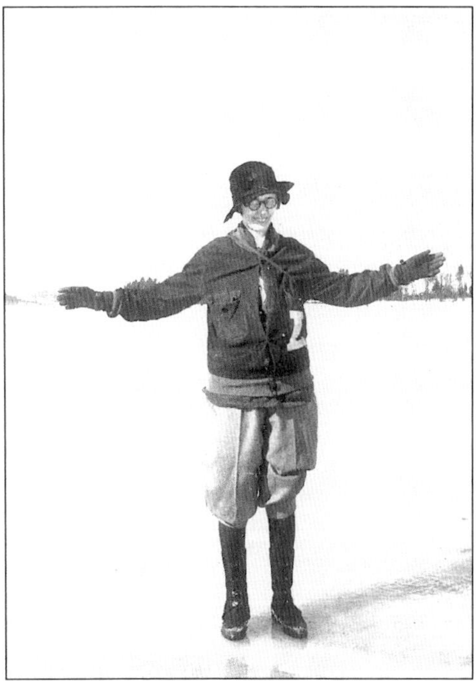

Those who knew Edith K. Proctor would have smiled to see her in this devil-may-care attitude on the ice at Dickinson's Lake. Proctor was usually seen at Ritter Memorial Library, where she dominated the scene as librarian for 35 years. In 1927, when this photograph was taken, both Proctor and the lake (now called Hickory Hills) were enjoying an uncomplicated youth.

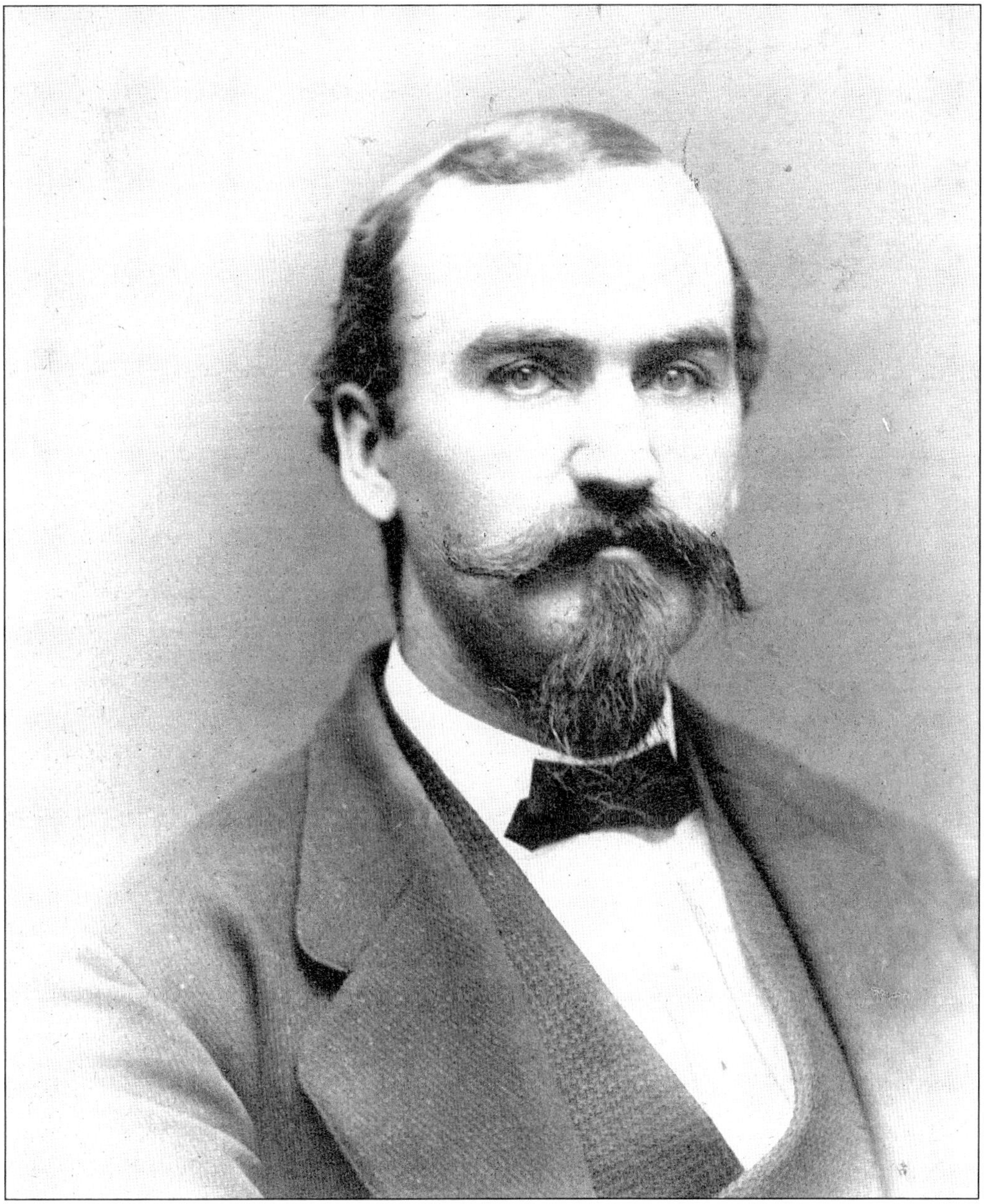

This photograph of James A. Litchfield (1844–1926) was taken c. 1868. Litchfield was born in Lunenburg. He became an apprentice to a Boston building and contracting business. In 1861, he joined the "Zonaves" (state guard). He enlisted in the Civil War on August 12, 1862, and served until 1864 in the 40th Massachusetts Regiment. He was later instrumental in getting proper pensions for Civil War veterans. After the war, he opened a grocery business in Boston and Somerville. He returned to Lunenburg in 1894 and built his house, Grovedale, on the corner of Massachusetts Avenue and Chestnut Street. Today, it is a funeral home. He later became the president of Old Home Week and the Memorial Association in town. Litchfield was also a member of Lunenburg and Fitchburg historical groups. He served as a representative in the Massachusetts legislature in 1899 and was on the committee responsible for the Fitchburg and Leominster Railroad and the state highway coming into Lunenburg.

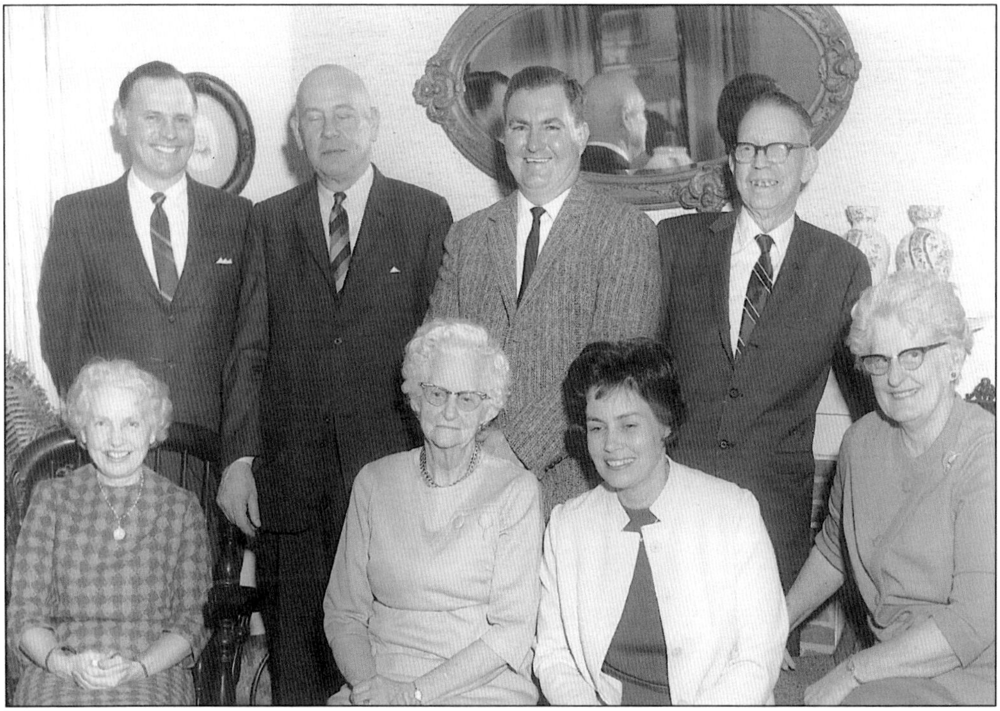

The Lunenburg Conservation Commission was established in 1961 and is a fine example of what can be accomplished by concerned citizens on a local level. Pictured from left to right are the following: (front row) Minnie M. Martin, Mrs. William R. Peabody, Mrs. Calvin Sholl, and Dorothy E. Millington; (back row) Willis C. Woodruff, H. Benjamin Normand, William J. Deming Jr., and Harold D. Harley.

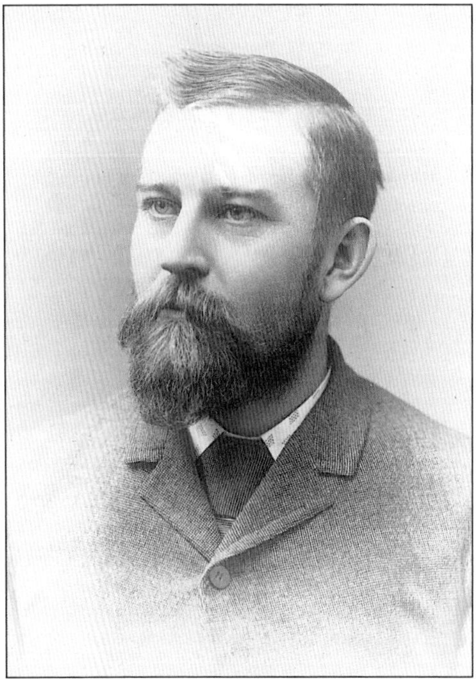

Warren Lewis and his brother Henry J. bought a general store from Sylvester Boutwell in May 1887. This store was previously the well-known store of Daniel Putnam. Warren Lewis sold the store to Flint H. Boutwell. When Lewis returned to Lunenburg in 1903, he bought back the store. He formed a partnership with his stepson, Carl E. Brown, known as Warren Lewis and Company.

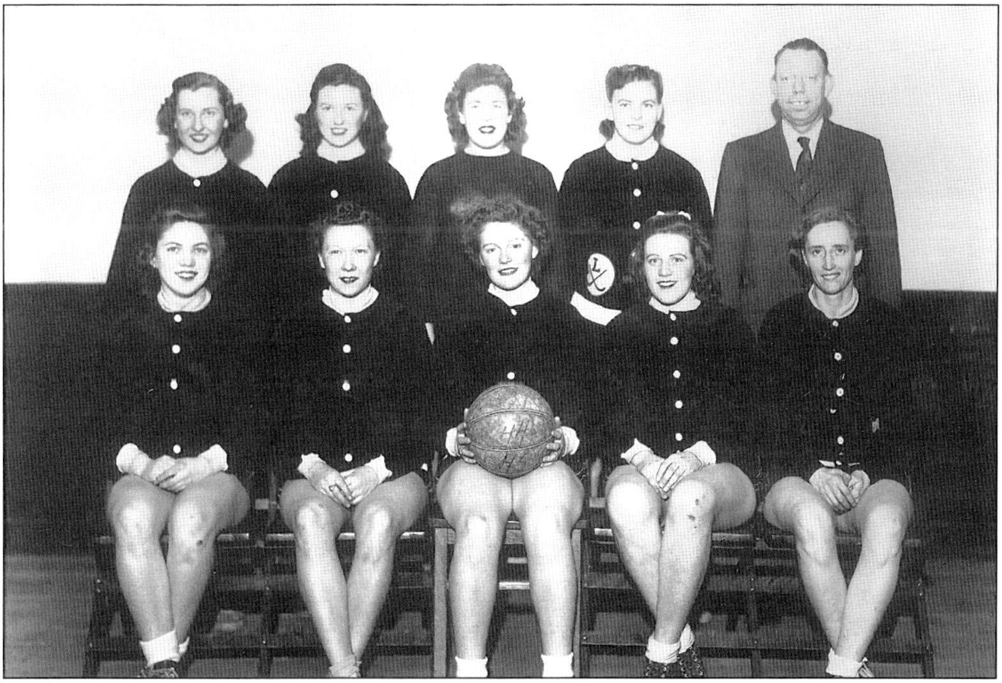

The Lunenburg Girls' Athletic Club basketball team (pictured here with their coach, Harold Harley) held a position of respect in the area for the team's successes on the court. The members of this 1945 team are, from left to right, as follows: (front row) Mary Padula, Sylvia Oksanen, Barbara Ward, Lil Griffiths, and Margaret Harley; (back row) Eleanor Bowles, Margaret Brown, Mary Bickford, Charlotte Harley, and Harold Harley.

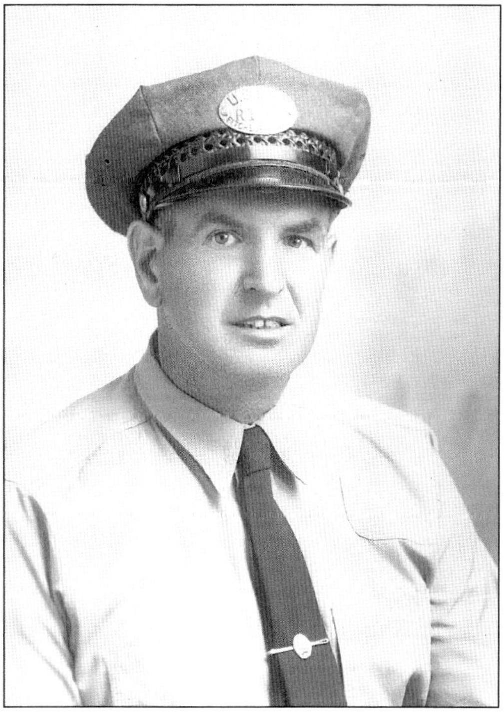

Pictured in this photograph is Walter Rinki, who lived on Howard Street in the northern part of Lunenburg. Rinki was a descendent of Gustaf Franti, who came to this country from Finland in 1901. Rinki was a U.S. postmaster for our town and served for many years. Rinki further contributed to our history in the role of selectman. (Courtesy of Dennis Rinki.)

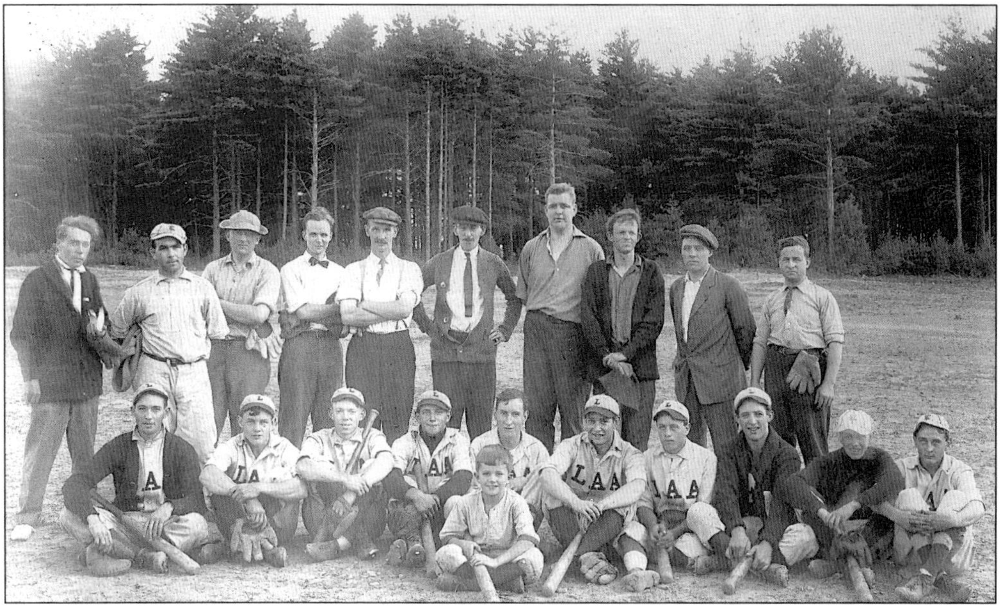

Marshall Park has served as a scenic background for Lunenburg athletes and their competitions ever since the land for the park was purchased from Edwin Marshall in 1912. In this 1914 photograph, the Lunenburg Athletic Association poses with a baseball team, whose members included two young men who later became well-known local figures—Harold Harley and Chet Page.

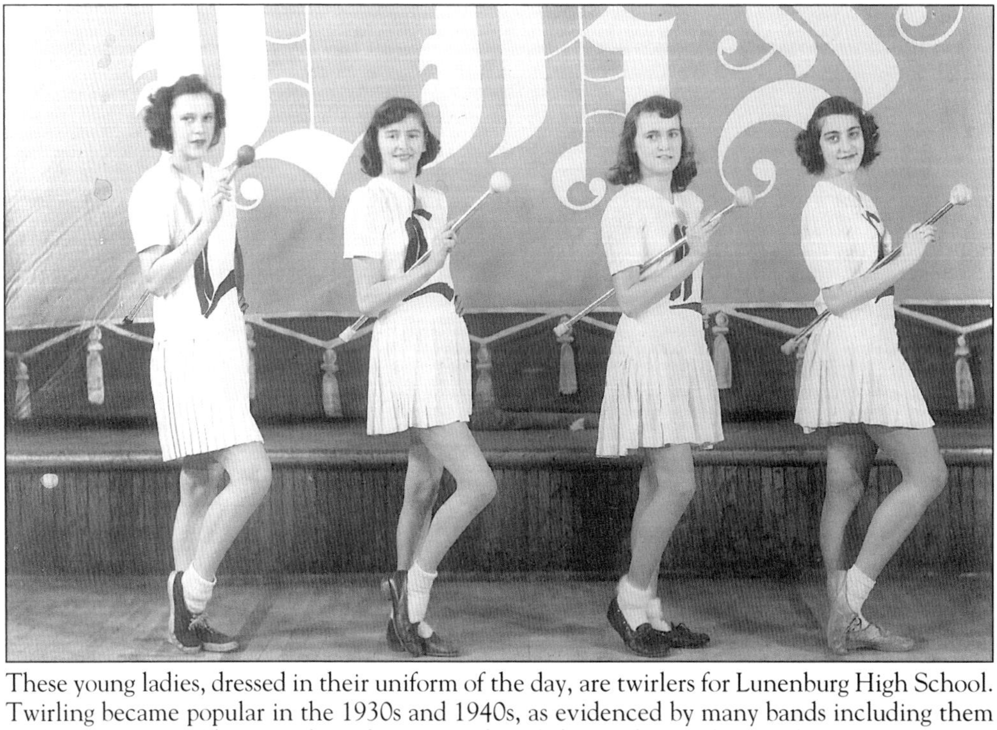

These young ladies, dressed in their uniform of the day, are twirlers for Lunenburg High School. Twirling became popular in the 1930s and 1940s, as evidenced by many bands including them in their programs. These twirlers of 1948 are, from left to right, Faith Temple, Auracy Proctor, Phillis Collelo, and Janice Liljegren.

This happy young rider is Lucina, daughter of Russ Hoisington, with her pony on the Hoisington Farm. Although farming is hard work, there is always a little time away from chores to enjoy some of the finer benefits of farm life. The road seen in the background is Lancaster Avenue near its intersection with Kilburn Street. (Courtesy of Diane DelliCarpini.)

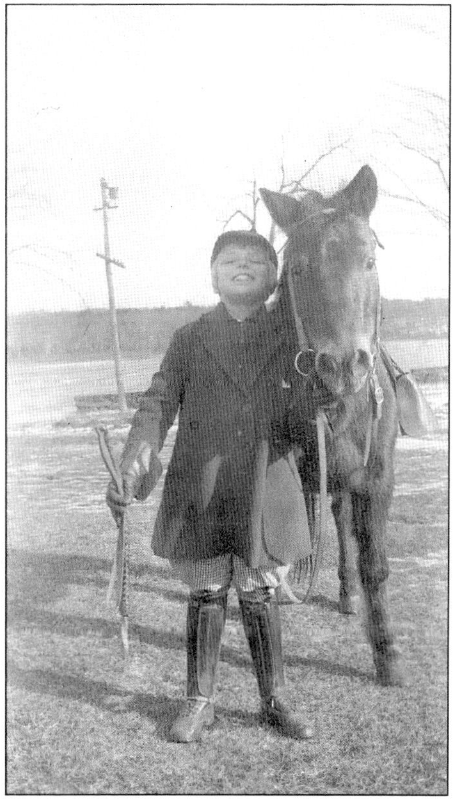

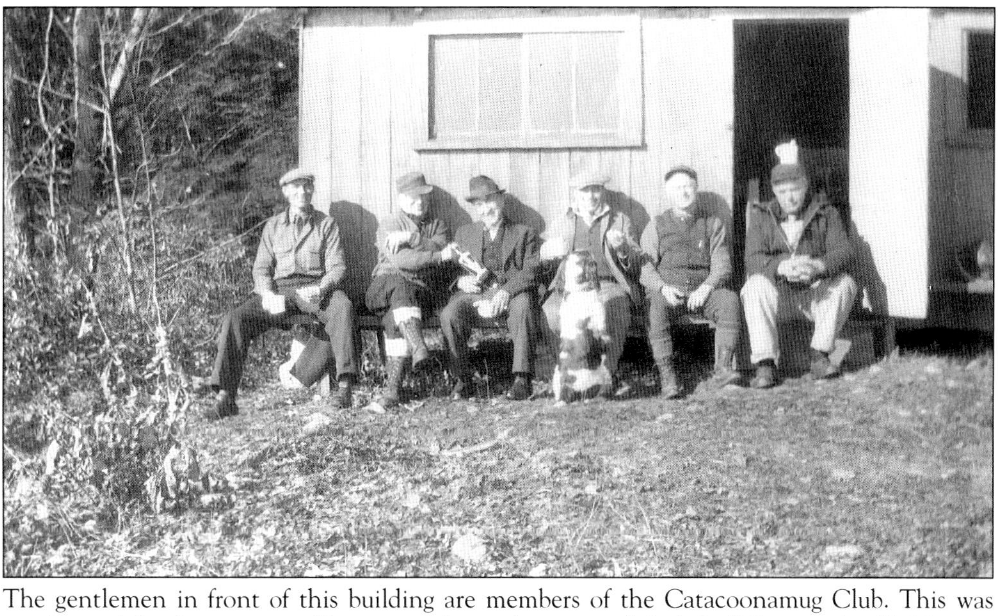

The gentlemen in front of this building are members of the Catacoonamug Club. This was a private club of sportsmen. Shown are the early stages of their building on the Hoisington property. The plans were to dam the stream running through the property, making a pond to raise fish and hunt in the surrounding woods. This club no longer exists. (Courtesy of Diane DelliCarpini.)

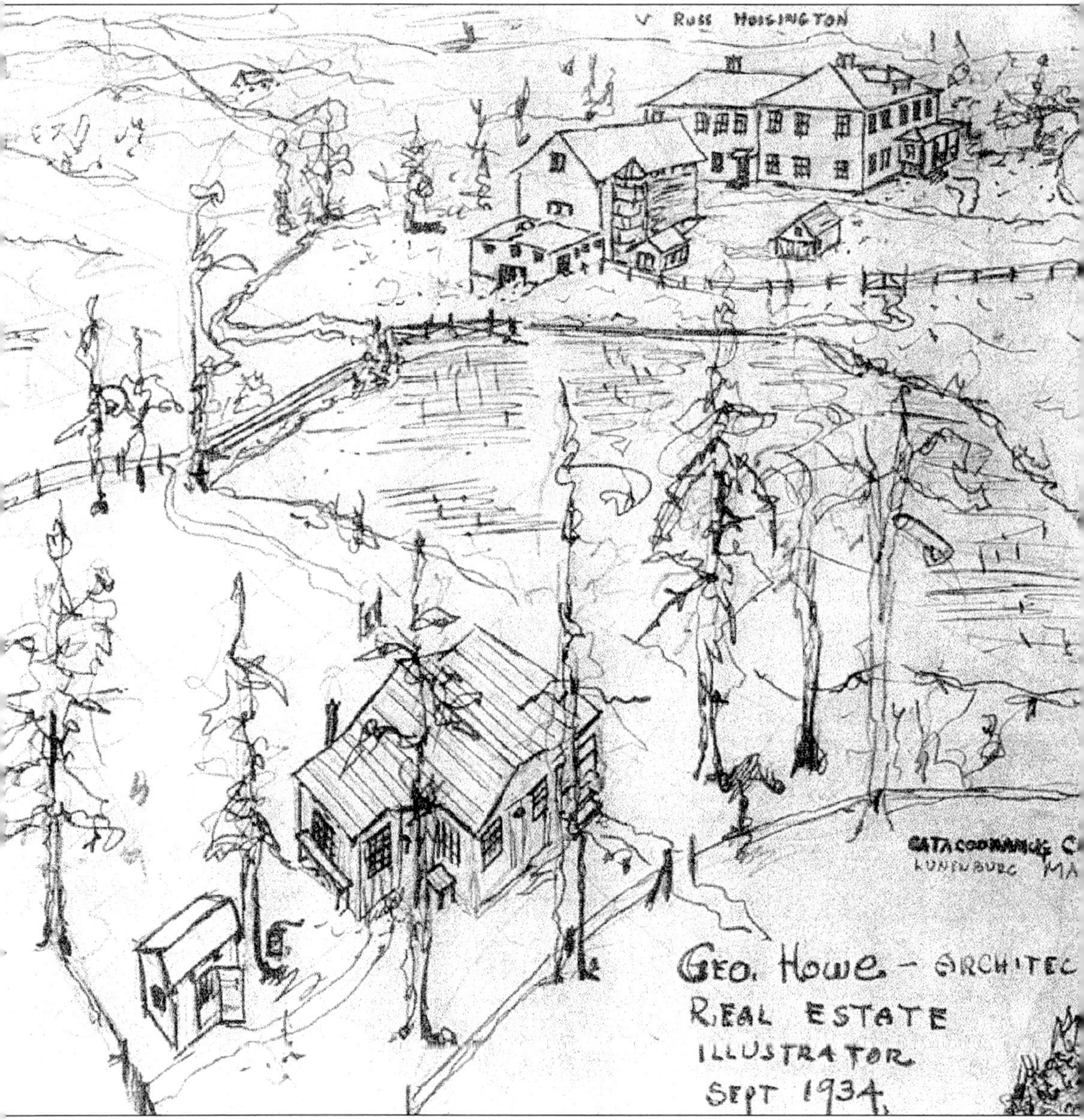

This architect's drawing by real estate illustrator George Howe gives a partial view of Russ Hoisington's property at the corner of Lancaster Avenue and Kilburn Street. The Hoisington House and barn are shown in the upper-right part of the photograph. In the lower-left portion of the photograph is the Catacoonamug Club with an outdoor water pump and outbuilding. The area between the barn and the club is a brook, which was dammed to form a small pond for fishing by its members. (Courtesy of Diane DelliCarpini.)

Three

SPECIAL EVENTS

One of the earlier popular events in Lunenburg was the Lunenburg Annual Fair and Cattle Show. There were exhibits of farm animals, fruits and vegetables, canned goods, home-baked treats, handworks, and quilts. The Farmers' Club, formed on September 23, 1848, presented these events. This club was the first of its kind in the United States. In 1861, during the Civil War, shows were postponed. The club revived in the 1920s and remained active for the next 10 years.

The Lunenburg Grange No. 169 was organized in November 1888. It was formed after the Civil War to aid farmers and to promote educational and social development in rural areas. Later, in 1895, the Farmers' Club presented all their property to the Lunenburg Grange, which in turn continued the fairs and shows.

May Day became a popular event in the early 1900s. It was a great honor to be chosen for this ceremony.

Old Home Week started in 1902 with the Massachusetts governor's proclamation to honor our heritage. There were special church services, pageants, parades, and patriotic programs in memory of days gone by. On July 29, 1903, Lunenburg held its first Old Home Week. It was held annually without interruption through 1935. Donations and some added town money funded these events. In 1928, our town's 200th anniversary was combined with Old Home Week. After the 200th anniversary, only Old Home Sunday was celebrated in the churches. Lunenburg Exchange Club revived it in 1967–1968. In 2003, we will be celebrating the 275th anniversary with a full year of activities.

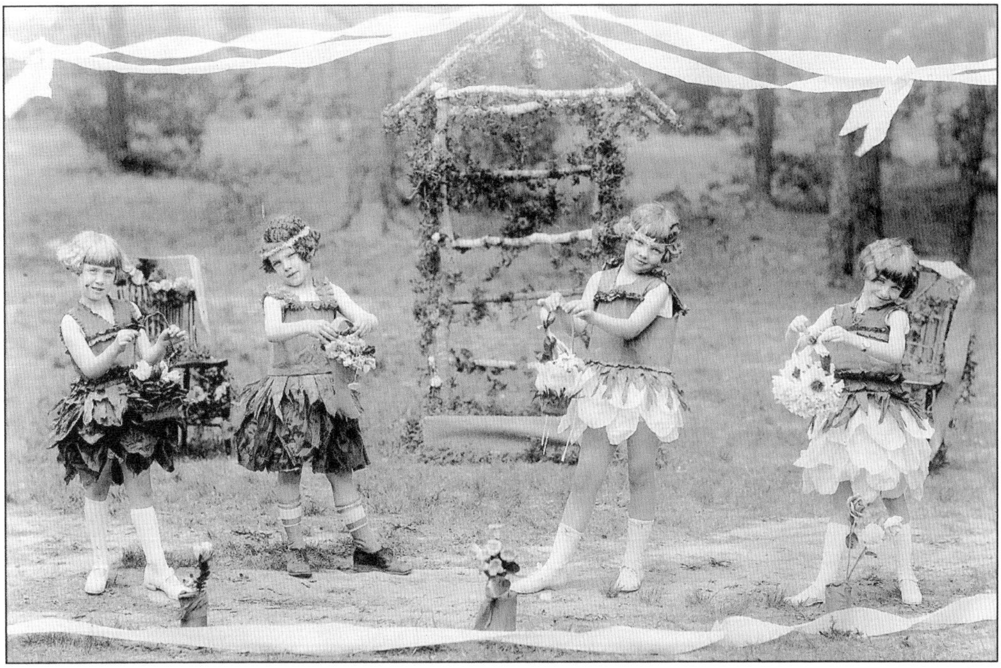

These children are showing off their may baskets on May Day *c.* 1920. May Day was, in this period, an important holiday. Note the costumes and crepe paper streamers in place for a maypole dance. It was a great honor to be chosen for this ceremony.

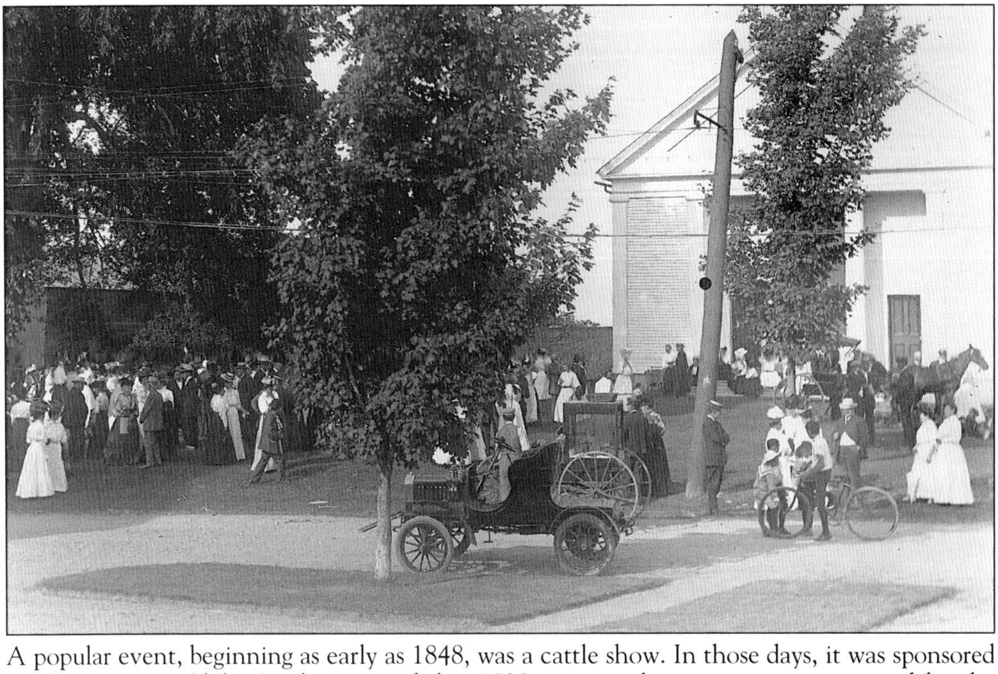

A popular event, beginning as early as 1848, was a cattle show. In those days, it was sponsored by the Farmers' Club. At the time of this 1920s picture, however, it was operated by the Lunenburg Grange. There were exhibits of farm animals as well as fruits and vegetables. Food was sold, and the Lunenburg Town Hall was filled with tables displaying canned goods, home-baked treats, handwork, and quilts.

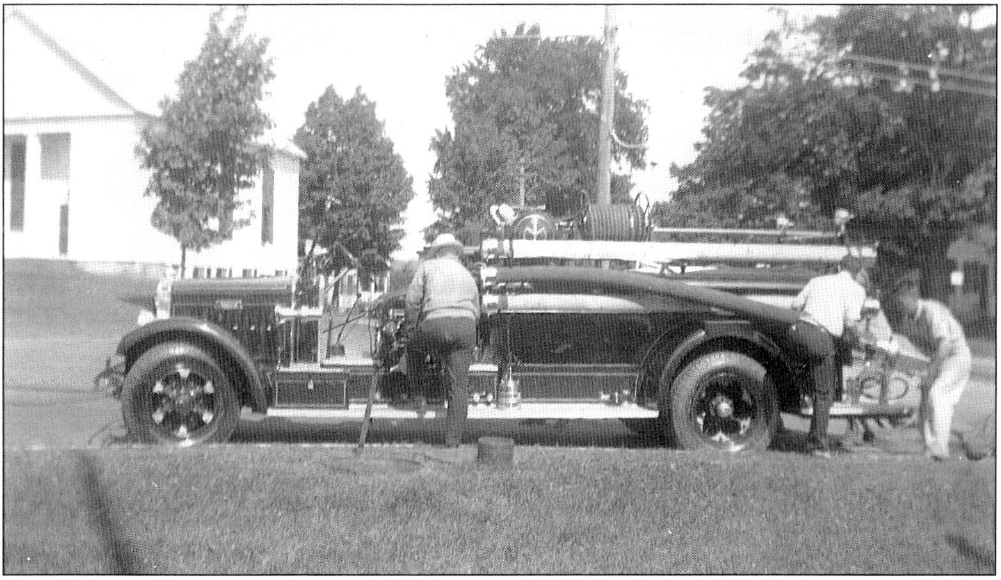

In 1935, the Lunenburg Fire Department acquired a new pumper fire truck. The men were so proud of their new piece of equipment they boasted about it. They claimed it was so effective it would be able to send a stream of water to the top of the town hall, one of the taller buildings in town. Naturally, some of the town folk wanted them to prove it. The challenge was accepted, and, one summer afternoon, they showed off its power. The top photograph shows the men at the upper common getting ready to attach one of their hoses to the underground water tank. The lower photograph shows them aiming the water at the steeple of the town hall. It was indeed a powerful piece of equipment for its time.

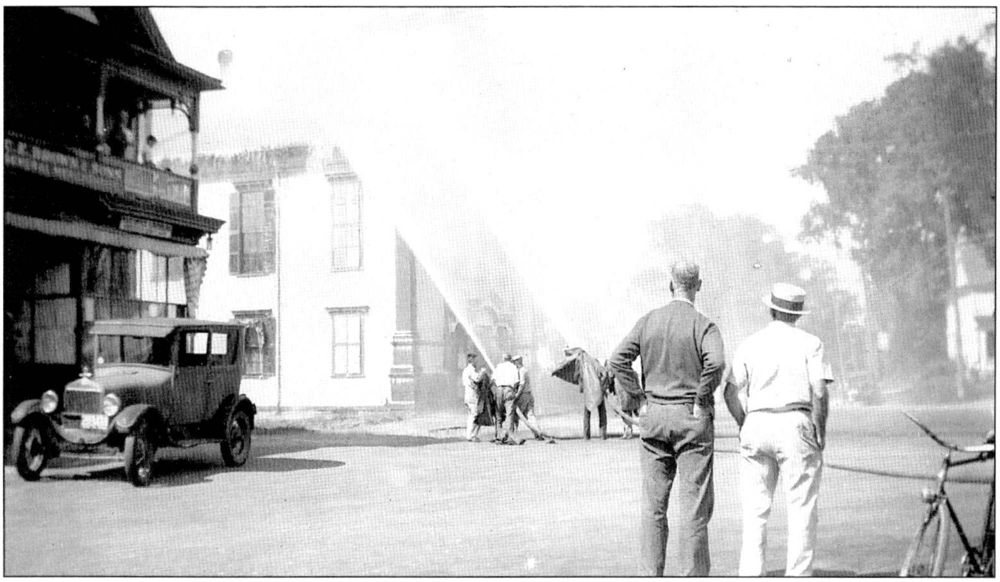

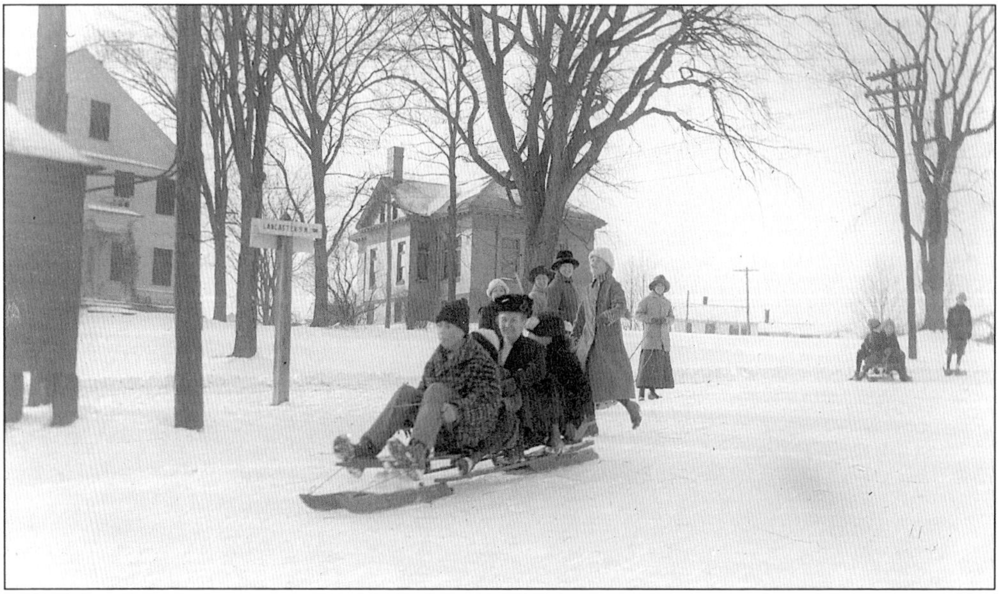

When winter came to Lunenburg, with its snowstorms, one of the most entertaining pastimes was sledding. Men, women, and children of all ages were participants. In this early photograph, taken beside the Ritter Memorial Library, are some old-fashioned sleds. In the background is a road sign with Lancaster Avenue printed on it. The white house on the left is the Abercrombie house.

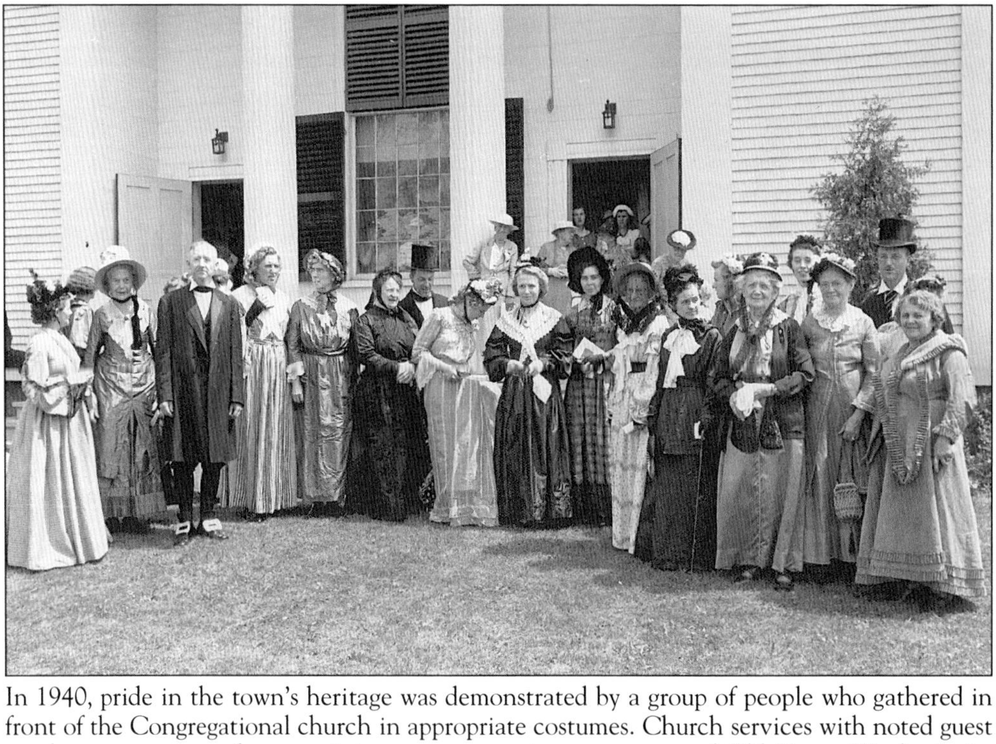

In 1940, pride in the town's heritage was demonstrated by a group of people who gathered in front of the Congregational church in appropriate costumes. Church services with noted guest speakers—sometimes former ministers—were an important part of Old Home Week. Attics were raided to find suitable clothing, and a good time was had by all.

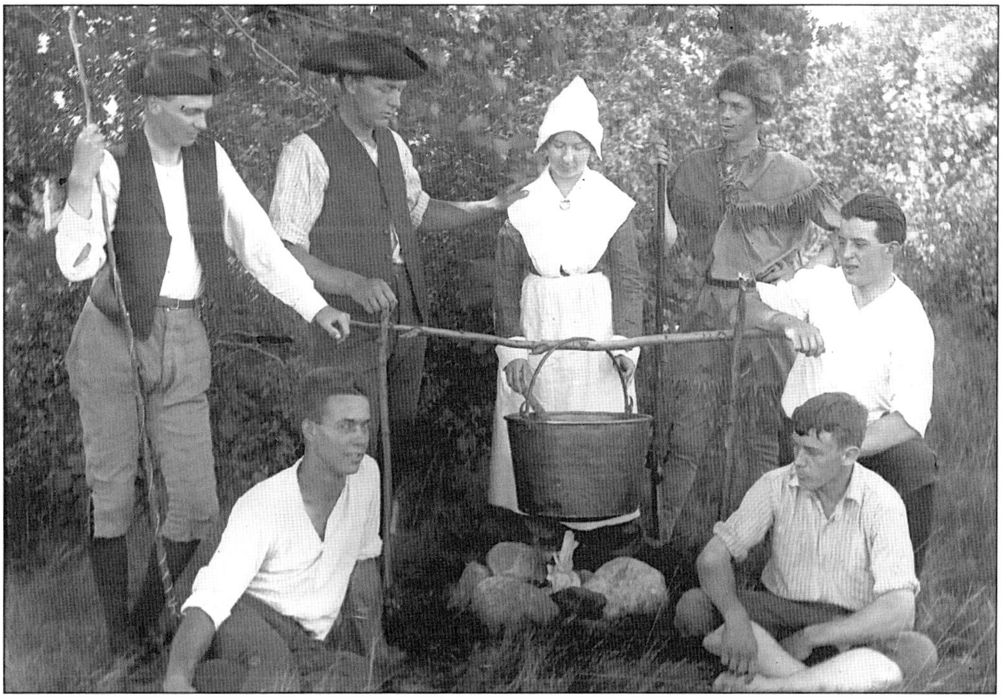

The 1915 pageant for Old Home Week featured these citizens reenacting an early ritual of Colonial homesteaders and hunters around the fire. Pictured from left to right are the following: (front row, sitting) Orvil Martin and Lewis Harrington Sr.; (middle row, kneeling) Chet Page; (back row, standing) John Gilchrest, Russ Hoisington, Marion Warren, and Sam Warren.

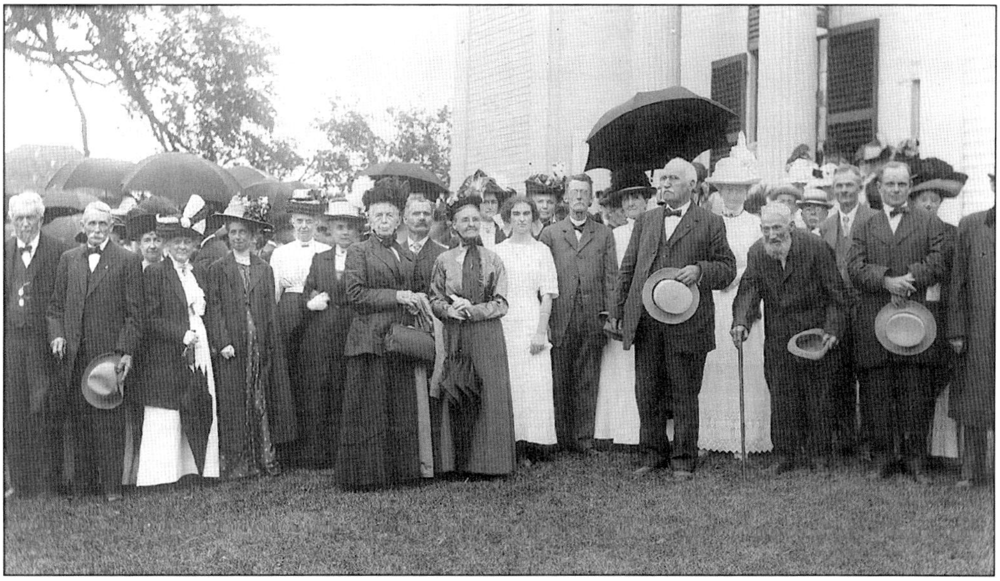

Lunenburg was diligent in its celebration of Old Home Week in the early years. Shown here is a gathering on the lawn of the Congregational church in 1912. On the program that week was a speech by Emerson W. Baker about his great uncle, George S. Boutwell. Raised in Lunenburg, George Boutwell helped organize the Republican Party and eventually became governor of Massachusetts.

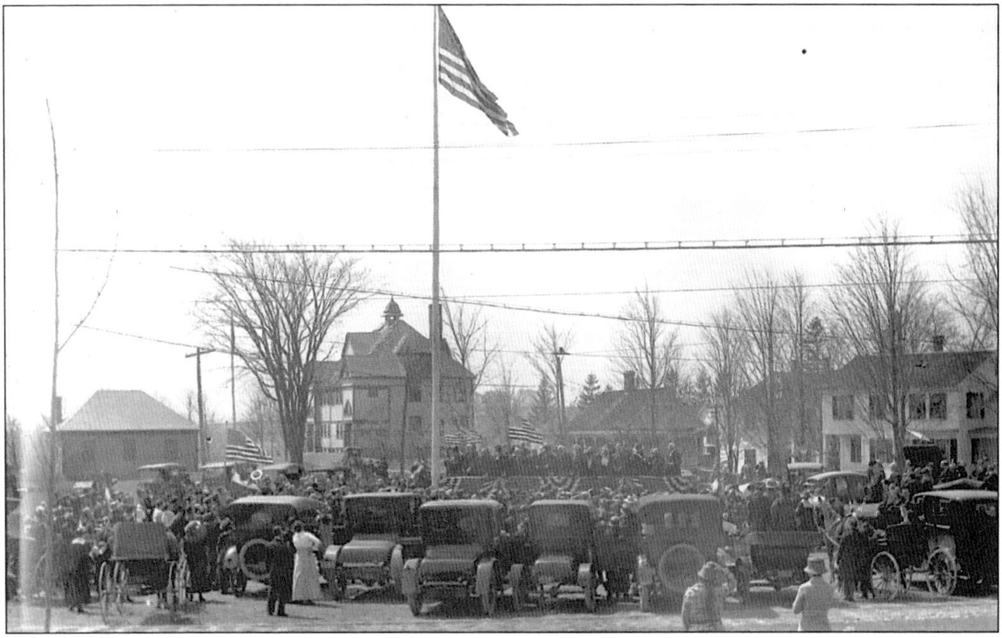

Old Home Day celebrations were something Lunenburg citizens took very seriously. They featured church services, patriotic programs, remembrances of days past, and noted speakers. Shown is a large crowd gathered on the center common, a row of veterans in a prominent position. The buildings, from left to right, are the fire station, Center School, the Susan Brown house, Ernest Proctor's house, and Lizzie Proctor's house.

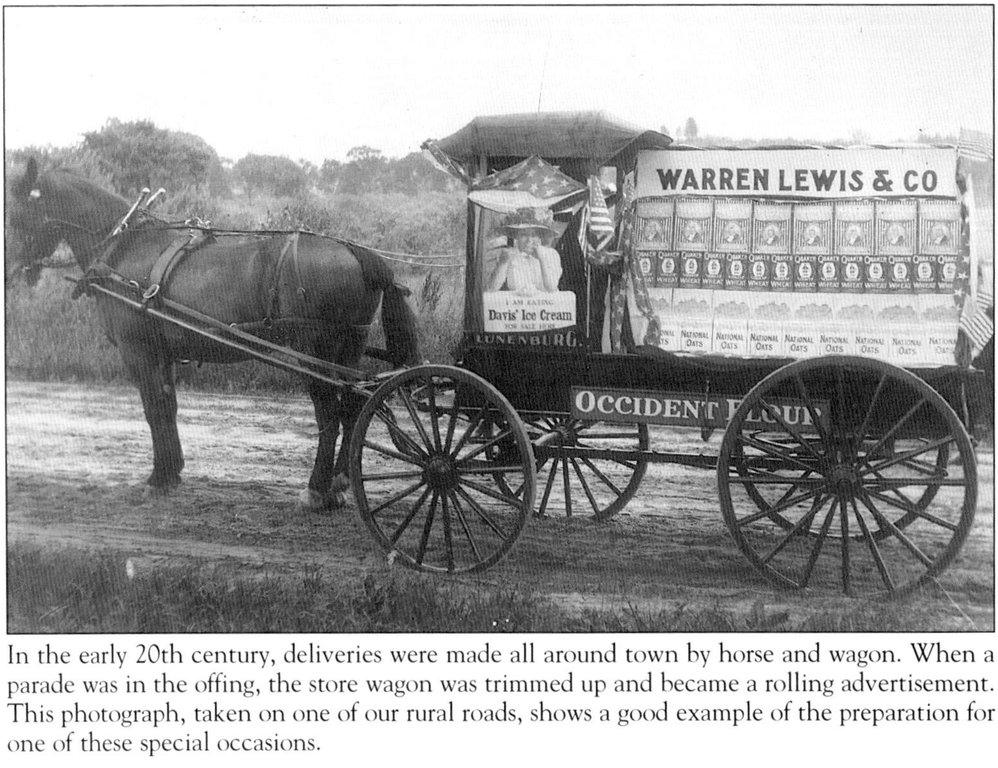

In the early 20th century, deliveries were made all around town by horse and wagon. When a parade was in the offing, the store wagon was trimmed up and became a rolling advertisement. This photograph, taken on one of our rural roads, shows a good example of the preparation for one of these special occasions.

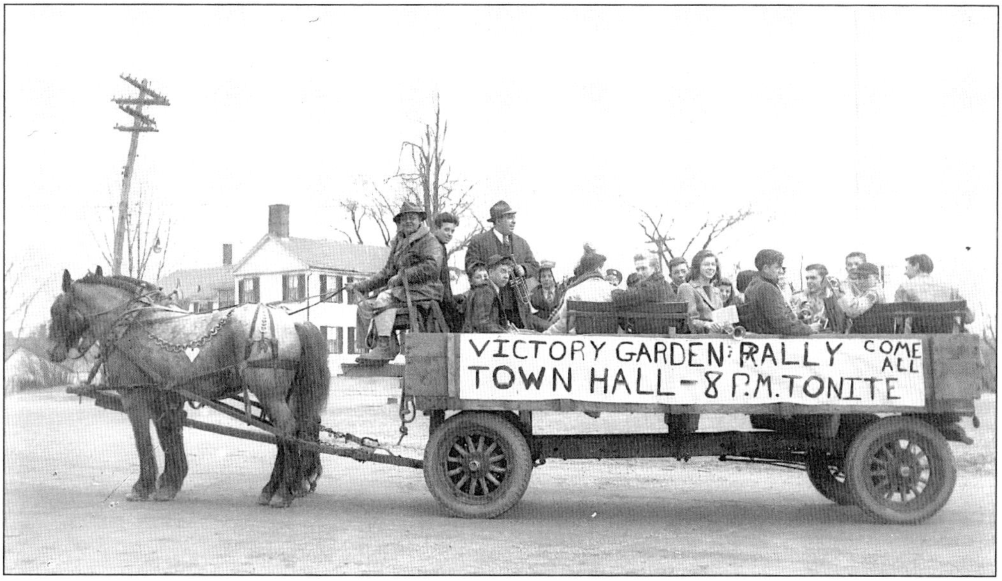

Victory gardens were another way for townspeople to support the war effort early in the 1940s. Pictured here is the high school band whipping up enthusiasm. The team and wagon were owned and driven by jovial and civic-minded local farmer Rosaire Chapdelaine, far left. Third from the left is high school director and band director Emanuel D'Ambrosio, known townwide as "D'A." (Courtesy of Elizabeth Burnap.)

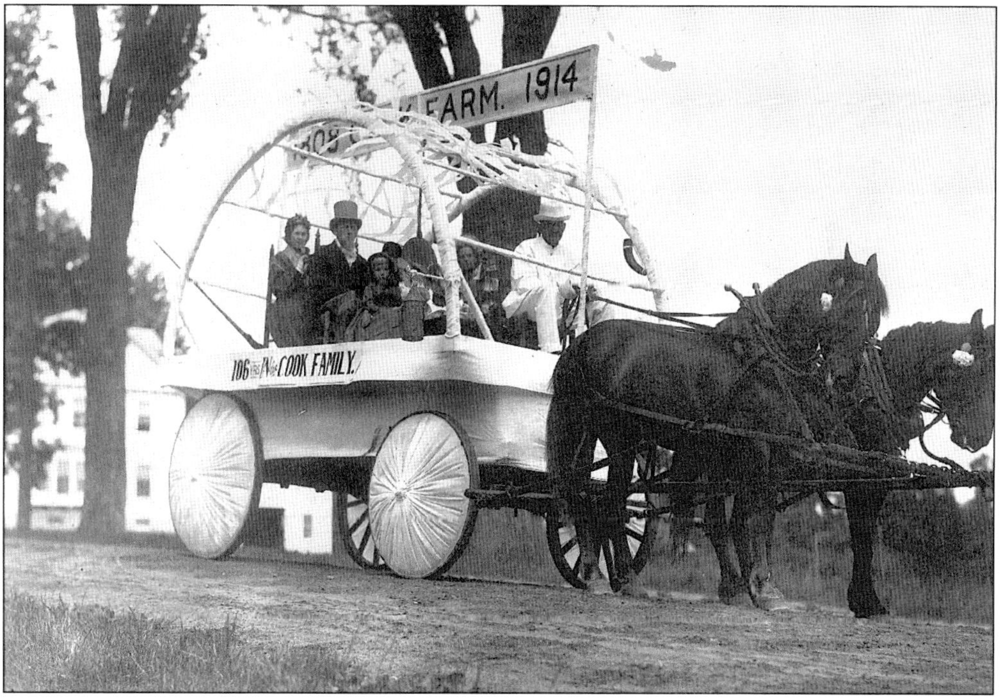

This float, entered in a parade celebrating the 1914 Old Home Week, belonged to the Cook family. The Cooks have been residents of Lunenburg since 1808. In earlier years, the Cook family ran a dairy farm delivering milk door to door. Later, milk was only sold from their farm. Lunenburg was the only town for a while not requiring pasteurization.

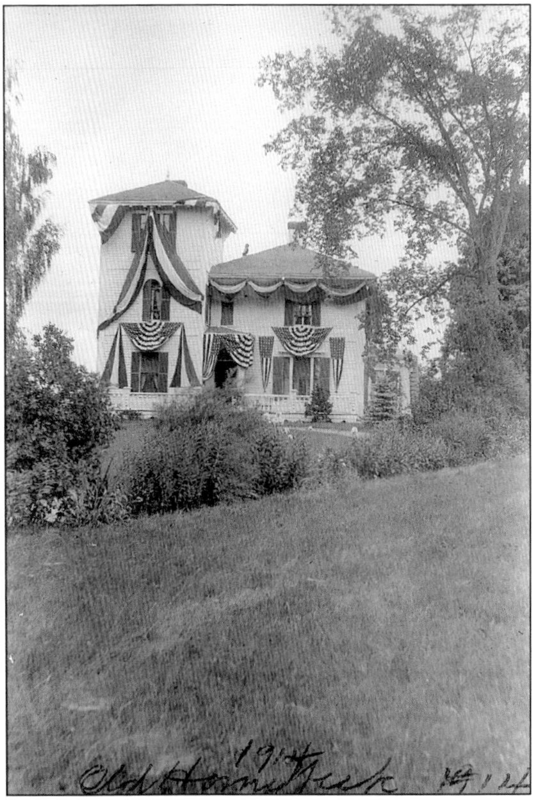

This photograph shows the Locke House (*c.* 1840) suitably decorated with bunting for Old Home Week in 1914. The house is thought to have been built before the Civil War, as evidenced by some of its features. There are many fireplaces and a brick oven in the kitchen, as well as brick-arched chimneys suggesting its age.

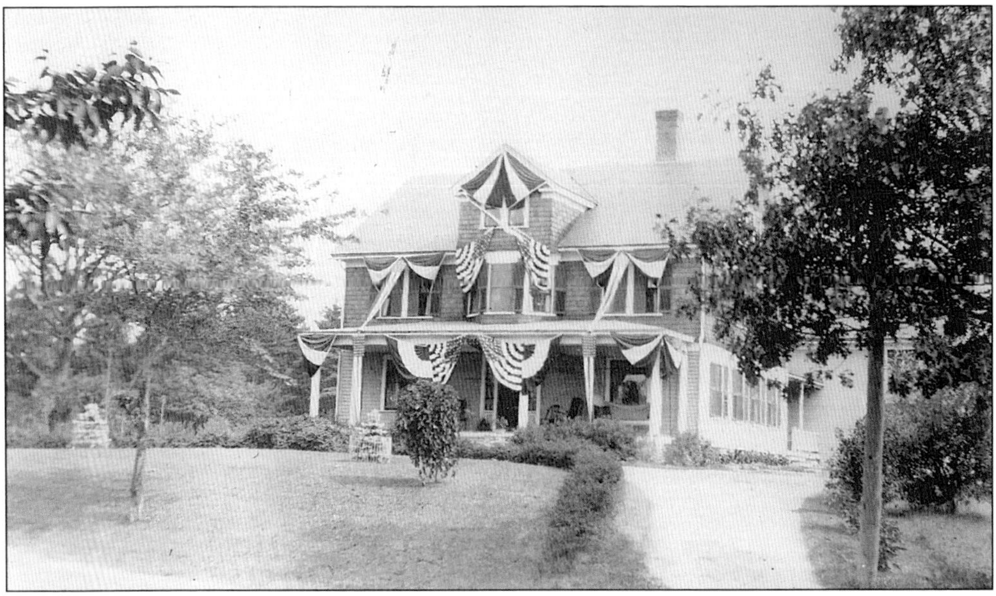

Early in the 20th century, one of the patriotic holidays was observed in colorful fashion by the occupants of this house at 871 Massachusetts Avenue. It was built by Warren Lewis in 1910. It was later occupied by "Chick" Woodward for many years. In recent years, it has been the property of the Norman Thompson family.

The town of Lunenburg went all out for its combined 200th anniversary and Old Home Week in 1928. Buildings in town were appropriately decorated and people came from far and near to take part in the festivities, parades, speeches, church suppers, reenactments, and other suitable activities celebrating Lunenburg's longevity. Free copies of Lunenburg's history were donated by May V. Estabrook in memory of her father and historian, A.C. Estabrook.

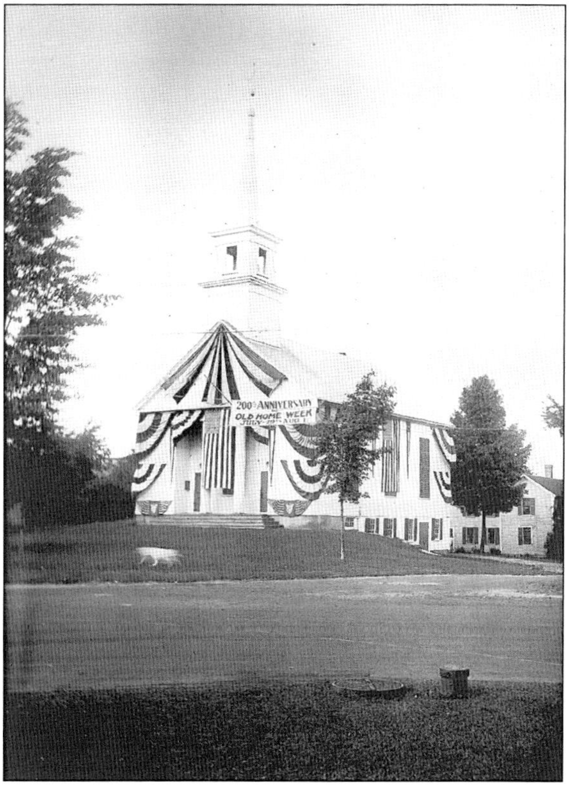

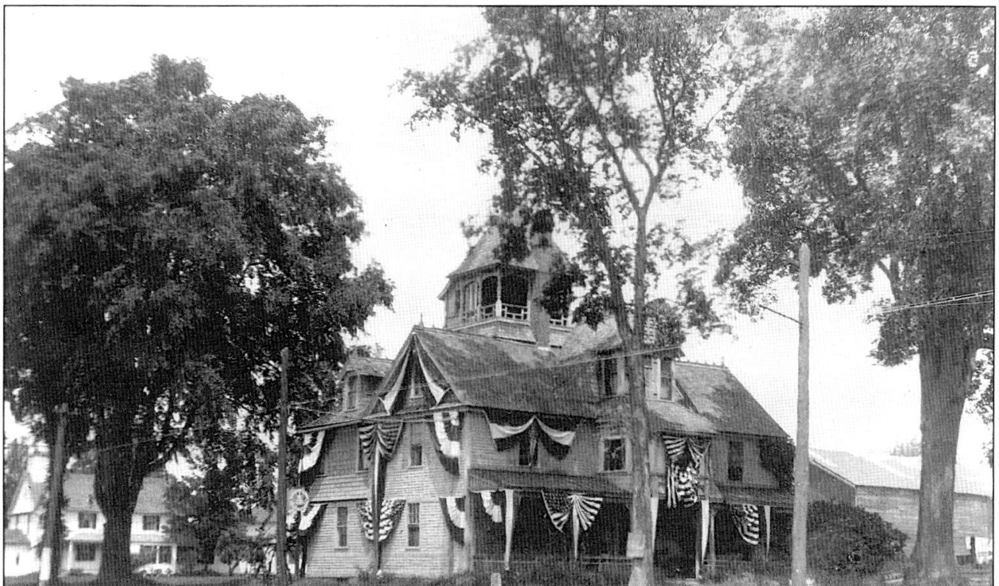

The Bellows' House, *c.* 1740, is pictured here in its original location, decorated for a town celebration. Originally owned by Col. Benjamin Bellows, it was inherited, along with 800 acres of land, by his son Col. Joseph Bellows. It was eventually given to the town by Arnold C. Dickinson and moved to a different location in 1937. Renovated, it now functions as the Eagle House Senior Center.

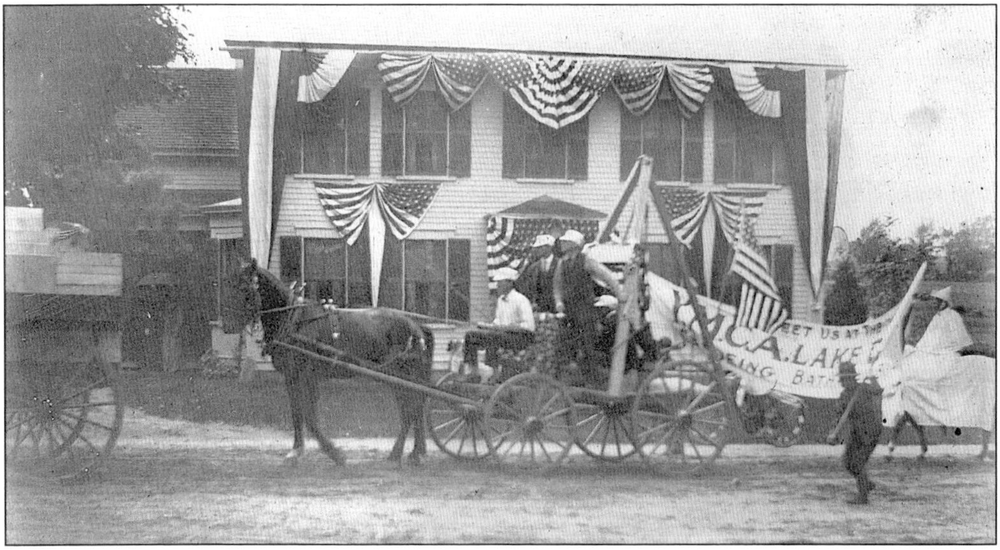

In midsummer 1928, the town held a gala dual celebration of the 200th anniversary of the incorporation of Lunenburg and the 27th Annual Old Home Week. The house in the background of the parade is the Marshall House, at the north end of Main Street. The population at that time was 1,875. Special church services were scheduled on July 29, 1928, and a full day of festivities on August 1, 1928. Included were band concerts at 10 a.m. and 4 p.m. There was a parade in the morning and an organ recital in the afternoon, along with athletic events, a speech by the lieutenant governor, and historical tableaus. Townspeople then banqueted in the Lunenburg Town Hall (below), played a ballgame at Marshall Park, and employed a third band concert in the evening. Along with the draped public buildings, many homes were decorated for the occasion.

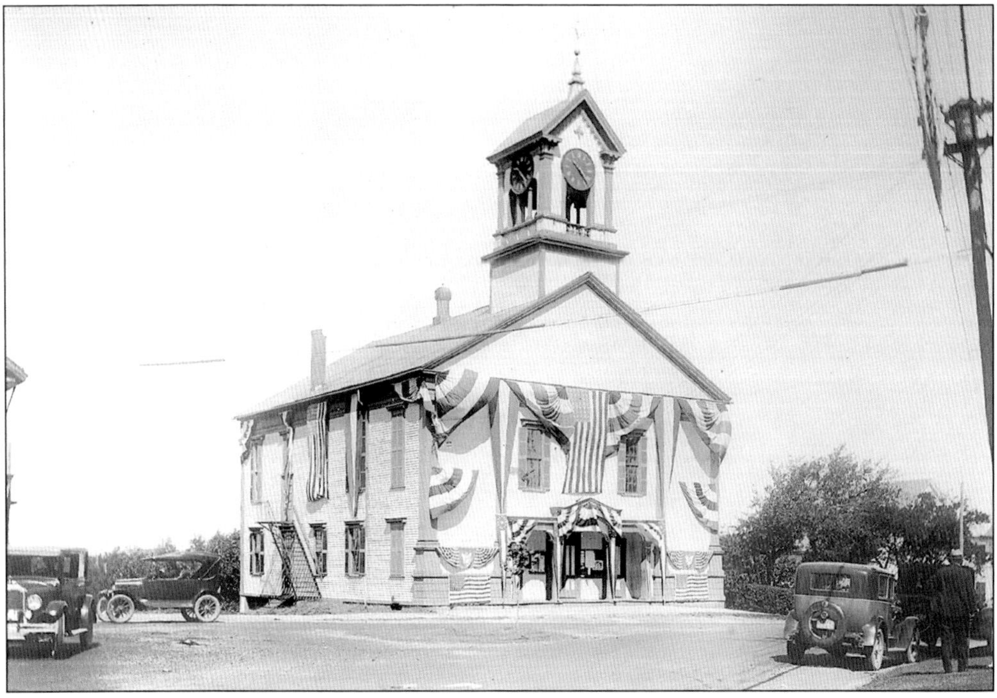

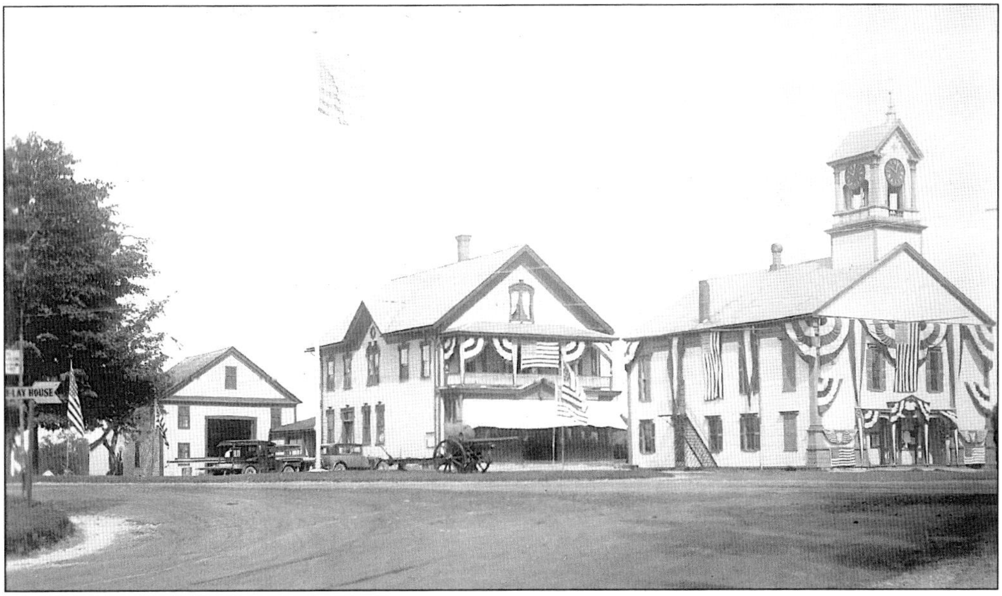

Brown's Store and the Lunenburg Town Hall are shown decked out in bunting in this 1928 photograph. In 1903, the Old Home Week Association was formed, and yearly observances were kept through 1935. This particular year coincided with the 200th anniversary of the town's founding in 1728 and, therefore, led to special events in addition to the regular Old Home Week features.

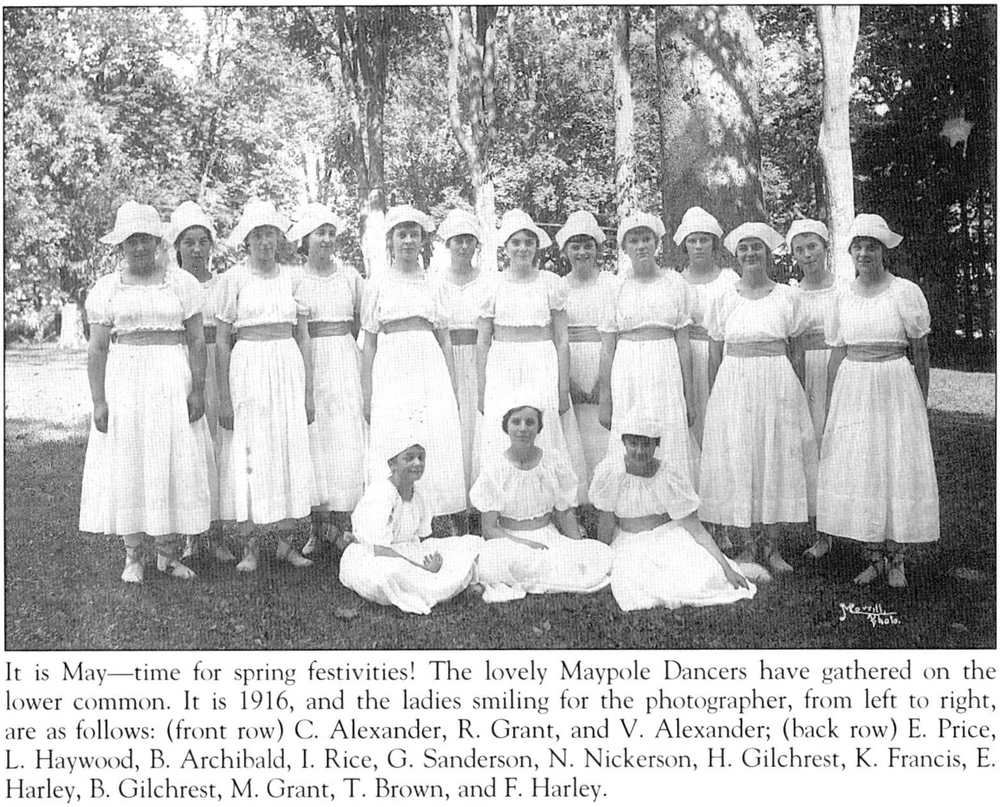

It is May—time for spring festivities! The lovely Maypole Dancers have gathered on the lower common. It is 1916, and the ladies smiling for the photographer, from left to right, are as follows: (front row) C. Alexander, R. Grant, and V. Alexander; (back row) E. Price, L. Haywood, B. Archibald, I. Rice, G. Sanderson, N. Nickerson, H. Gilchrest, K. Francis, E. Harley, B. Gilchrest, M. Grant, T. Brown, and F. Harley.

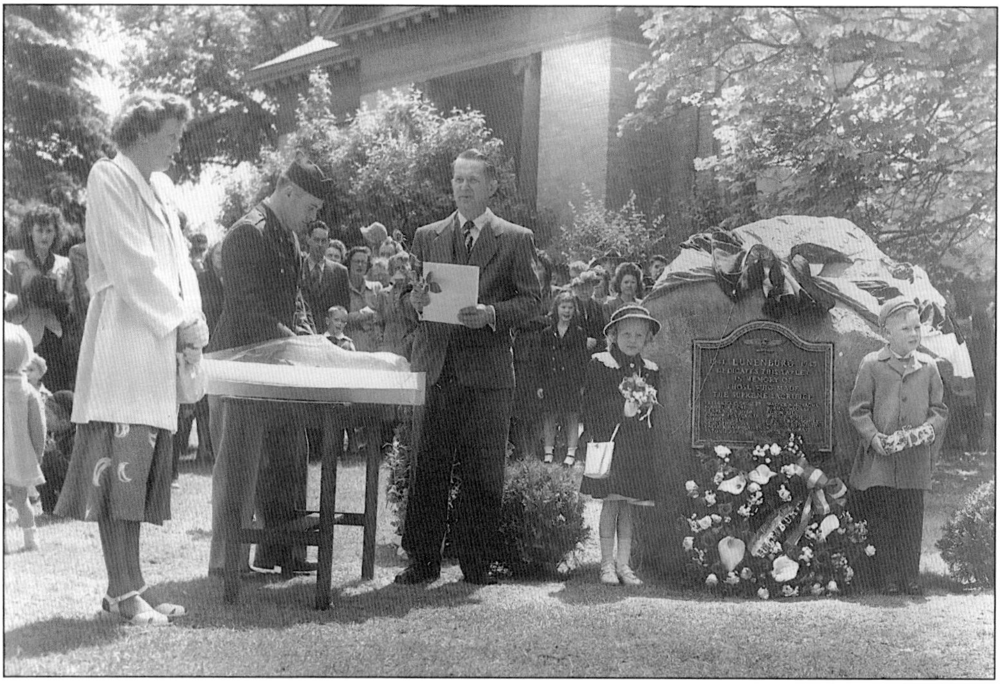

Memorial Day in 1949 saw the dedication of a monument honoring Lunenburg men who lost their lives in World War II: F. Cross Jr., W. Cross, C. Dyer, J. Fortune Jr., R. Gale, K. Gove, R. Haapalainen, A. Jones, W. Monaghan, J. Palonen, E. Rill, W. Rill, L. Schultz, N. Tonseth, and W. Waye. Selectman Eino Toko presents Mrs. Jorma Palonen with a token of the memorial service, as her young daughter Elizabeth stands beside the memorial stone.

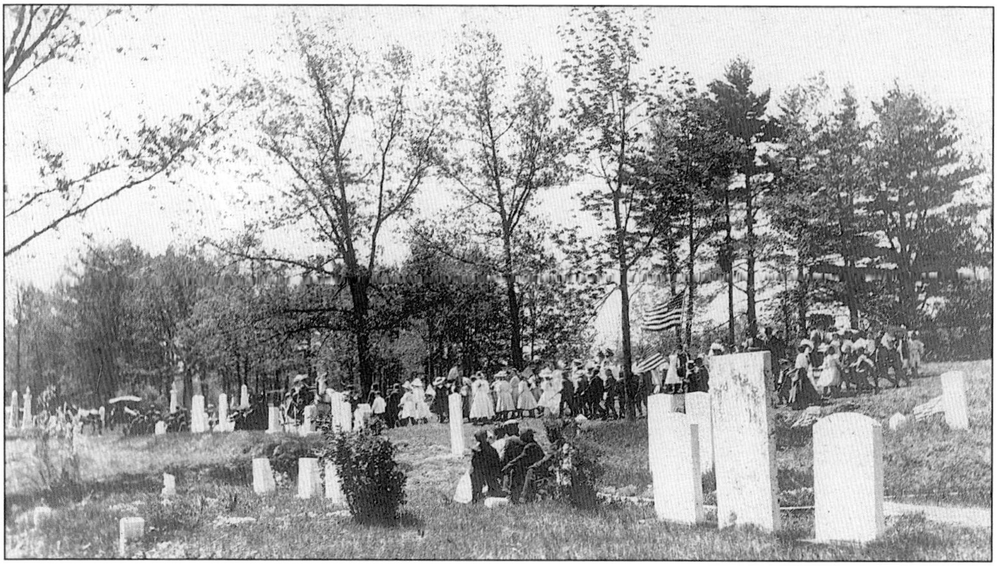

The Soldiers' Memorial Association, formed in 1872, directed Memorial Day ceremonies for the next 103 years. A procession was led by the town band of veterans' groups, town officials, various organizations, and schoolchildren. All took part in ceremonies at the North and South Cemeteries. They returned to the town hall for prayer, speeches, patriotic recitations, singing, and a light lunch.

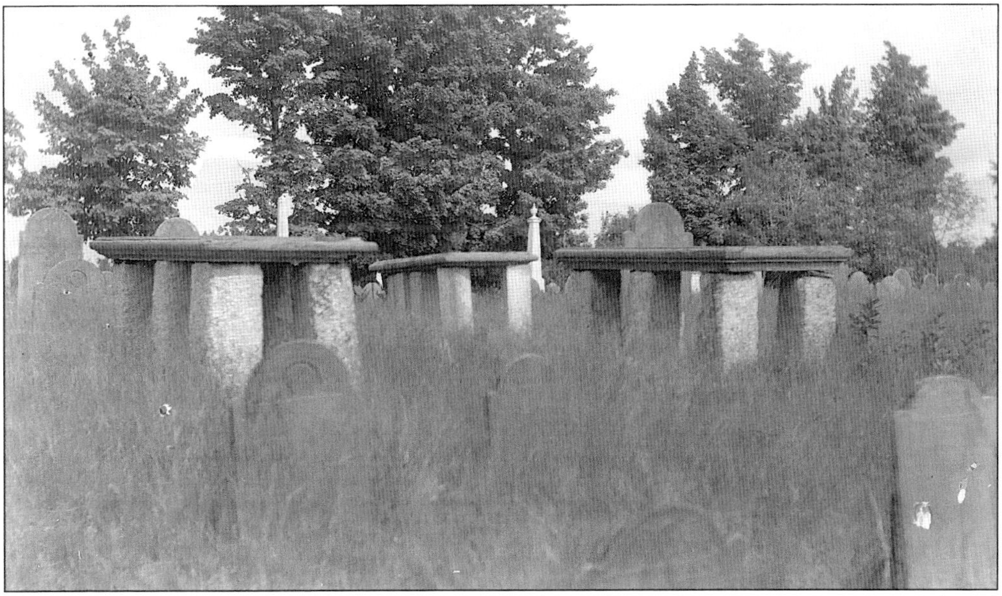

Parts of the South and North Cemeteries are the least changed areas in town since Colonial times, aside from the neatly trimmed grass one sees today. The three table stones pictured are in the oldest section of the South Cemetery. Here lie three early ministers. Table stones, from left to right, are those of Rev. Samuel Payson, Rev. Zabdiel Adams, and Rev. David Stearns. Copious biographical material is carved into the top surfaces.

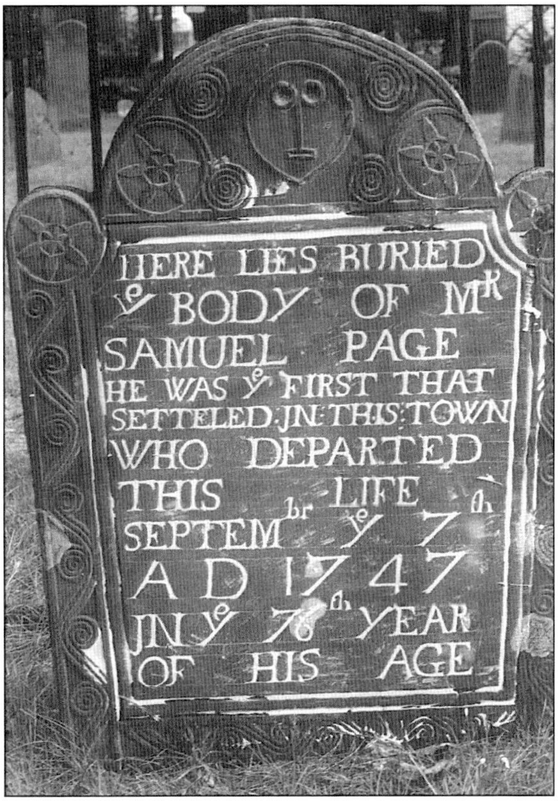

This is the tombstone of Lunenburg's original settler, Samuel Page, who came to this town in 1718. He was buried in the South Cemetery in 1747. This marker is still viewable today. A wrought-iron fence encloses the burial site. A bronze marker has also been placed on Samuel Page's grave. In 1976, opposite the entrance to the cemetery, the town placed a granite marker noting the site of his farm.

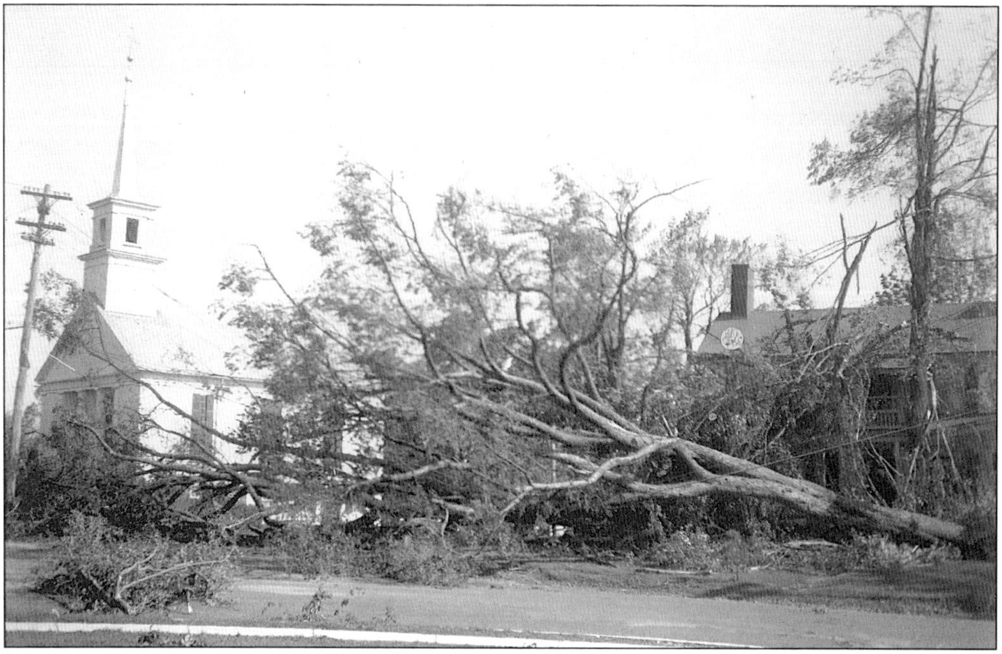

On September 21, 1938, the appearance of Lunenburg was greatly altered by a hurricane. Huge elm trees that had graced Lunenburg Center for many years crashed down, along with innumerable other trees and telephone poles. This photograph, taken from the Ritter Memorial Library lawn, shows one of the fallen elms. The United Parish church can be seen beyond and the Corner House, on the right.

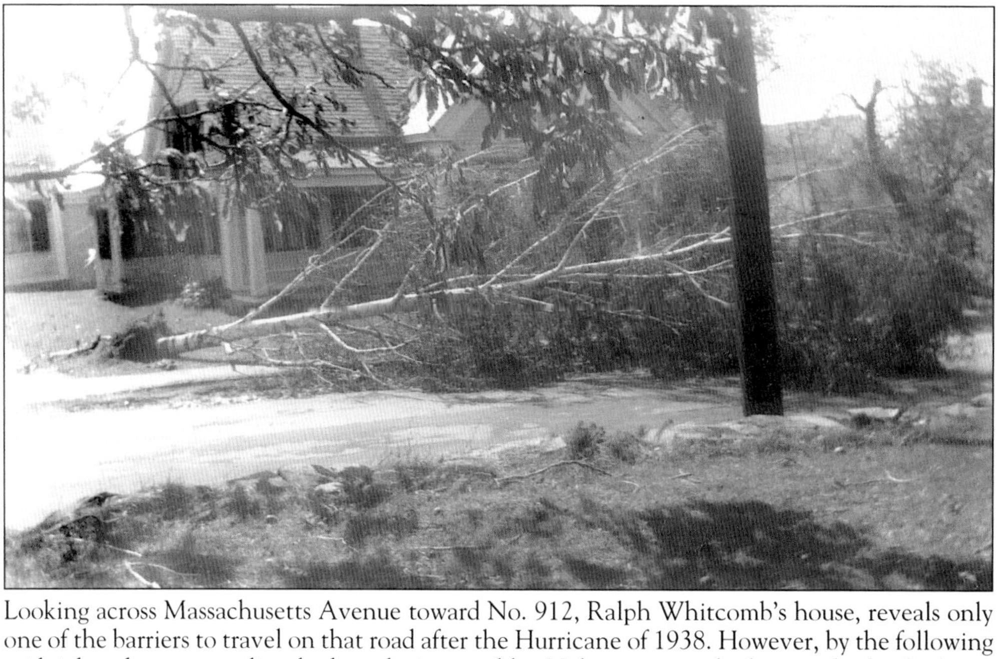

Looking across Massachusetts Avenue toward No. 912, Ralph Whitcomb's house, reveals only one of the barriers to travel on that road after the Hurricane of 1938. However, by the following midnight, the state police had made it passable. Volunteers pitched in with the highway department, cutting up fallen trees. It was weeks before power and telephone service could be restored to every home.

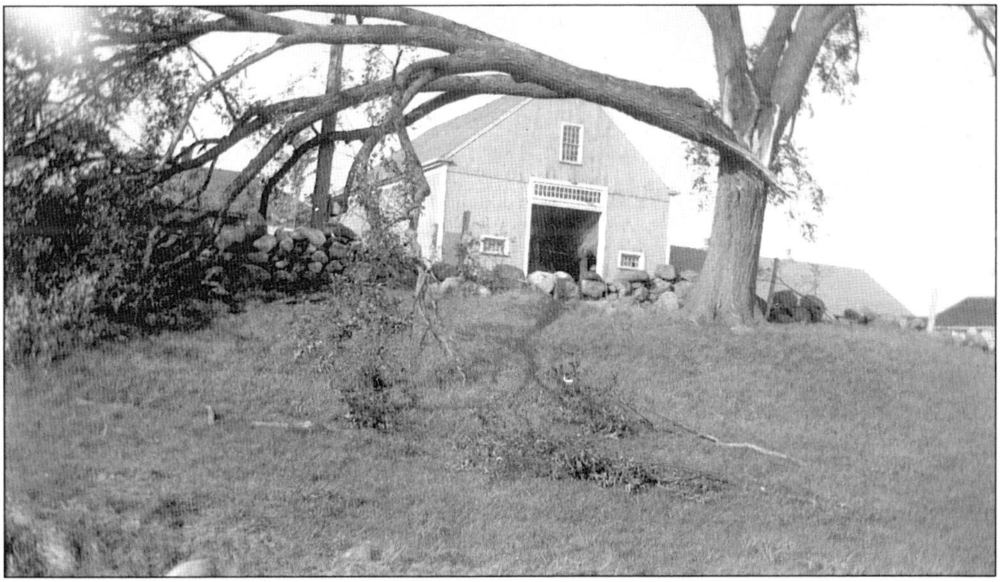

The Cook Farm still stands on Mulpus Road, no longer graced by the huge elm split by the hurricane. In the weeks following the storm, families who had not yet modernized their homes led more normal lives than their relatively modern neighbors. Wood stoves for cooking and heating, and old-fashioned kitchen sink hand pumps were newly appreciated and generously shared.

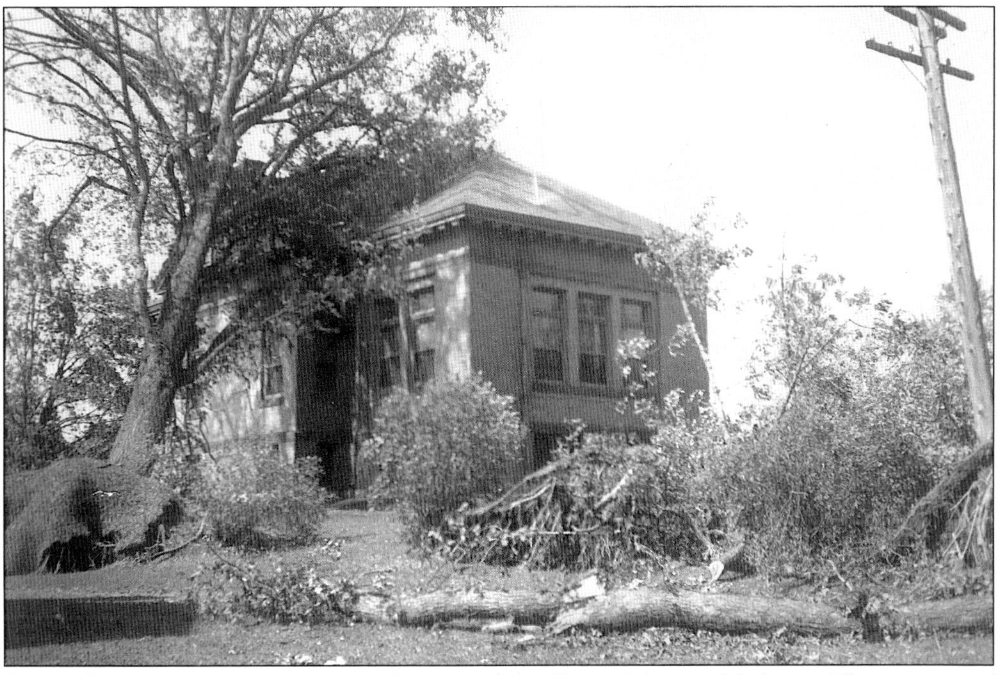

A very large tree came to rest on the rear of the Ritter Memorial Library. The exterior of the library at that time was still the original sandstone, and there was no addition on the side toward Lancaster Avenue. Townspeople were fortunate that the fall weather, after the hurricane, was mild, allowing the opportunity to repair damaged roofs, chimneys, and broken windows.

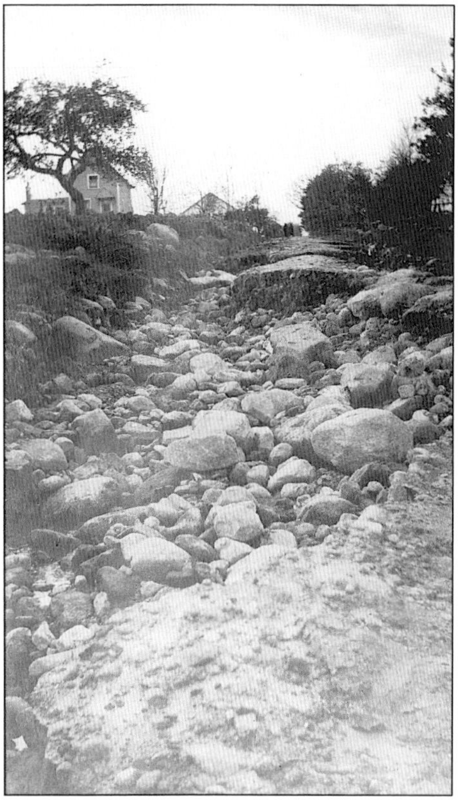

In 1927, a flood washed out many town roads. As few side streets were paved at that time, they were easily destroyed down to the bedrock. A small stream that flowed into Mulpus Brook was able to scour out the road in front of 189 Howard Street. Pictured is the old Timothy Howard Farm, dating back to the Kilburn map (K-231).

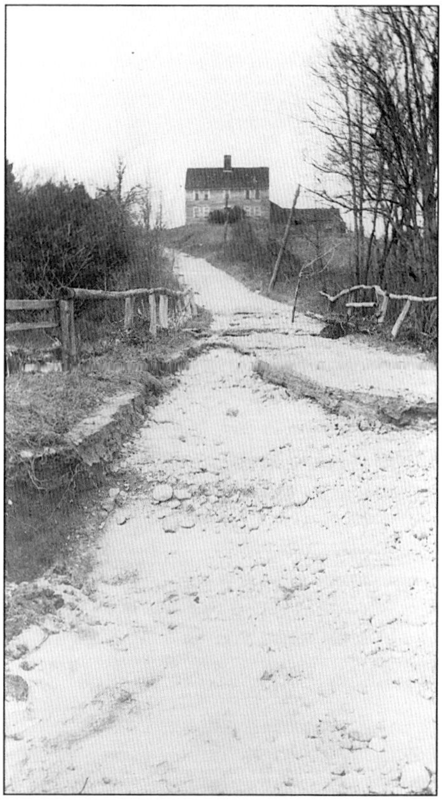

A washout from the 1927 flood is pictured here at 300 Holman Street. Mulpus Brook was crossed by an old stone bridge at this point. The house on the hill beyond, now the property of Sandra Lane, was owned by Henry Dunsmore. Dunsmore had a sawmill a short distance from the brook. Water was directed to the mill via a short channel. The Dunsmore house (K-248) appears on the old Kilburn map.

Four

Street Scenes and Travel

This chapter brings together some scenic areas of Lunenburg and looks at how our residents traveled to surrounding towns and neighborhoods. Landscape scenes of farms, streams, bridges, lakes, and different modes of travel are included.

In his deed research of early Lunenburg roads, William R. Bingham tells us, "The acceptance of roads was a pretty much hit or miss affair in olden times. The written descriptions in early town records cannot be easily researched. More often than not, the town didn't get a deed for the property taken. Some roads were never constructed." Only a dedicated researcher like Bingham can make heads or tails of early road patterns. Roads were discontinued and new ones built as easily as houses were moved in the earlier years.

Bridges often deteriorated and needed replacement, sometimes in a more suitable location. Development of the town over the years led to many changes, often a result of growth of neighboring towns or state, new techniques, new materials, new methods, or better inventions. Seasons of the year also had its impact on travel.

There is an aerial view of Lunenburg taken in 1948. Although limited in scope, it portrays the center of town. The large lake at the top of the photograph is man-made by one of our former residents, Arnold Dickinson. Dickinson was president of Sikorsky Aircraft Manufacturing Company. It is part of our community known as Hickory Hills. It was built as a reservoir. Later, it became a summer community and is now occupied by many year-round residents.

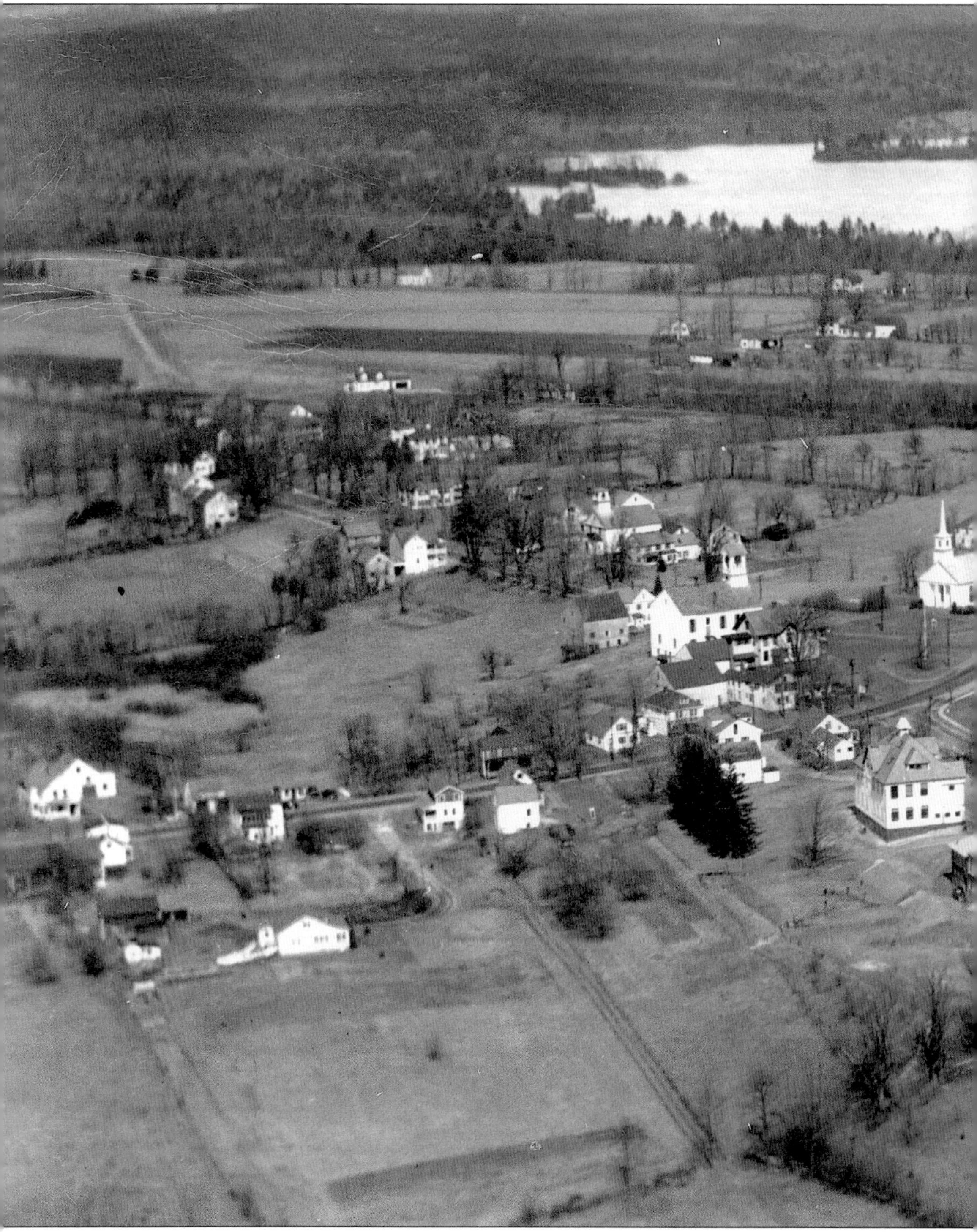

This aerial view shows Lunenburg Center as it appeared in 1948. Note the old Center School, where the Lunenburg Historical Society stands today. Note also the Lunenburg Fire Station before its 1976 addition. The library on the corner is barely visible. The open fields between

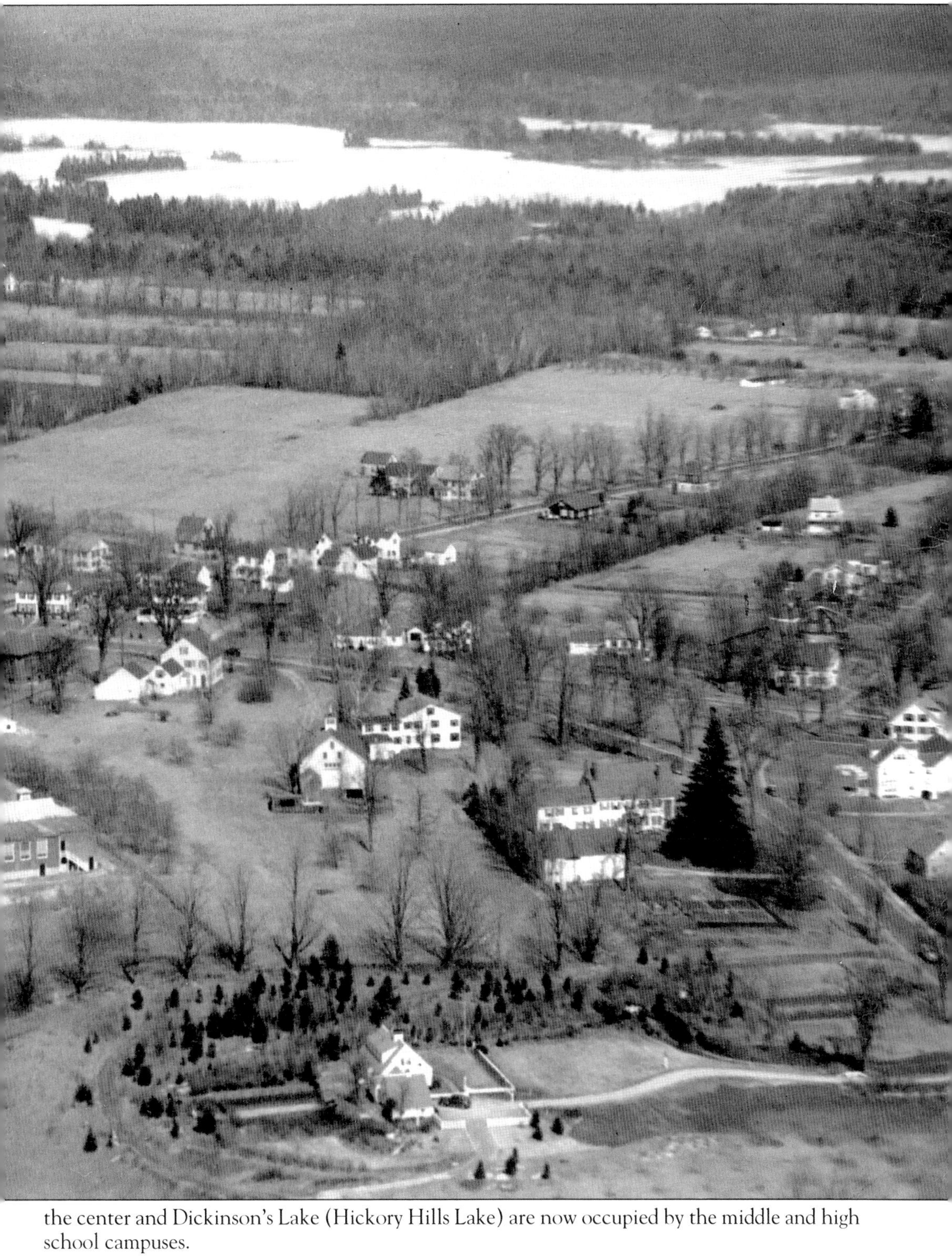

the center and Dickinson's Lake (Hickory Hills Lake) are now occupied by the middle and high school campuses.

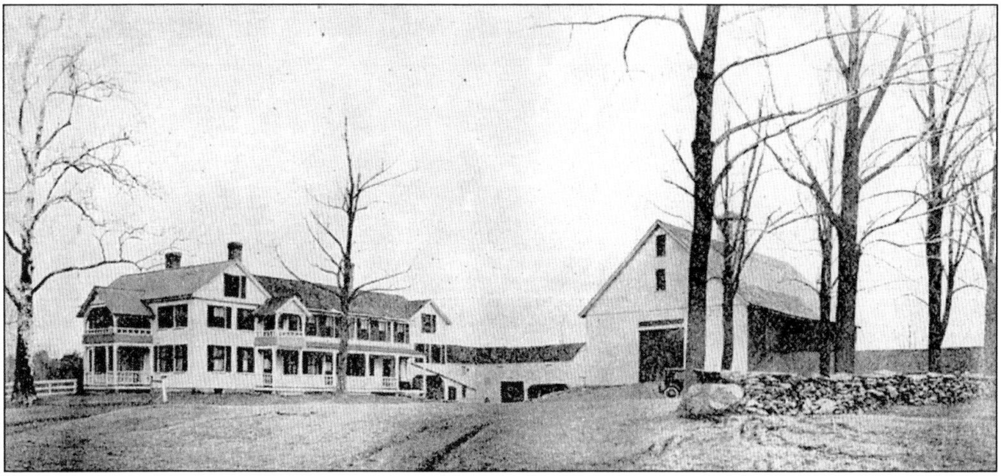

This beautiful farm scene shows the Old Goodrich Homestead, located at about 991 Lancaster Avenue and currently owned by the Stillman family. The original house was built by Phillip Goodridge. The present house was built on the same property in 1825 by Joseph Goodrich. The scenery is unique with a wonderful view, a dirt road, and a row of large trees. This farm is still in operation today. There is a dairy store, recently opened, next to the homestead where milk is sold. The photograph below shows the view from the homestead looking west at one of their pastures with Lake Massapoag in the valley. A buttonwood tree stands in the foreground. The stone wall is characteristic of those built during these times. Farmers usually dug the stones out of their working fields and put them to good use. (Courtesy of Nancy L. Bigelow.)

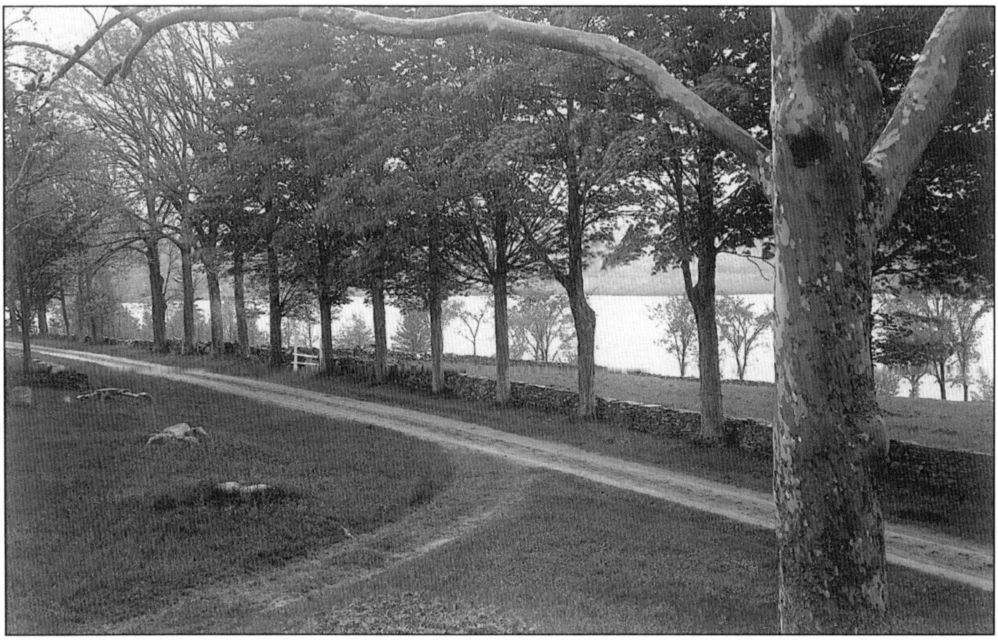

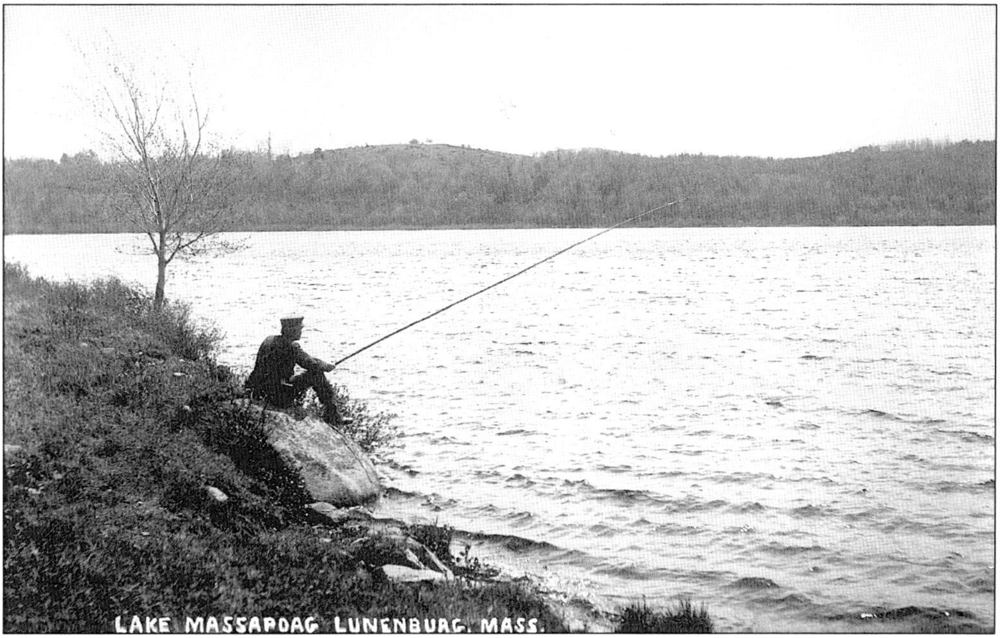

Over the years, Lake Massapoag has been a site to visit for a relaxing and peaceful day. In this photograph, Norman G. Bigelow takes some spare time from his many farm duties to fish and enjoy the scenery. Bigelow's mother was a Goodrich who married a Bigelow, and the Goodrich farm later became known as the Bigelow Farm for several years. (Courtesy of Nancy L. Bigelow.)

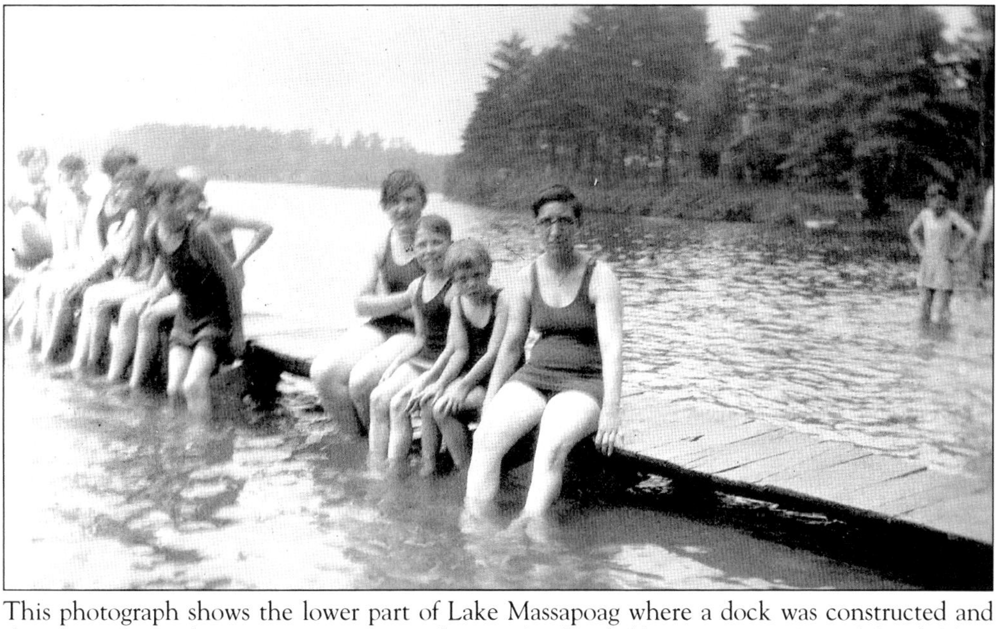

This photograph shows the lower part of Lake Massapoag where a dock was constructed and the American Red Cross gave swimming lessons for the children in town. One of the children having her first swimming lesson is Lucina Hoisington, whose family lived farther north on 612 Lancaster Avenue. (Courtesy of Diane DelliCarpini.)

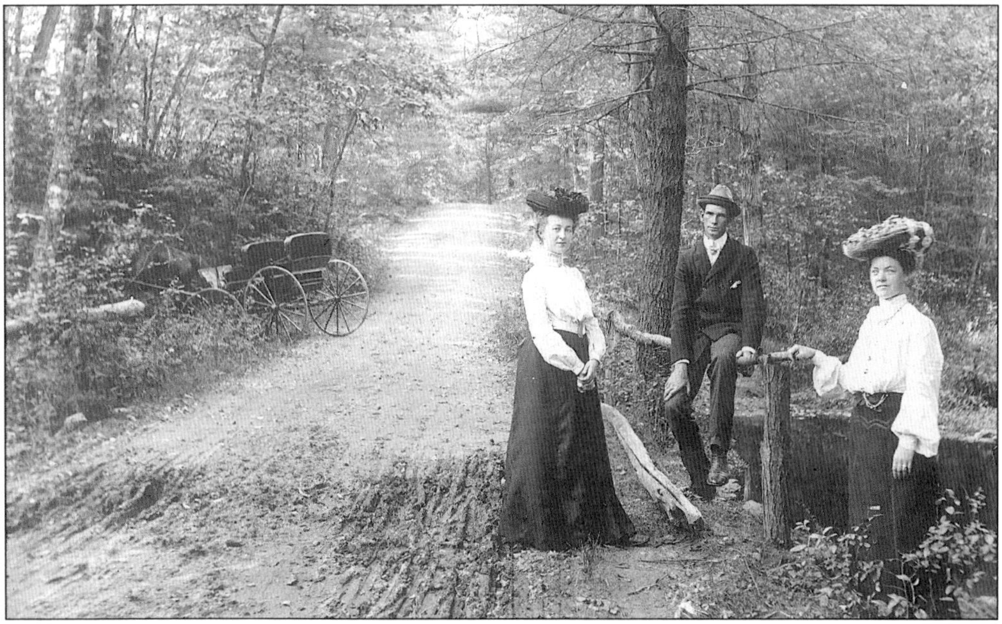

Harry and Bertha Francis and their friend Mrs. E.H. Bryant are seen here posing in their Sunday best at the bridge on Holman Street. Their buggy can be seen to the left, with the horse grazing nearby. The first mention of a street, later to become Holman Street, is found in the early records of March 1, 1784. This photograph shows a section from Northfield Road to Chase Road with the bridge over Mulpus Brook.

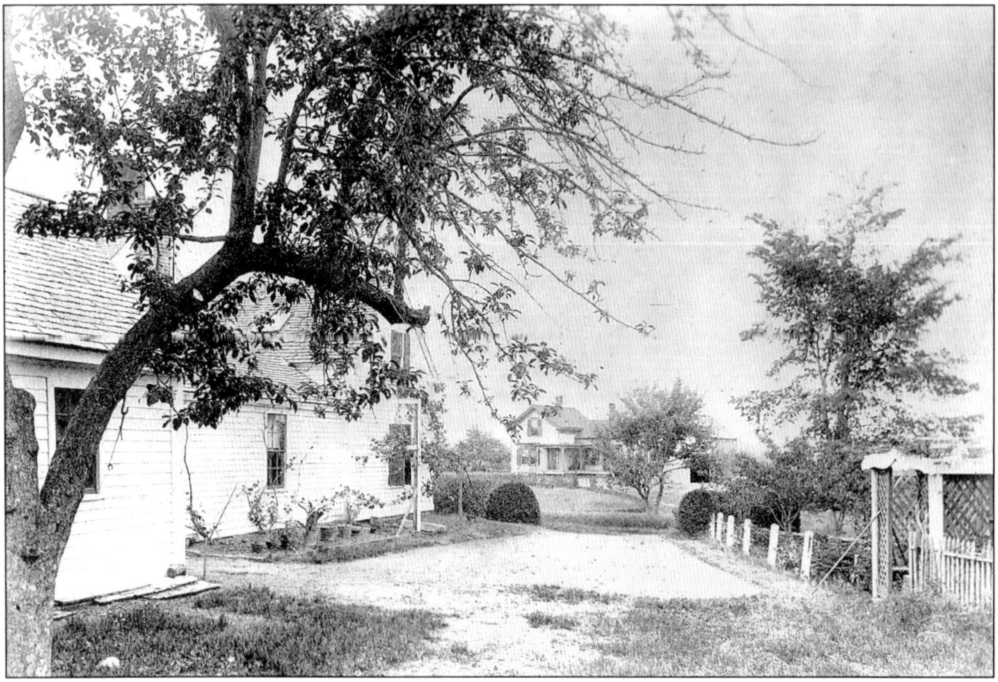

This delightful scene was taken on Arbor Street. The building on the left is the Arad Wood house (K-113), located at 90 Arbor Street. Looking across the road from Arad Wood's driveway is the John Gilchrest house, located at 83 Arbor Street.

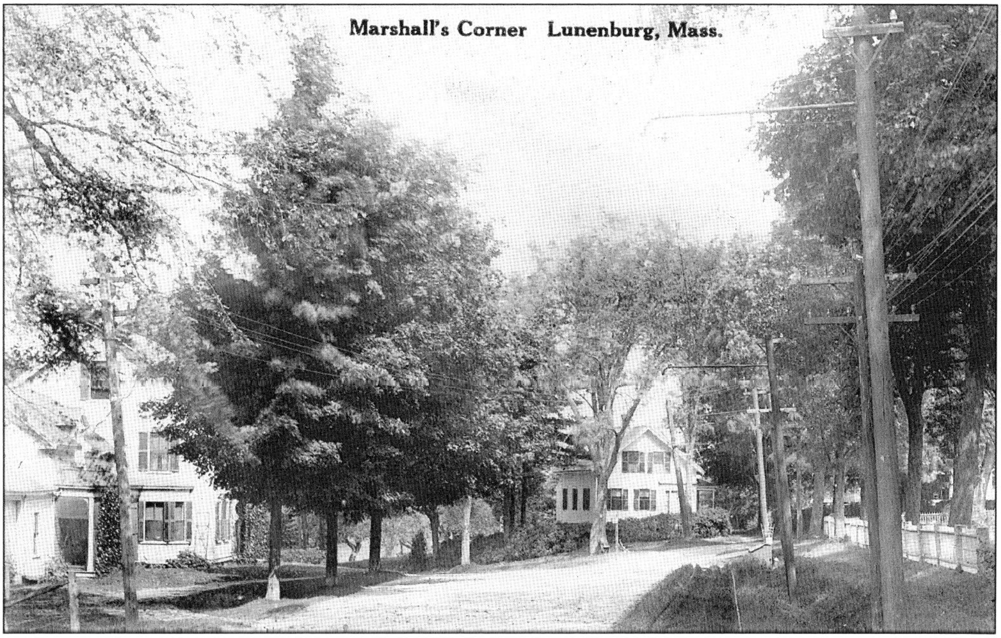

At the northern end of Main Street stand these two houses, and, on the right, the fence of a third, looking much as they did early in the 20th century. The Marshall Cottage (right), at 3 Oak Avenue, was built in 1852. The Edwin Marshall House (left), at 91 Main Street, was built c. 1790 and named for the man who was born in the Marshall Cottage and later moved to this house.

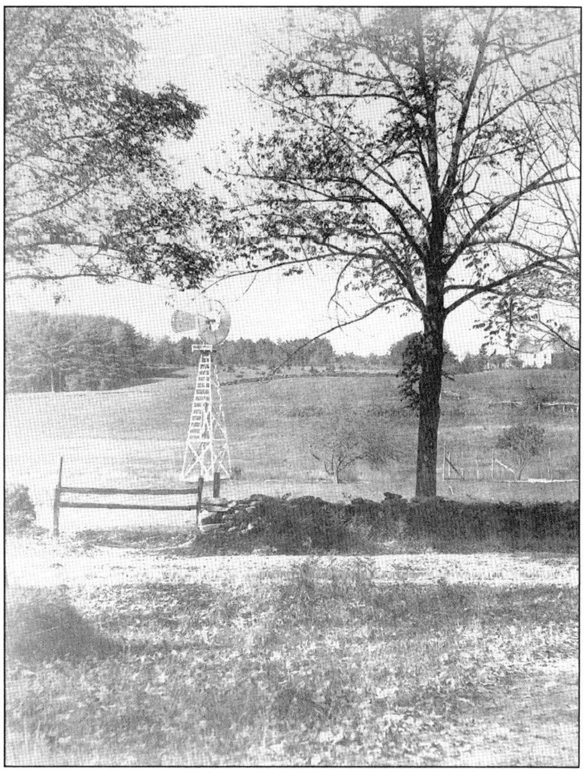

One hundred years ago, when Lunenburg was just a quiet little town with a population of about 1,000, one could stand directly behind the house at the end of Main Street (corner of Highland and Chestnut Streets) and be charmed by this pastoral scene. Today, the rambling stone wall, the windmill, and the meadow are all gone. However, the house in the distance is still there but no longer visible from this angle.

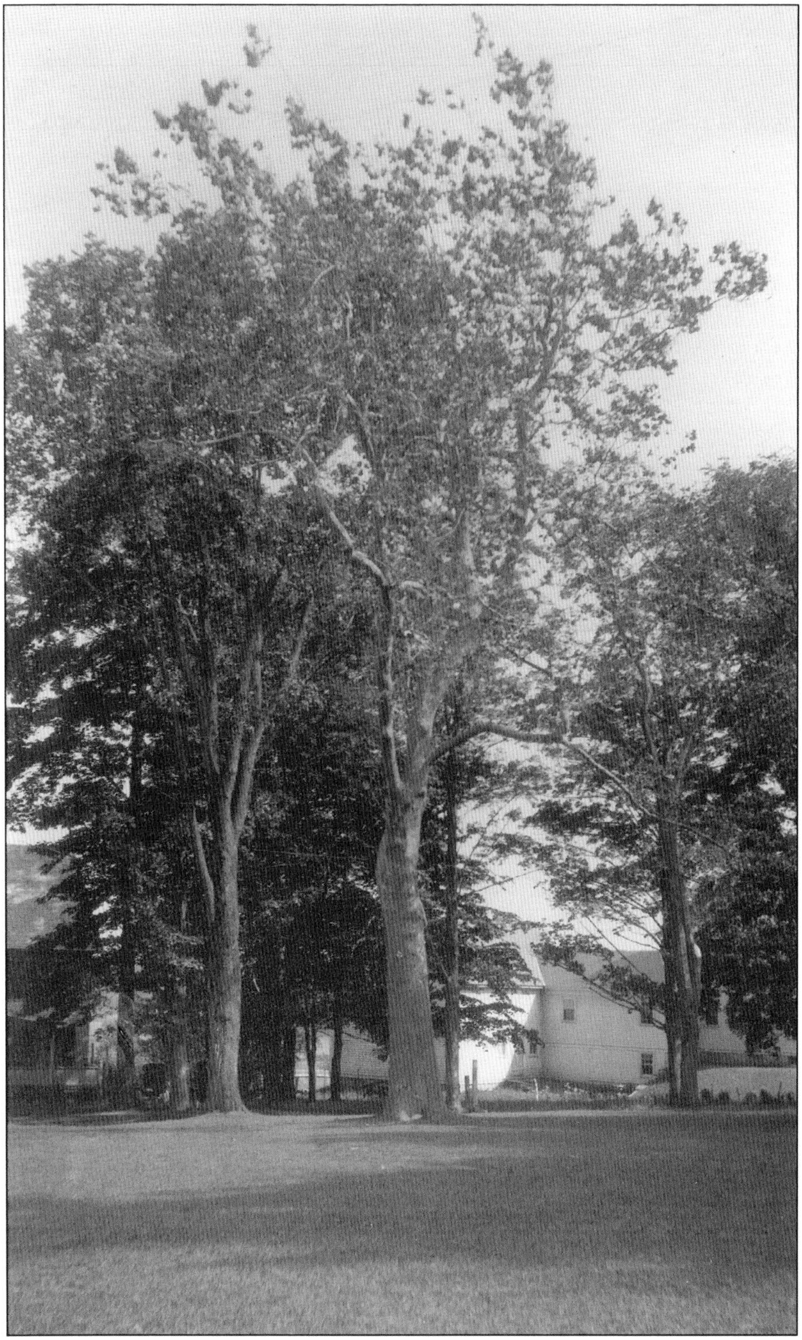

Pictured is our historic Liberty Tree, planted by Capt. John Fuller on the lower common on April 19, 1775. This common served as a training field for the 27 men of the Lunenburg Militia under Captain Fuller. The tree survived until March 5, 1938, at which time it was deemed unsafe and cut down. G. Barry Whitcomb crawled through the entire length of this rotted tree, which had a circumference of 12 feet. The spot on which this magnificent tree stood is today marked by a granite watering trough purchased with funds given to the Village Improvement Society by Benjamin Jones.

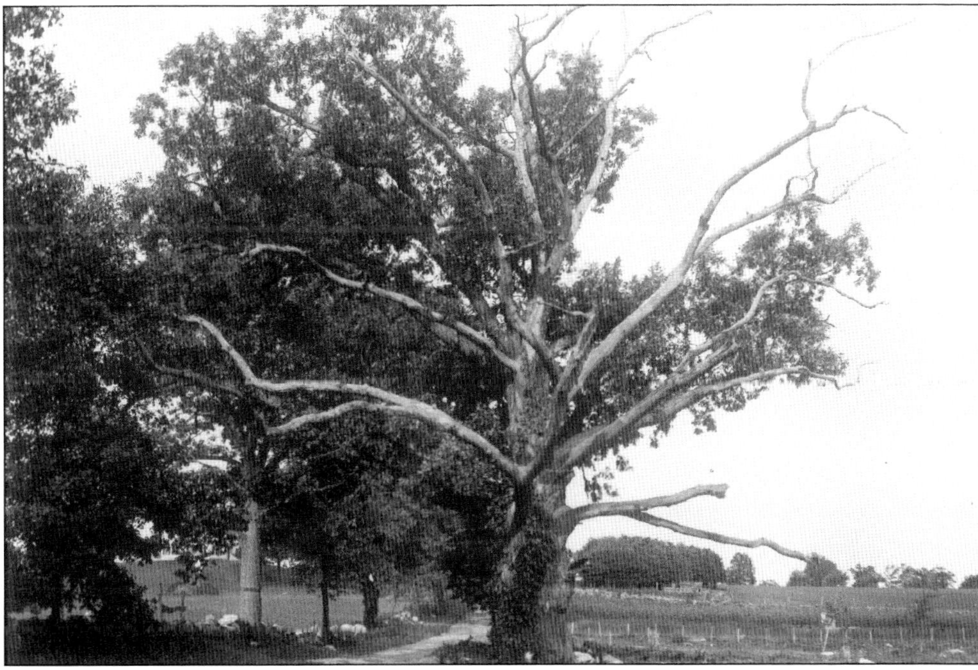

The King Arthur Oak once stood on Beal Street near the Pilgrim Covenant Church. It was a magnificent tree with a height of 70 feet, a circumference of 16 feet, and is said to have a spread nearly 100 feet. It supposedly got its name from a prank someone played by nailing a King Arthur flour sack to it.

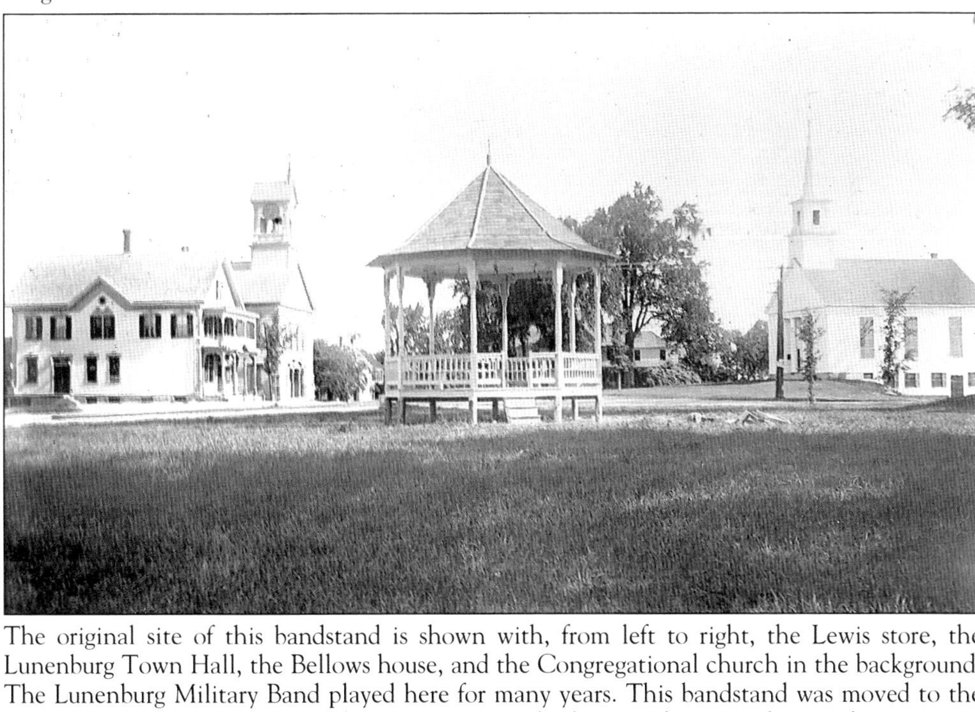

The original site of this bandstand is shown with, from left to right, the Lewis store, the Lunenburg Town Hall, the Bellows house, and the Congregational church in the background. The Lunenburg Military Band played here for many years. This bandstand was moved to the lower common to make way for the Ritter Memorial Library and remained in use for 100 years, at which time a new bandstand was built.

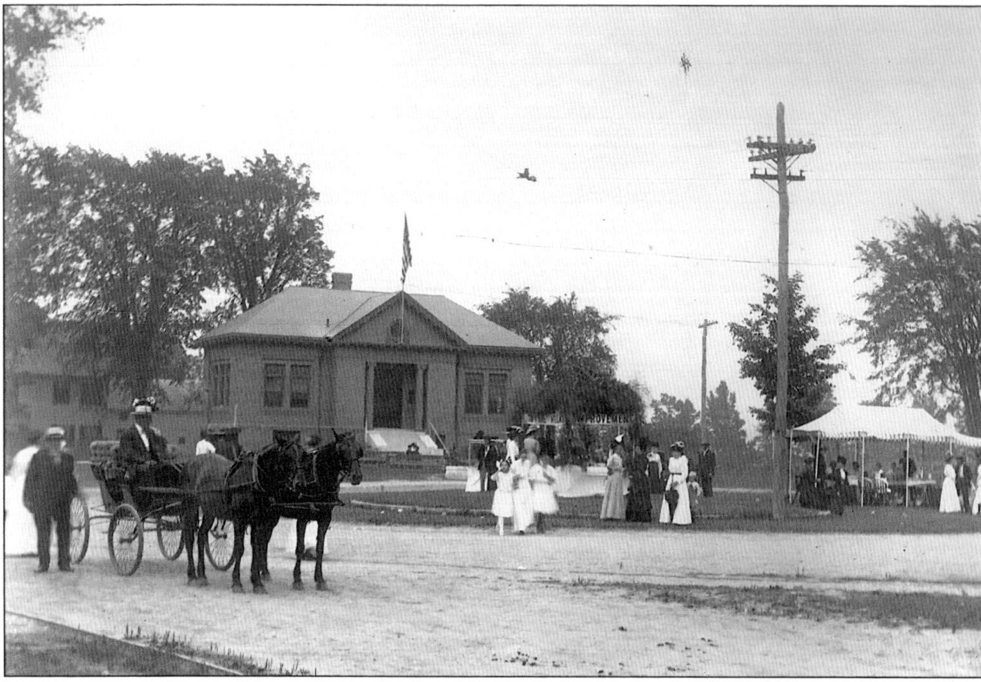

The center of Lunenburg experienced many changes over the years. The above scene gives the reader an idea of one of them. This 1914 scene shows the Ritter Memorial Library with its beautiful granite steps. The trolley tracks traverse the road, and horse and wagon is still a popular mode of transportation. It is interesting to see how our town has evolved.

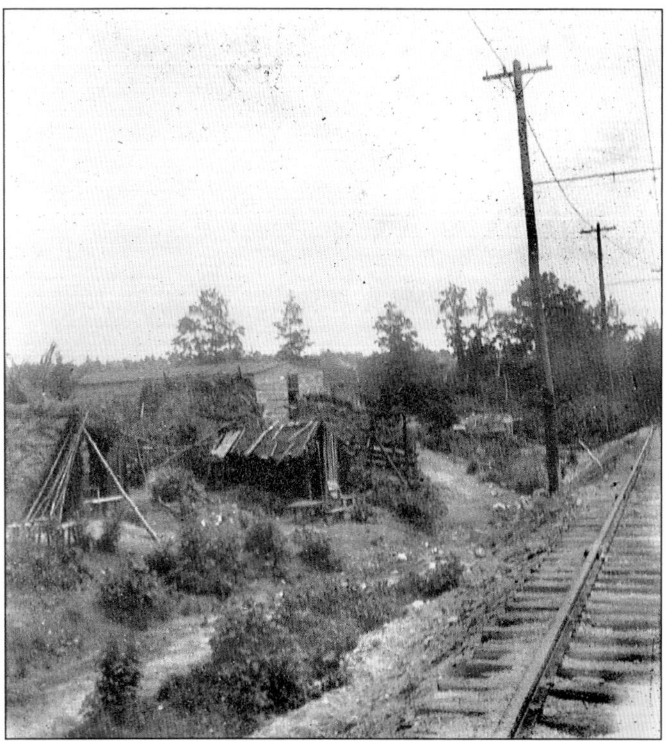

At the beginning of the 20th century, railroad lines were laid from North Leominster to Shirley. They passed through Lunenburg, paralleling the Shirley-Leominster Road. During the building project, Italian laborers lived in this camp. It became known as "Little Italy." This camp was located near the site of the present Pioneer Industrial Park.

About a mile into the woods, north of Northfield Road, behind the Maplewood Golf Course, is a glacier-created natural wonder: Table Rock. Local hikers of all ages, Girl Scouts, Boy Scouts, campers, and family trekkers have marveled at not only the three-legged "table" but also the massive ledge on which it stands. Many thin-bodied daredevils have traversed the lengthy crevice, defying the danger and potential trap.

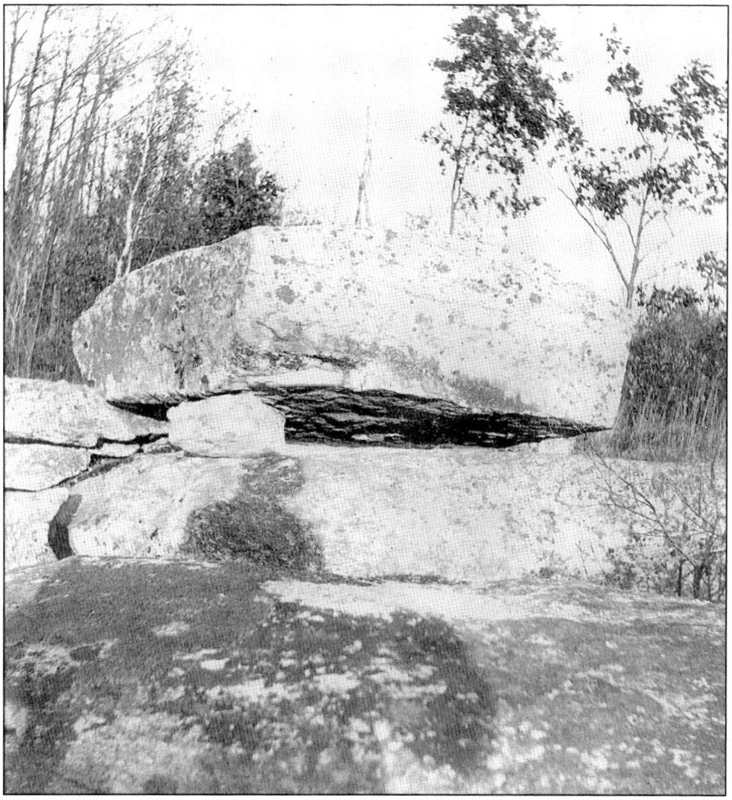

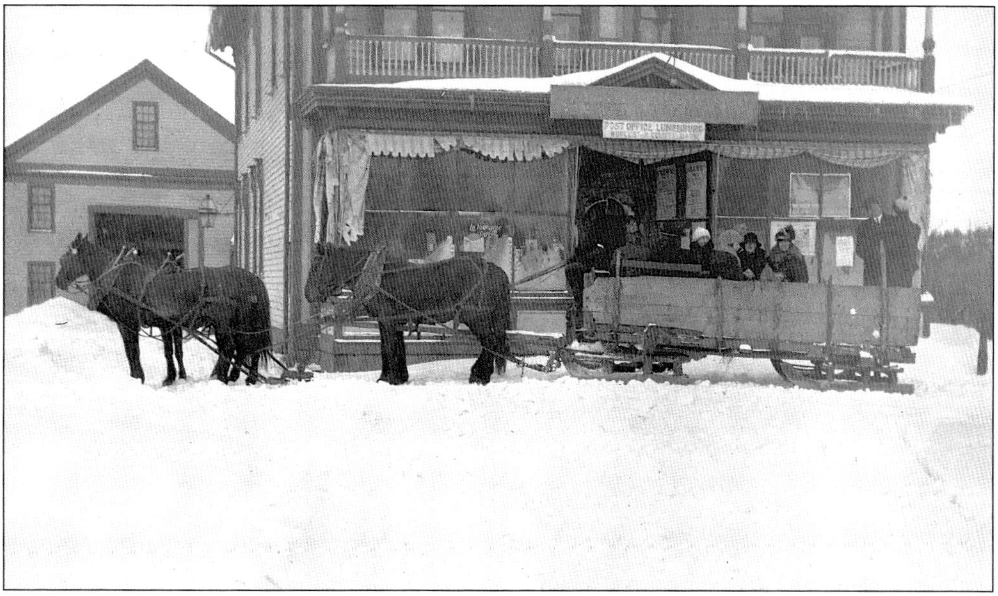

During heavy winter weather, this form of transportation may have been more reliable than the trolley. This vehicle with four-horse hitch, pictured in front of the Warren Lewis General Store and Post Office, was called a "barge." It would be equipped with wheels in milder weather. Barges frequently carried groups to meetings in surrounding towns and to social occasions, such as barn dances. Schools also used them to transport children.

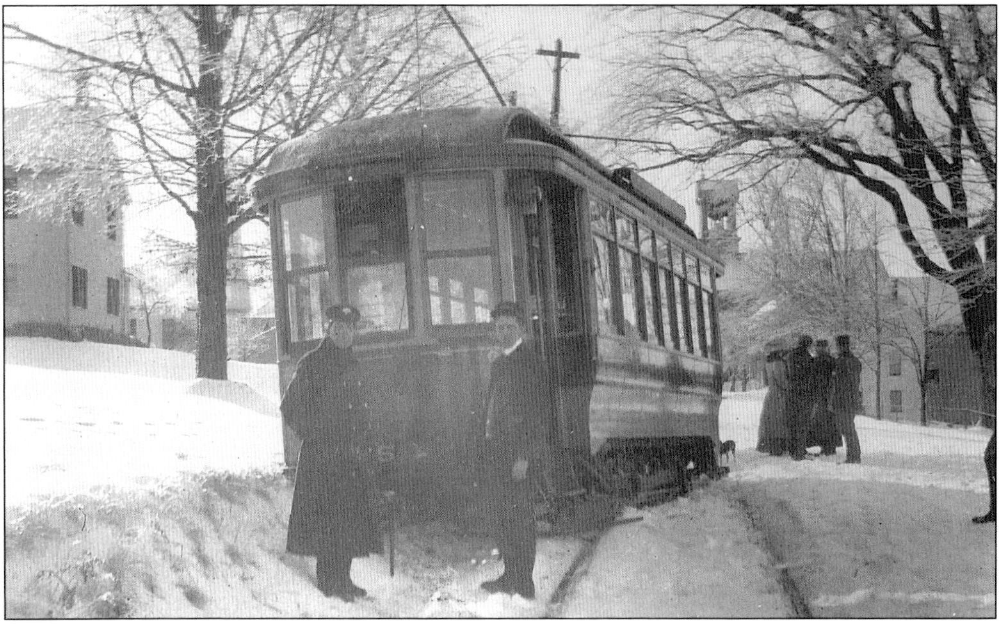

The trolley jumped the track on Main Street after a snowstorm in 1912. Since no one was hurt, the driver and the investigating police officer were able to smile for the cameraman. Eight years later, a larger storm's drifts were so high that the trolley became stuck on Leominster Road, where it remained for two or three months. Finally, the entire town mobilized and dug out the tracks.

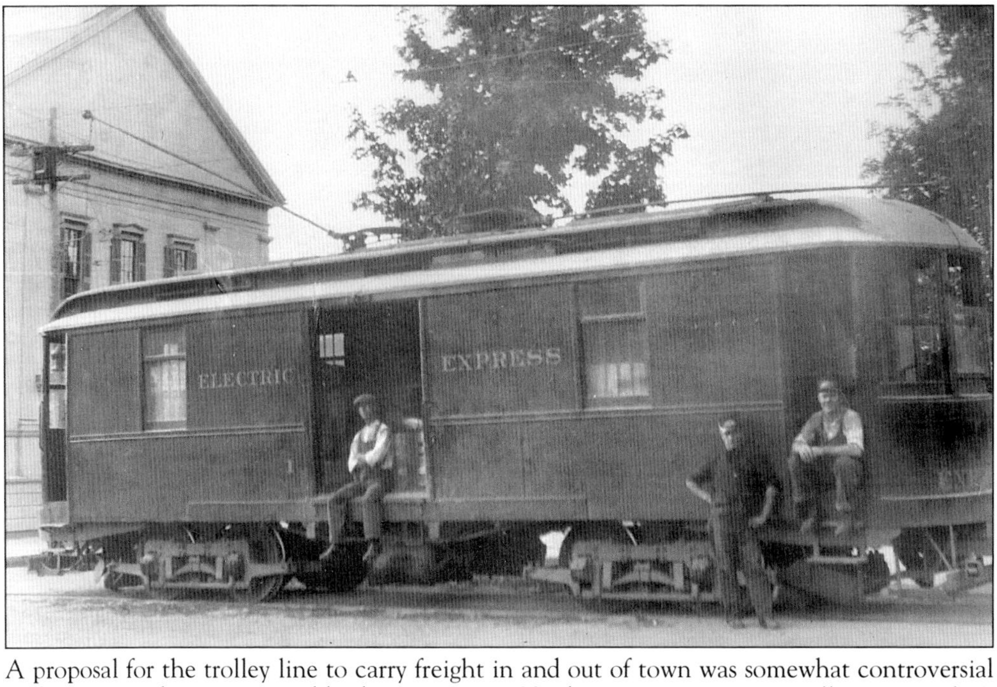

A proposal for the trolley line to carry freight in and out of town was somewhat controversial and occasioned numerous public hearings in 1903; this service was eventually permitted. A spur line for freight ran between Warren Lewis's store, now Honey Farms, and the Lunenburg Town Hall. Trolley service was discontinued in 1925, when it became obsolete with the use of cars, trucks, and buses.

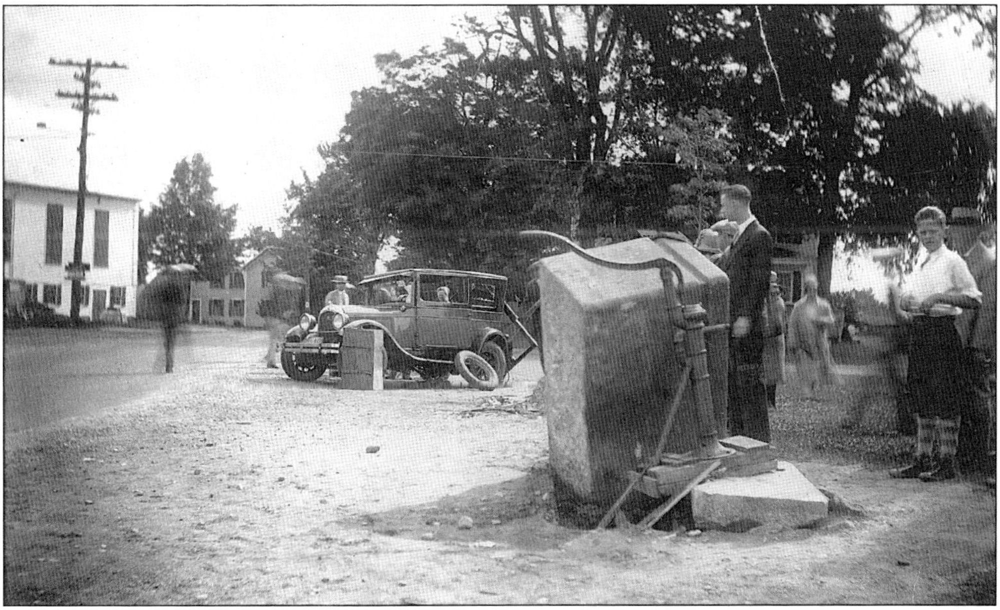

When the wooden watering trough was replaced with a granite one in front of the Ritter Memorial Library, it became the target of the newly invented automobile. So many cars ran into the trough that it was moved to the lower common. This photograph shows the trough tipped on end with half of the base resting against the front left wheel of the car. The whole right side of the car was destroyed.

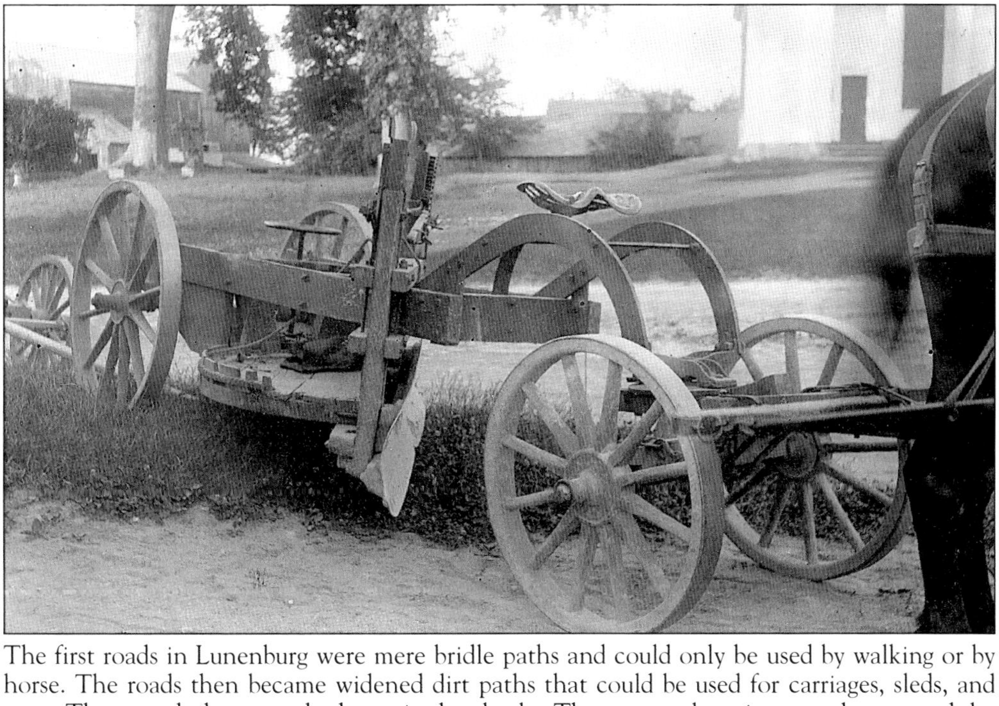

The first roads in Lunenburg were mere bridle paths and could only be used by walking or by horse. The roads then became widened dirt paths that could be used for carriages, sleds, and carts. These roads, however, had certain drawbacks. The carts and carriages made ruts, and the soil would be pushed to the side. Road scrapers, pulled by horses, were needed for maintenance. Shown here is a typical scraper.

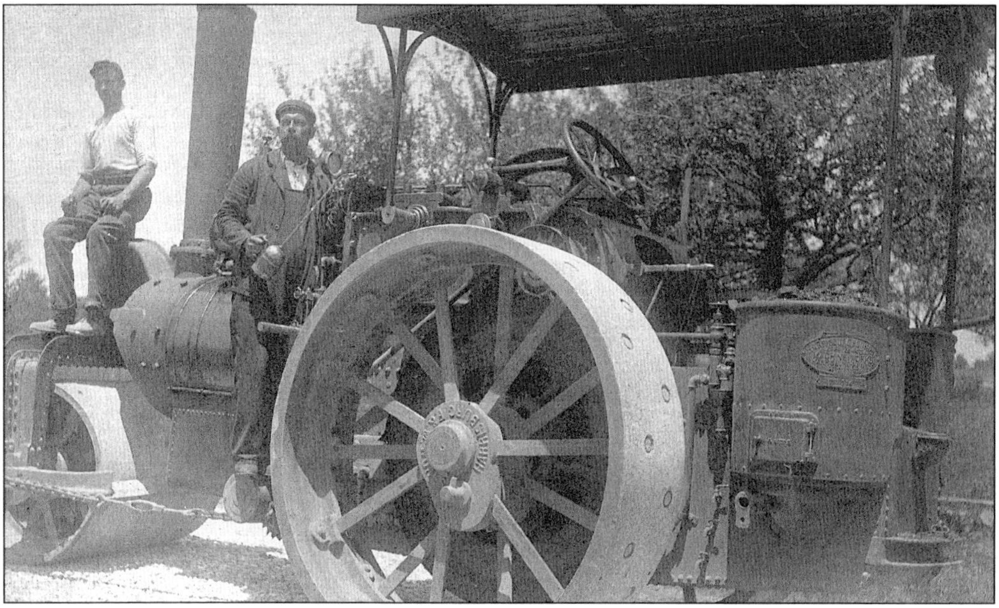

This new steamroller, used in the early 1900s, replaced men using shovels and hired teams to clear snow. They found it much easier to roll and pack down the snow after a storm. It was also useful for dirt-road maintenance. The town bought two of these steamrollers in 1905 for the total sum of $187. Motor-driven highway equipment eventually led to the necessity for a town barn on West Street for storage.

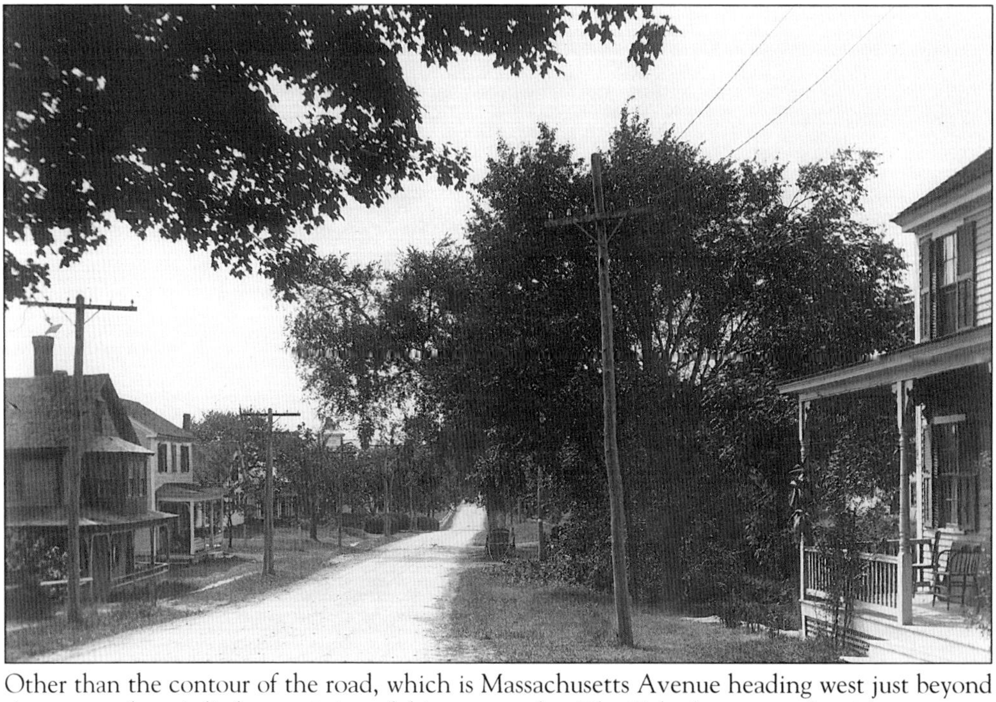

Other than the contour of the road, which is Massachusetts Avenue heading west just beyond the center, there is little remaining of this scene today. The Tyler house, on the right, was torn down. Its site will be used for a new post office. The first two houses on the left burned (the farther one in 1964), and newer houses have been built on these lots.

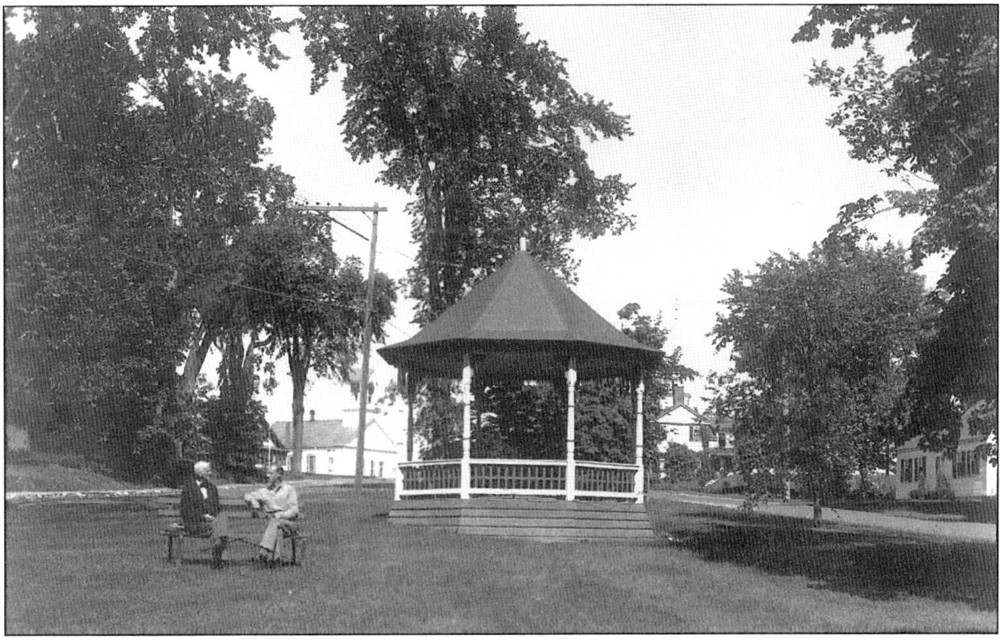

This bandstand, built in 1905, was originally located on the site of the present library. It was moved to the lower common in 1909. It was lighted by electricity taken from the trolley line on Leominster Road. When the trolley went up the hill during a concert, lights dimmed and musicians could not read their music. A new bandstand was erected in 1998, and the old one moved to the home of the Ebersoles.

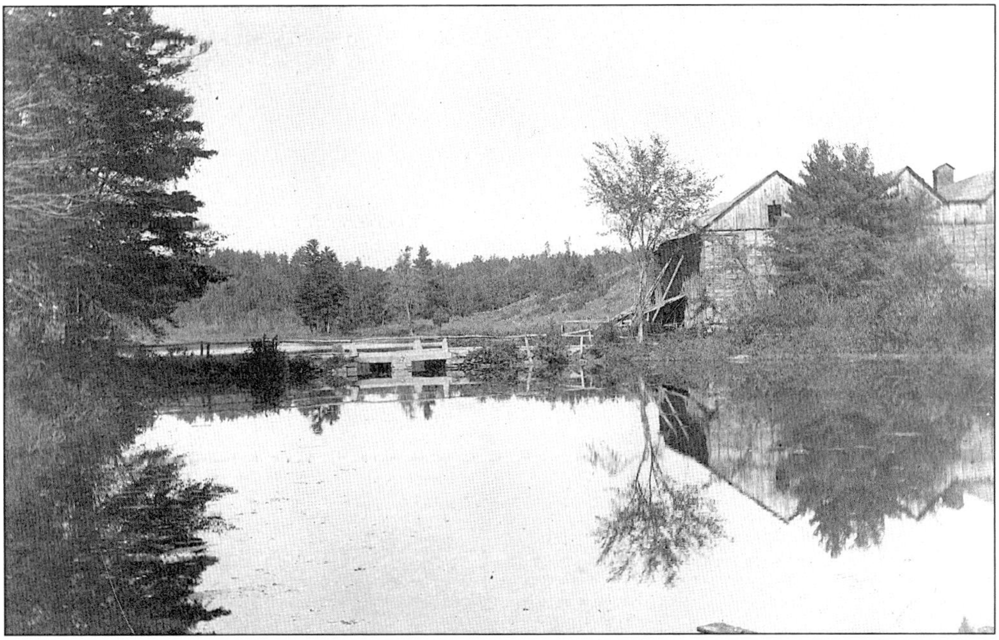

This tranquil scene shows Baker's Pond. The bridge in the distance crosses over Baker's Brook and is part of Young's Road. The building to the right is Green's Icehouse. Many Lunenburg children enjoyed ice-skating here over the years and shared some of its cool surroundings during the summers.

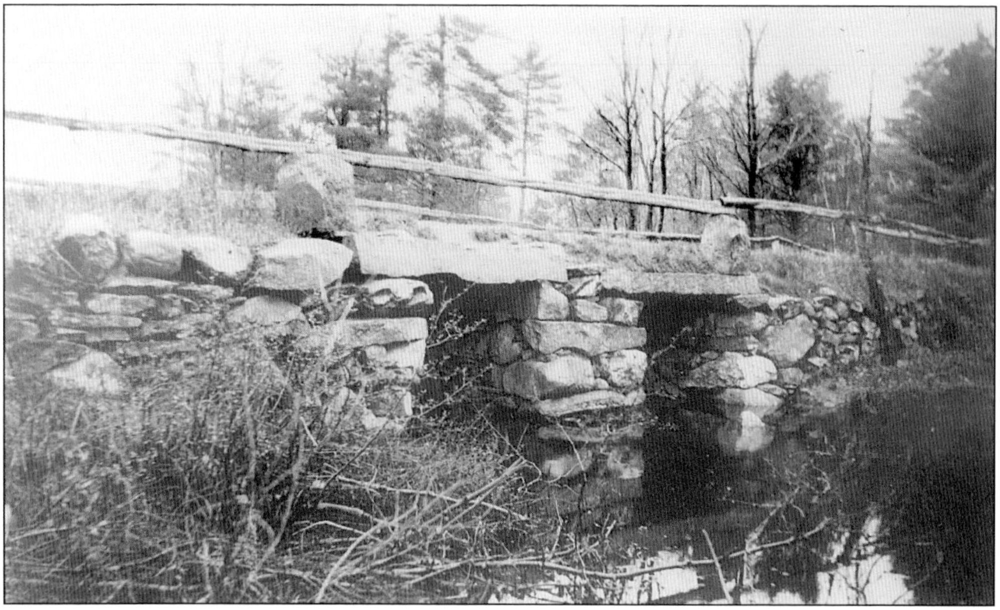

Hickory Hills Lake was formed in 1925, when the Dickinson family built a dam and spillway beside Townsend Harbor Road, on the other side of this bridge crossing Mulpus Brook. This picture was taken in the same year. The dam backed up the water of Mulpus Brook to create a lake covering more than 200 acres. Until the development of Hickory Hills in the early 1950s, it was Dickinson's Reservoir.

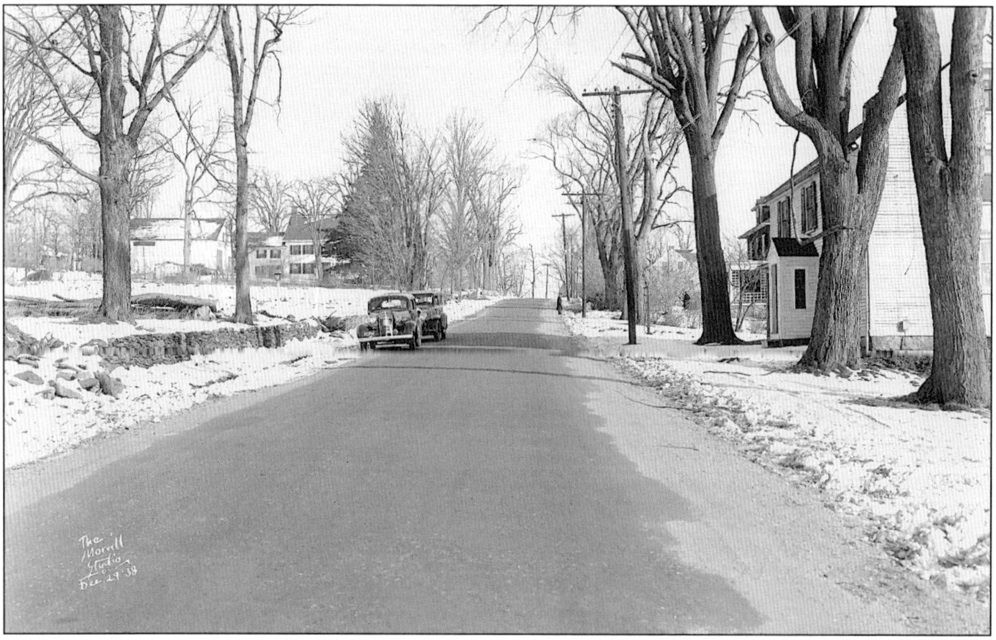

This street scene, taken in December 1938, shows Leominster Road in a view looking north from an area near the intersection of West Street. These houses are all standing, as well as others built since. The many elm trees are survivors of the destructive Hurricane of 1938, which roared through Lunenburg three months earlier, but the battering they took is evident and most of them were gradually destroyed by Dutch elm disease in following years.

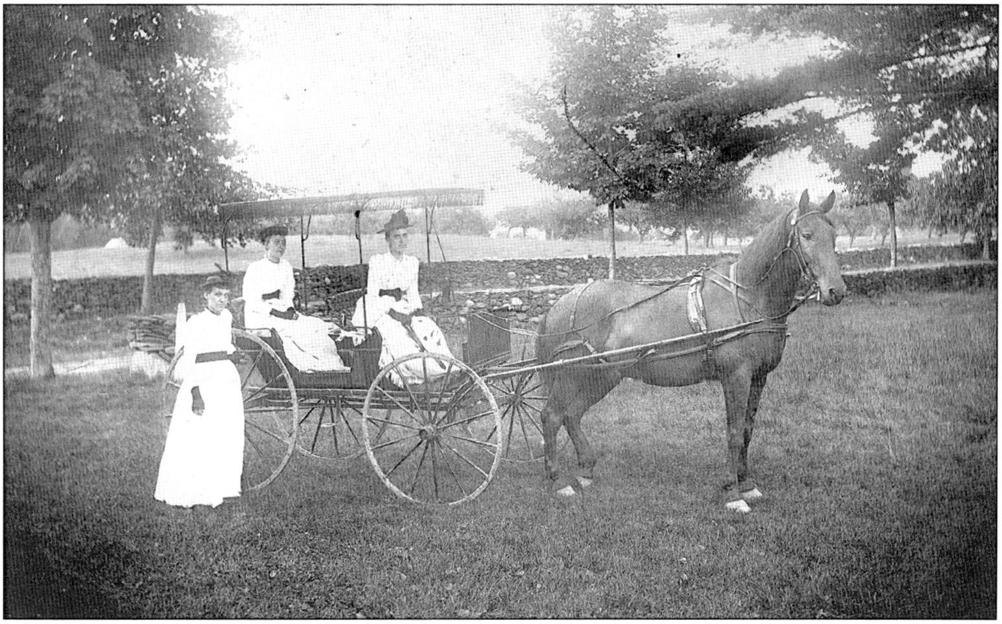

All set for a lovely afternoon tour of the town, these elegantly dressed Litchfield family ladies and their friend pose for an August 13, 1892 photograph prior to their departure. From left to right are Emma L. (Litchfield) Eaton, Florence E. Baxter, and Nellie F. (Litchfield) Brown. Their patient horse is named Prince. Their carriage is well suited for the occasion. Chestnut Street is pictured in the background.

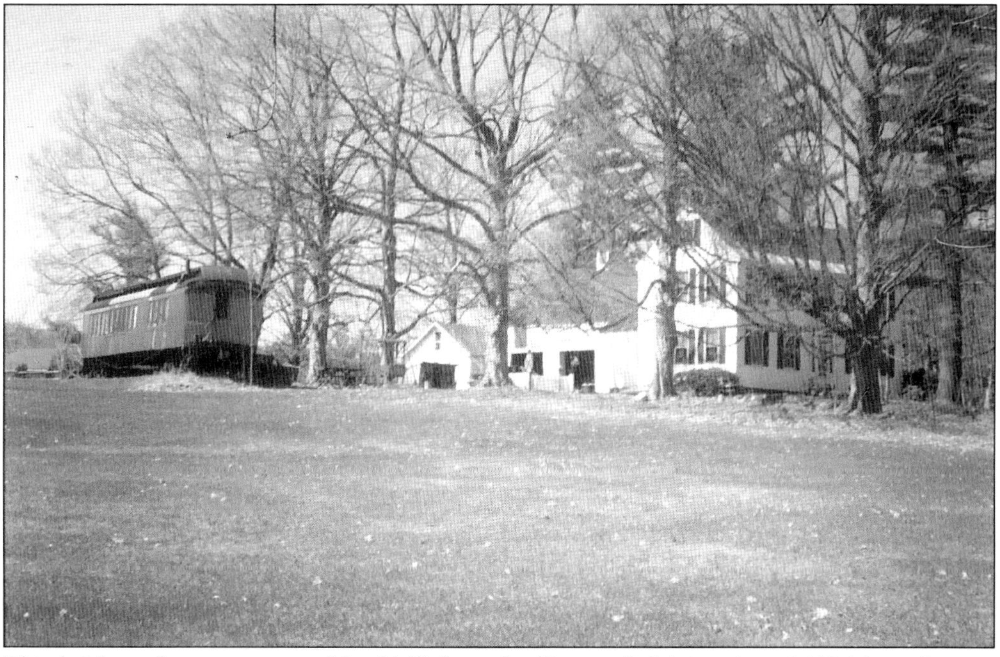

This bright-red passenger car, No. 3149 from the Boston & Maine, is at 1442 Massachusetts Avenue. The 68-foot, 43-ton car came to town on the railroad tracks and was then loaded on a truck flatbed and carried eight miles, where it was placed beside an 1875 Colonial house. Two years went into remodeling the interior with electric lights, heat, and vintage seats.

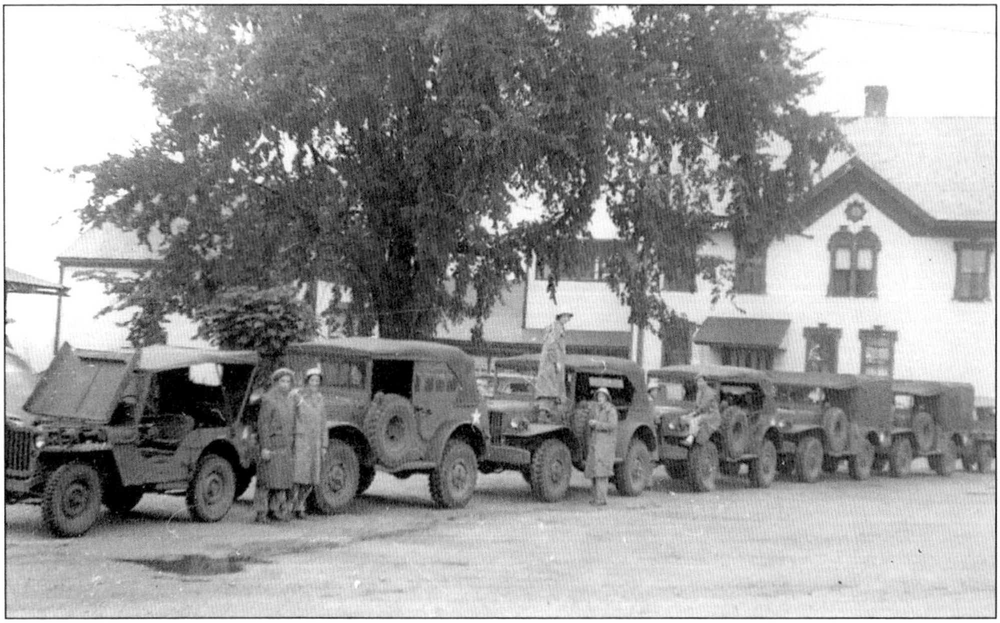

During World War II, soldiers from many states were stationed at Fort Devens in Ayer. Due to our proximity to Ayer, many convoys stopped in Lunenburg for brief periods. Lunenburg residents opened their homes to these soldiers who were far from their own homes. This view shows one of Devens' Jeep convoys stopping along the upper common in Lunenburg.

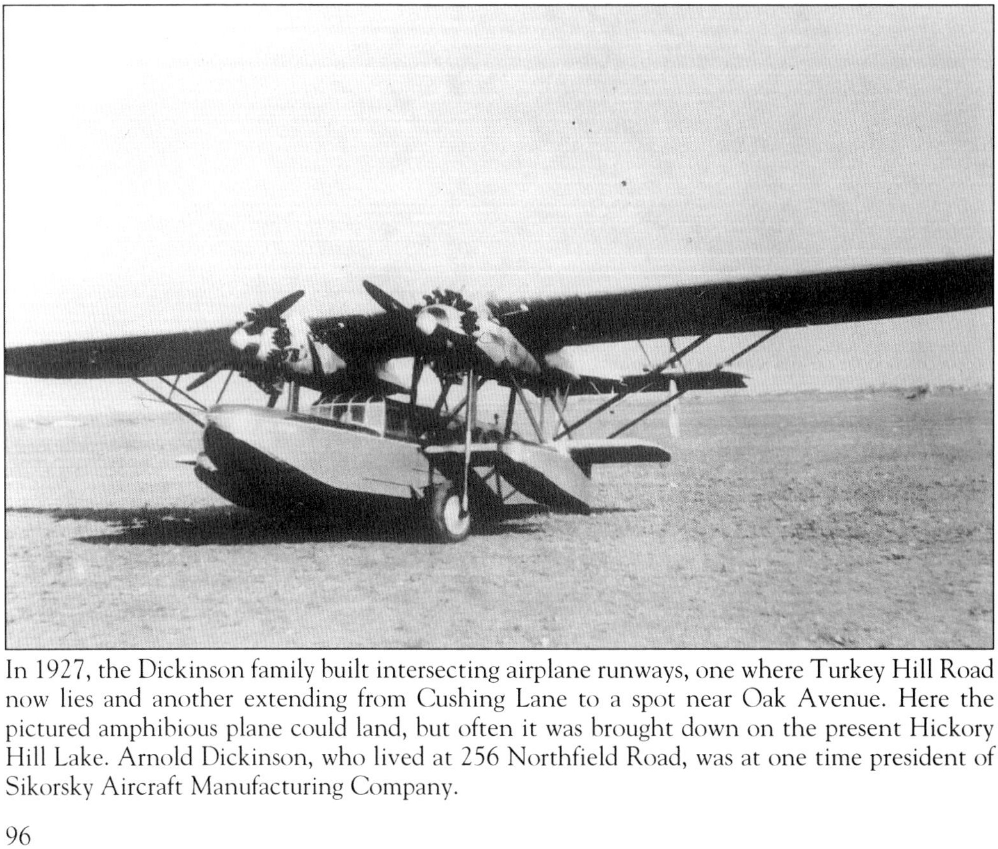

In 1927, the Dickinson family built intersecting airplane runways, one where Turkey Hill Road now lies and another extending from Cushing Lane to a spot near Oak Avenue. Here the pictured amphibious plane could land, but often it was brought down on the present Hickory Hill Lake. Arnold Dickinson, who lived at 256 Northfield Road, was at one time president of Sikorsky Aircraft Manufacturing Company.

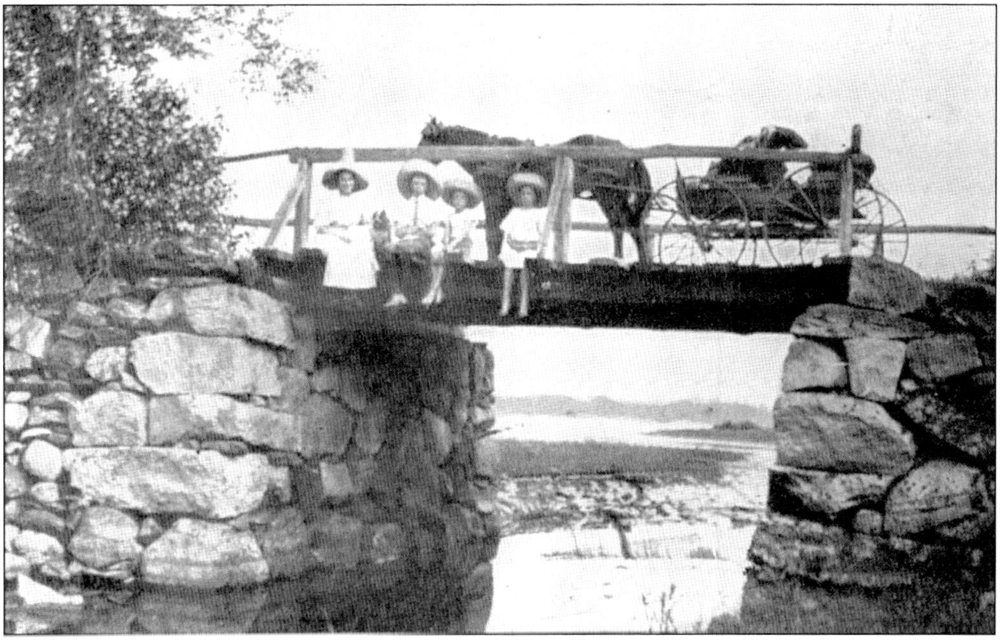

This *c.* 1900 photograph captures a quiet summer scene at the Old Houghton Bridge over Catacoonamug Brook on the north end of Shirley Reservoir, adjacent to Houghton Mill Pond. A sawmill operated here until 1898. The horse waits patiently while its young travelers relax and enjoy the view, before continuing their journey.

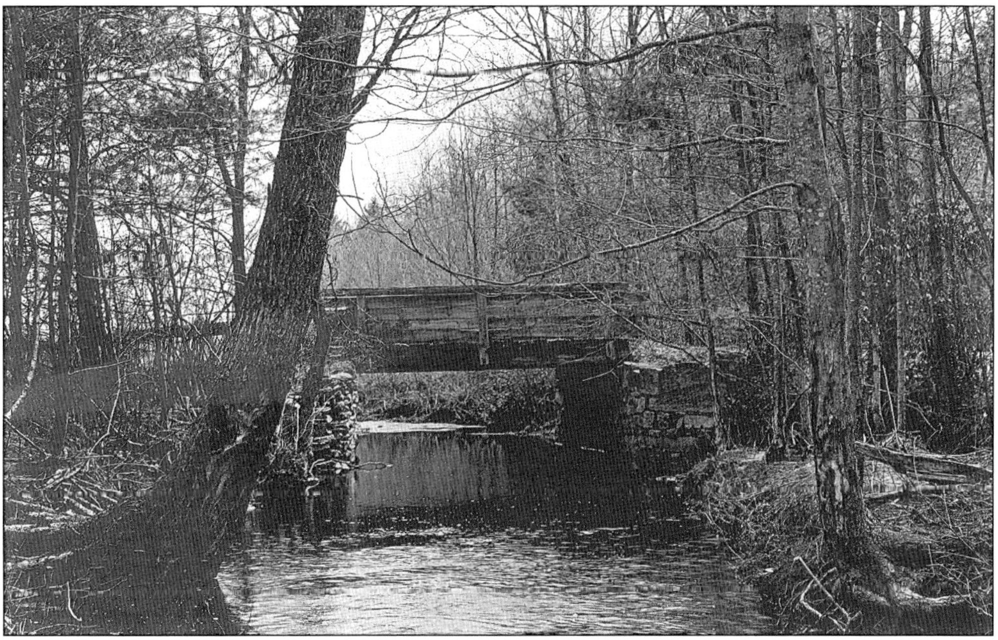

In earlier times, townspeople could travel down Gilchrest Street beyond its present end and circle the north perimeter of what is now Hickory Hills Lake. Gilchrest Street crossed Mulpus Brook on this old wooden bridge. Although this bridge survived the flood of 1936, Arnold Dickinson, owner of the property, later replaced it with an arched bridge. The new bridge, in turn, washed out sometime after 1952.

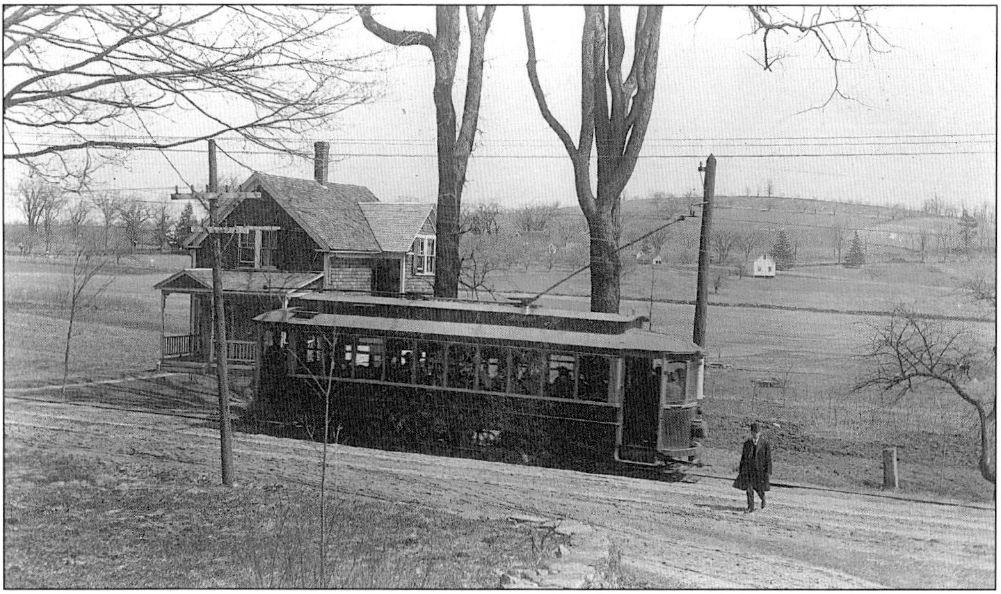

This photograph shows a trolley car on Leominster Road, just north of West Street. The Fitchburg–Leominster Street Railway line ran from Whalom Park, through Lunenburg Center, to the end of Main Street. The Fitchburg and Leominster Street Railway opened for passenger travel on August 7, 1901. The Lunenburg Military Band was honored to be among its first passengers. Service ended in 1925.

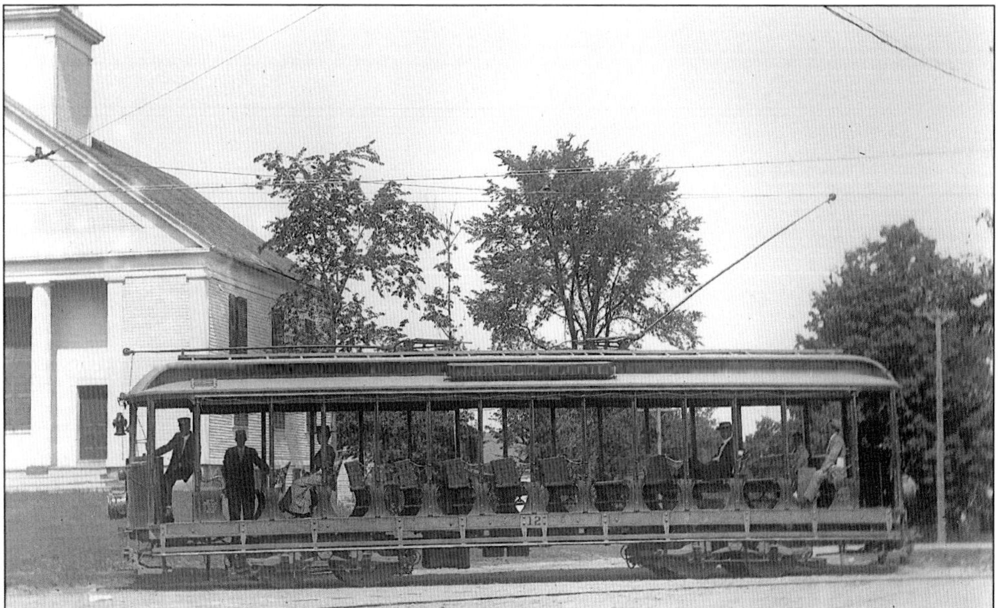

During the warmer weather, the trolley service in Lunenburg changed to cars more suitable to the climate. This photograph illustrates the trolley car used during these times. It is an open-air vehicle transporting summer customers. It gave the rider a better view as well as a cooler one. You might wonder how pleasant it was on rainy days.

Five

BUSINESSES

Business in Lunenburg was the outgrowth of the economic needs of our early settlers. The first businesses began on farms to provide food for our inhabitants. As the population increased, gristmills became a necessity. Sawmills provided lumber to build houses. Water was needed to provide power to run these mills. Most of the water came from ponds and brooks. Mulpus Brook was the principal source.

A jig mill on West Townsend Road provided stock for chairs and spinning wheels. Abel Cook built an "up-and-down" sawmill before circular saws were available. A cotton mill was built at the outlet of Whalom Lake. Bookbinding and printing was carried on in several locations. One of these printed polyglot Bibles. Woodworking was abundant in Lunenburg. Bureaus, grandfather clock frames, mirror frames, and even coffins were produced. In 1830, there was a cooper's shop. The abundance of wood brought the trades of builders and carpenters. Blacksmiths provided horseshoes and farm tools. Basketry and box making were soon to become a popular industry. Many women and children began straw hat making for farmers and field hands. Hat making became a cottage industry. The Civil War brought an end to this industry.

The lack of plentiful waterpower and railroads led to the demise of most industries. In the late 1800s, Lunenburg once again became an agricultural center. Today, it is a bedroom community for the larger surrounding cities.

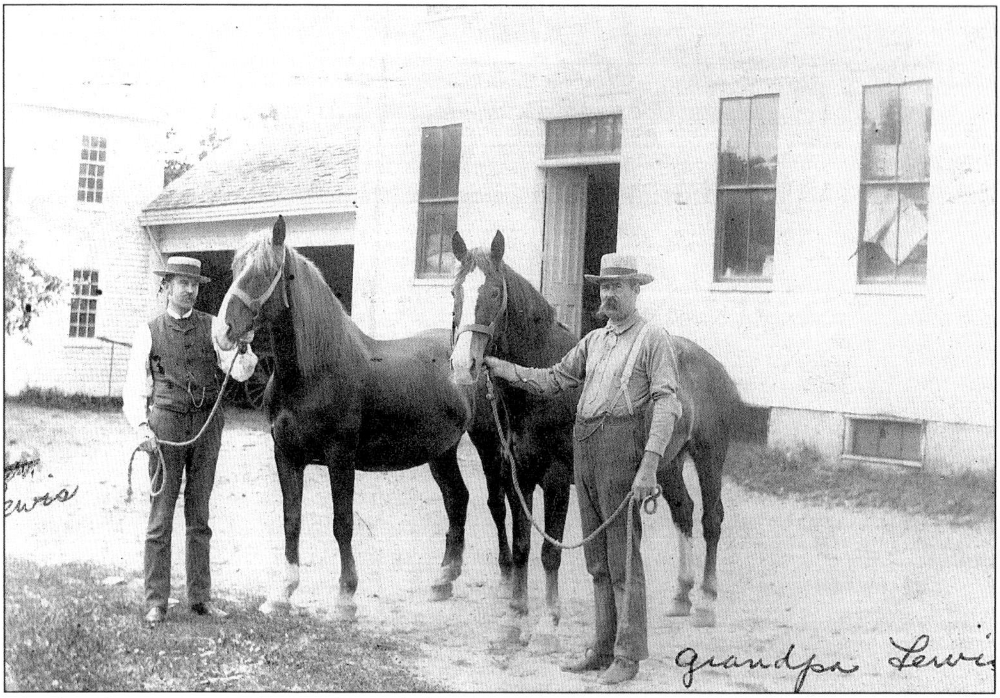

This handsome team of horses, being held by Henry Lewis (left) and Grandpa Lewis, was used with a wagon to make store deliveries for Warren Lewis's store in the center of town. In the background is the side of the store with the barn in back.

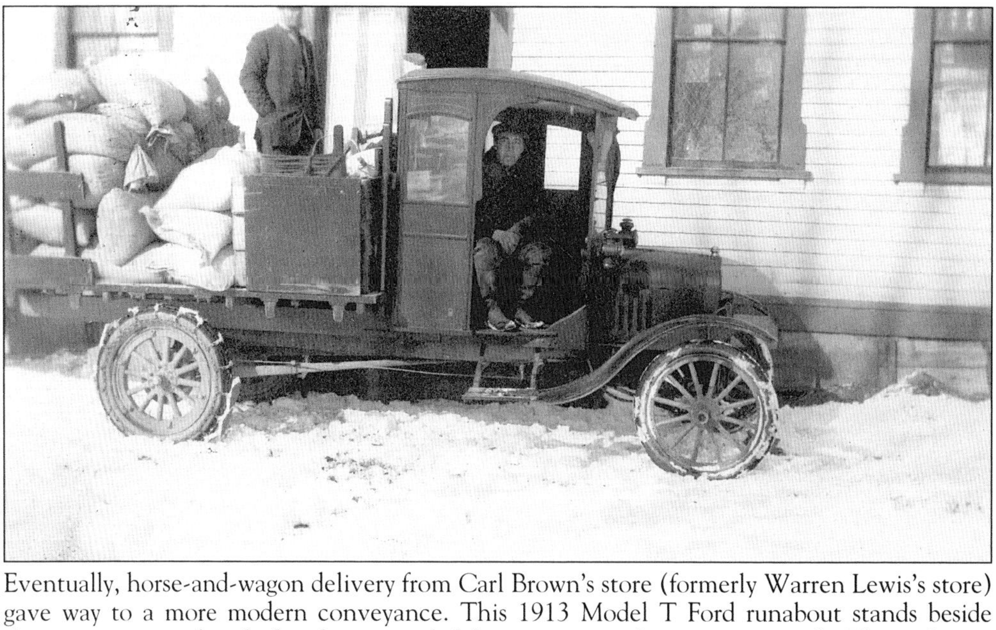

Eventually, horse-and-wagon delivery from Carl Brown's store (formerly Warren Lewis's store) gave way to a more modern conveyance. This 1913 Model T Ford runabout stands beside the store, equipped with the chains needed for winter travel on country roads. The pickup is loaded with grain sacks and is on its way to provide feed for animals in Lunenburg and the surrounding communities.

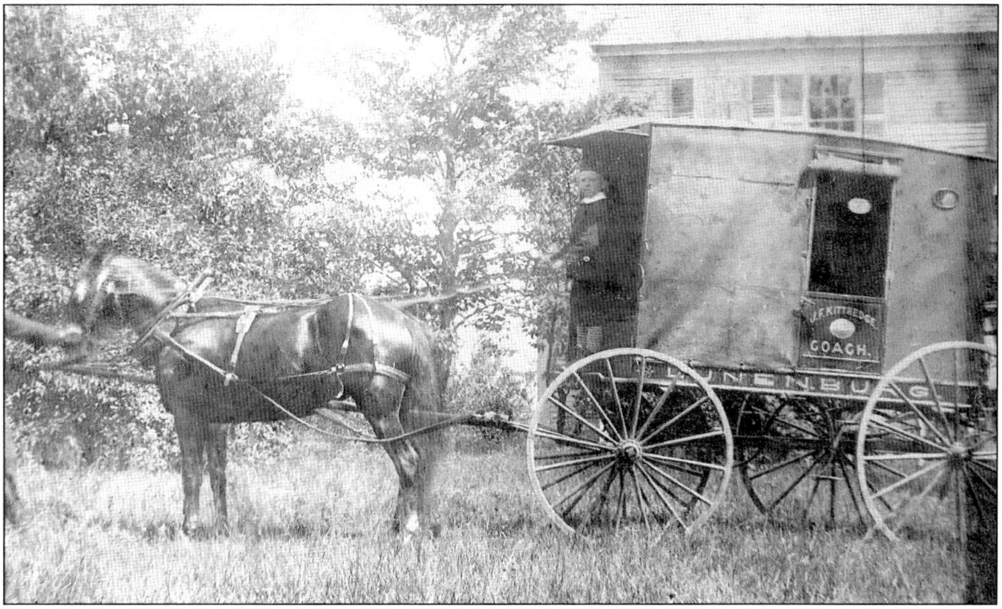

As communication among early communities began to grow, so did the volume of mail. At one time, it was carried by a stage known as the Harvard, Lunenburg and Winchendon Stage. In this photograph, we see a later mail coach, owned by J.F. Kittredge and used to transport mail from the town of Lunenburg to the post office in Fitchburg.

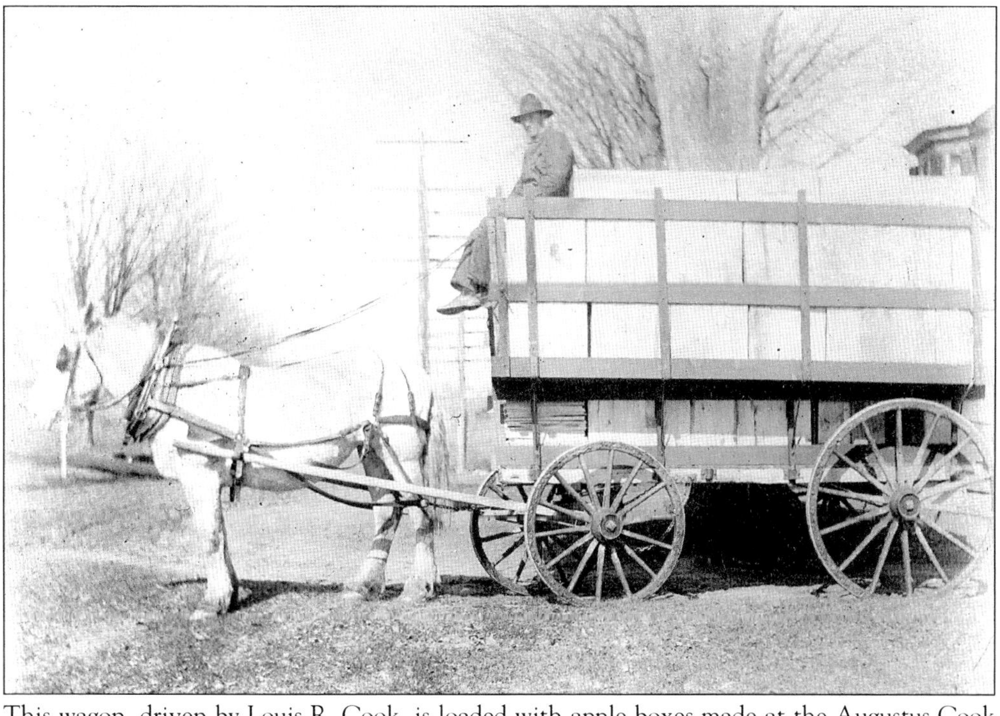

This wagon, driven by Louis R. Cook, is loaded with apple boxes made at the Augustus Cook sawmill. The mill, located on Mulpus Brook near Hunting Hill, closed down c. 1921. It was the last of several early mills along the Mulpus. Custom sawing and box making were carried on here, using both waterpower and steam power.

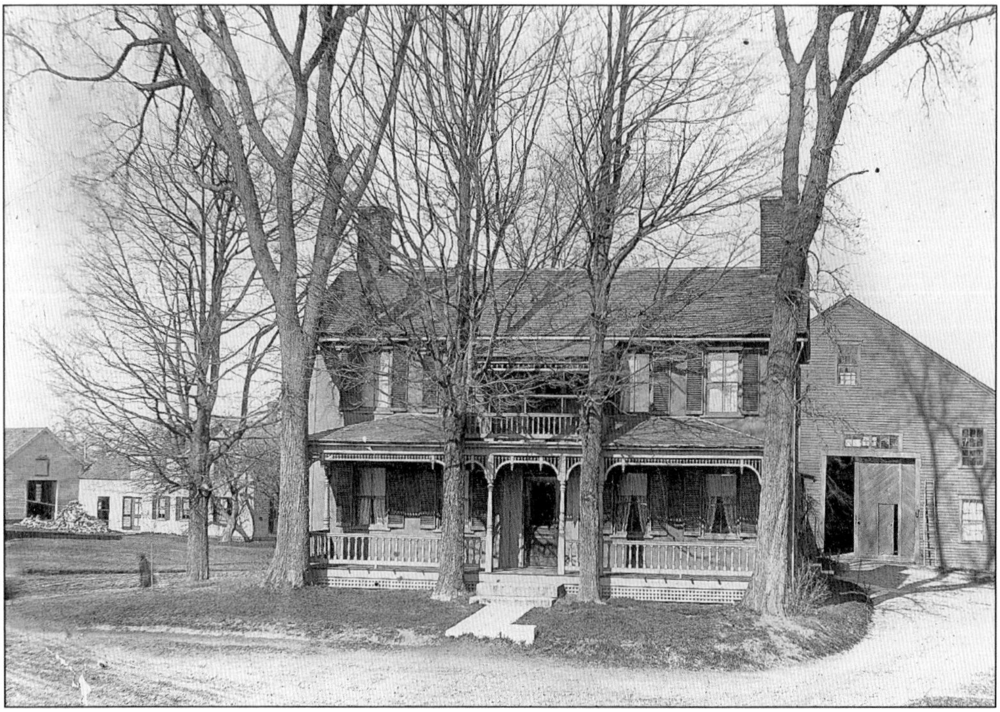

At 3 Lancaster Avenue stands the A.K. Francis House (K-3), better known as the Corner House. It was built in 1798 by Col. Edmund Cushing, who did bookbinding here. Over the years, numerous business here have included bandbox making, shoemaking, an antique shop, a telephone office, a gift shop and restaurant, an apothecary, a credit union, and a yarn shop. This view dates from the early 20th century.

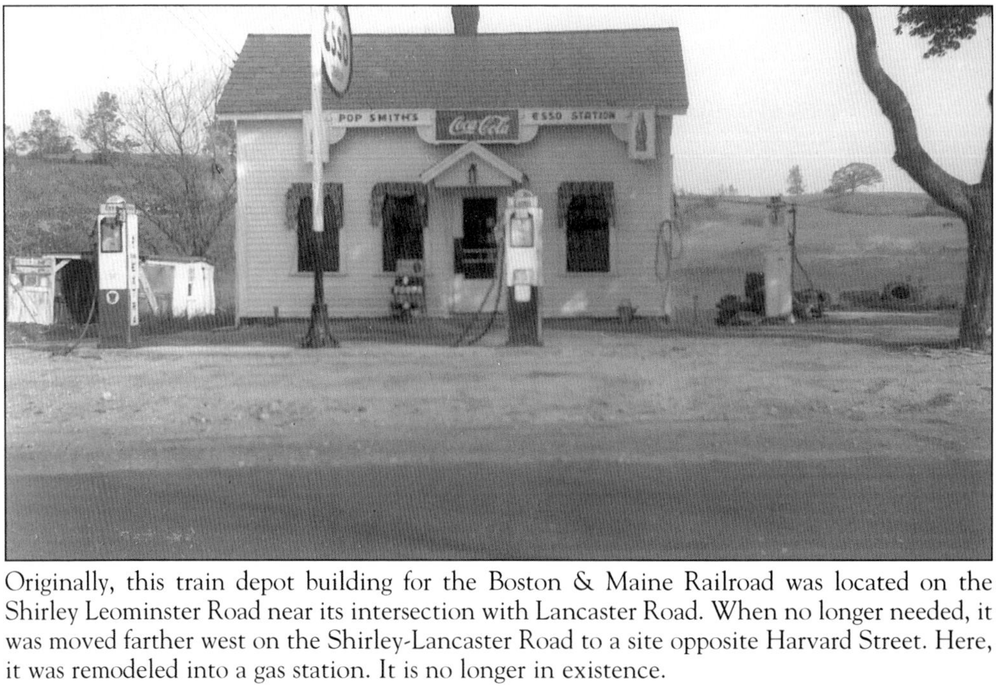

Originally, this train depot building for the Boston & Maine Railroad was located on the Shirley Leominster Road near its intersection with Lancaster Road. When no longer needed, it was moved farther west on the Shirley-Lancaster Road to a site opposite Harvard Street. Here, it was remodeled into a gas station. It is no longer in existence.

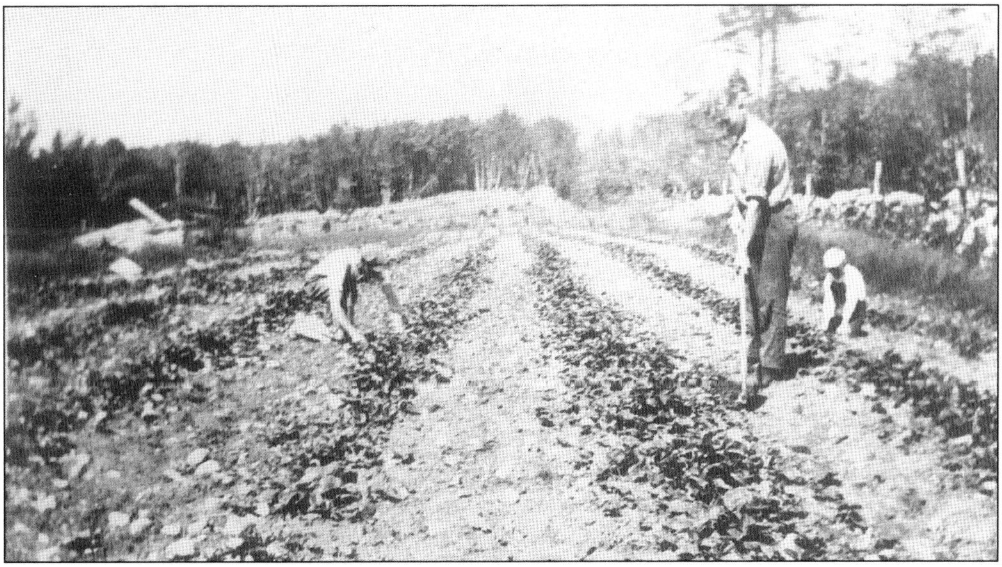

Many Finnish immigrants settled in the northern section of Lunenburg, and most worked farms where they settled. One of the main crops raised was strawberries. Pictured here are the fields of the Lahti family on New West Townsend Road, where strawberries thrived. They raised turkeys, silver fox, and milking cows. Today, they have a greenhouse and an extensive tree farm. A pond was recently added. (Courtesy of Barbara Lahti.)

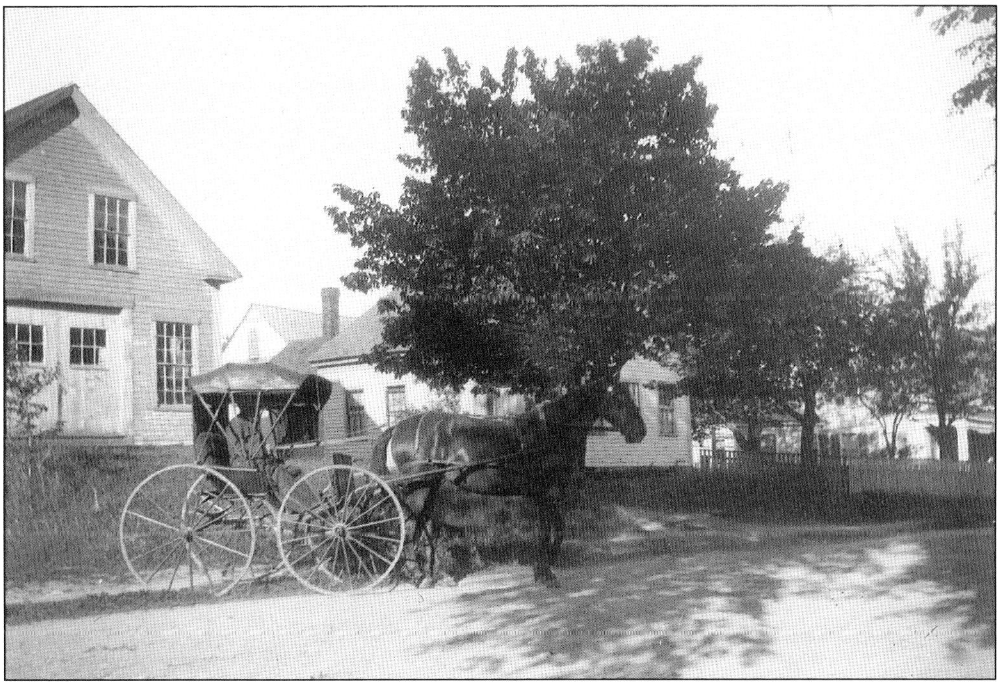

The building on the left was George Alan Jewett's Wheelwright Shop. It was located on 920 Massachusetts Avenue. Jewett built wagons, moved houses, and did repair work for the blacksmith Thomas Archibald. He hung the bells in both the Lunenburg Town Hall (1878) and the Congregational church (1889). After his death in 1904, his shop was moved to 184 Highland Street.

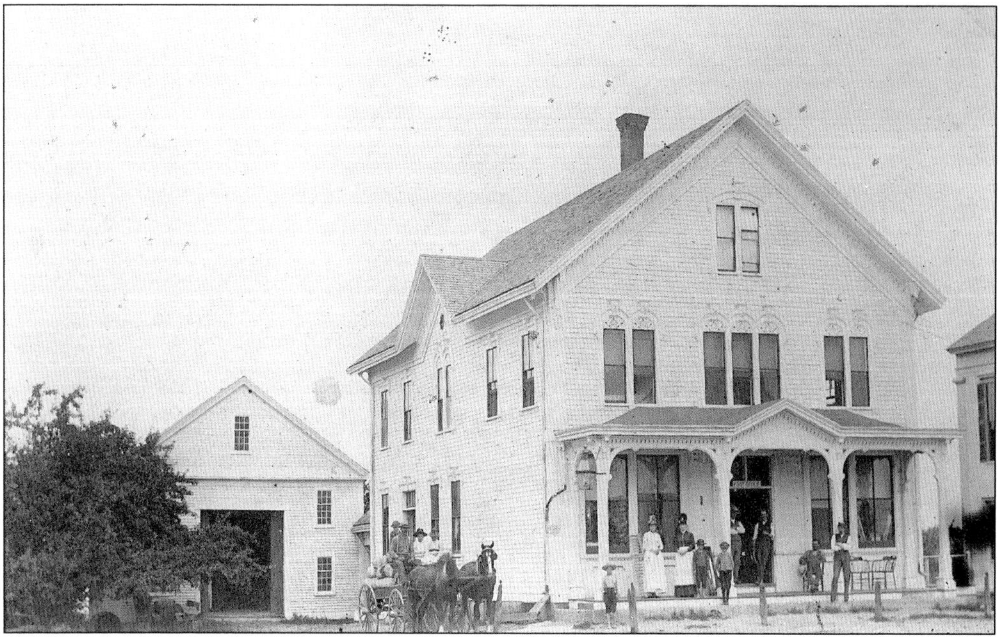

This photograph, taken in 1888, shows the general store in the center of town. It is currently called Honey Farms and has been altered over the years. The store, built in 1868, was originally owned by Daniel Putnam and contained the post office. In 1915, it was purchased by Carl Brown. Brown served as postmaster, and his son Earle succeeded him. The post office remained in this store until March 1956.

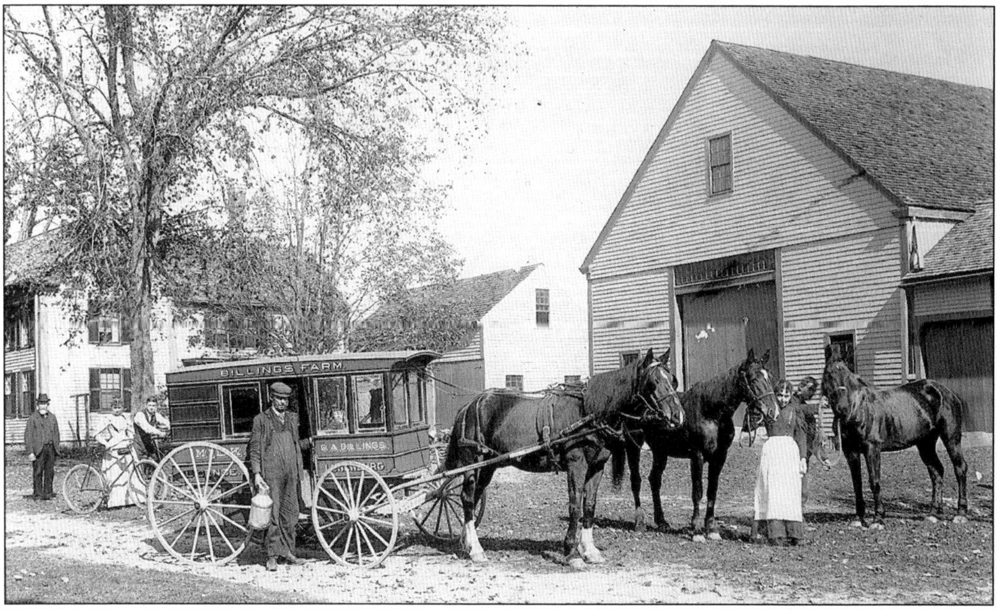

Pictured here is the Billings Farm, c. 1897, located at 629 Lancaster Avenue. From left to right are George Billings, Mary "Mamie" and Arthur Billings (with bikes), Alden Billings (standing by milk wagon), and Ida Billings (holding horses). The buildings are situated on what was an original land grant in Lunenburg and typifies a working farm prevalent during this era. (Courtesy of Mary Bingham.)

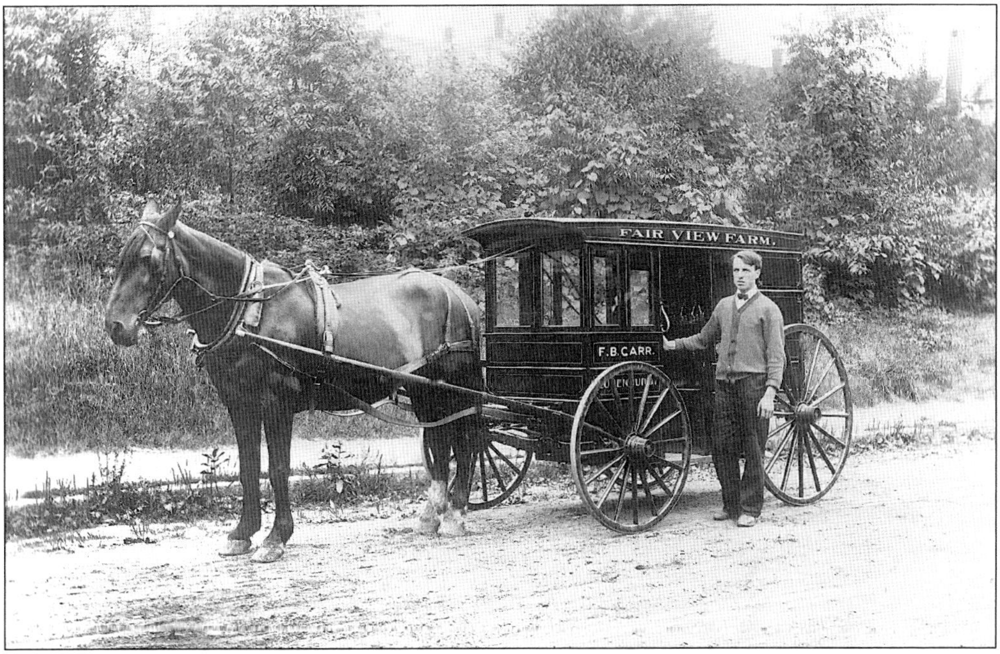

In the earlier years of Lunenburg's development, farmers needed horse and wagon to deliver their goods to the people. The Fairview Farm, owned by F.B. Carr, was no exception. Fairview was a dairy farm and well known for providing its customers with one of the staples of life. It was necessary to provide milk year-round, and the farmers had to accommodate their wagons for this purpose. The upper photograph shows one of their wagons used in warmer times. The lower photograph shows their wagon equipped with sled runners for travel in the snowy winters. Milk was carried in large milk cans and then poured out into containers that their customers provided. This made it possible to deliver only the amount needed by each customer.

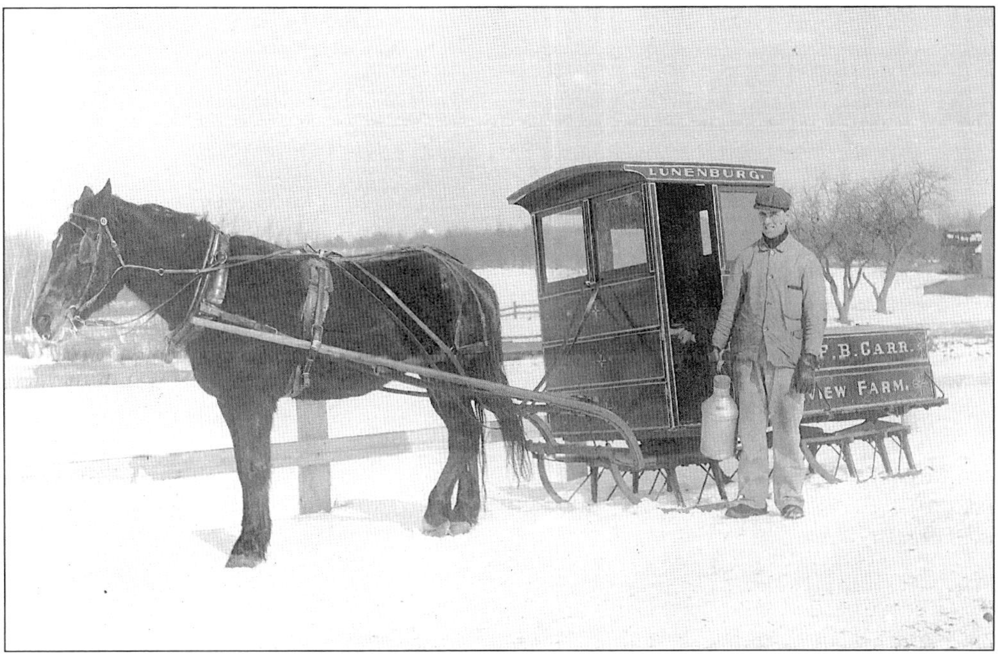

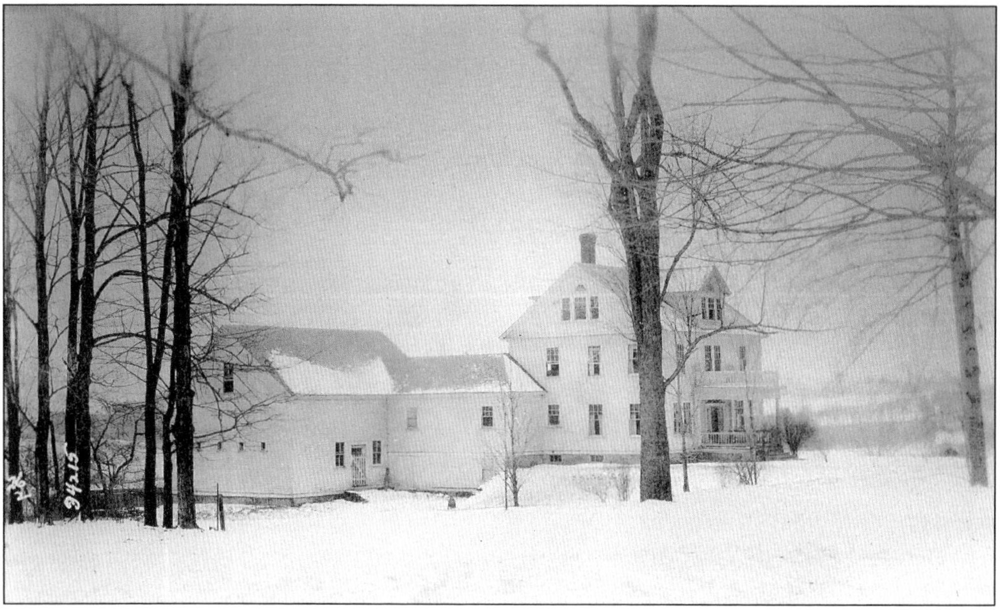

Six generations of the Goodridge family operated a farm on lower Lancaster Avenue—an original land grant when the town was settled. In 1910, Norman G. Bigelow, a sixth-generation member, moved to the center and built this house. Here he continued to farm and keep dairy cattle for many years with his sons.

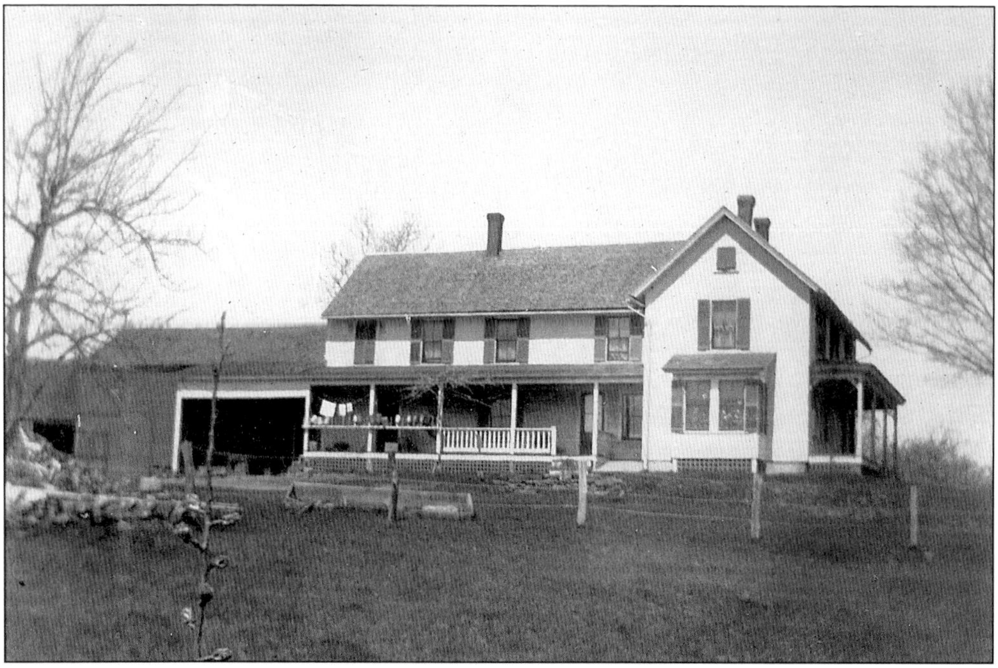

This house once stood at 598 Leominster Road, where Cherry Hill Farm is now located. Oliver Goodrich built an earlier house here in 1782. The house pictured was a later one built on the same site in 1914 and was known as the H.R. Houghton Farm. This house was destroyed by fire.

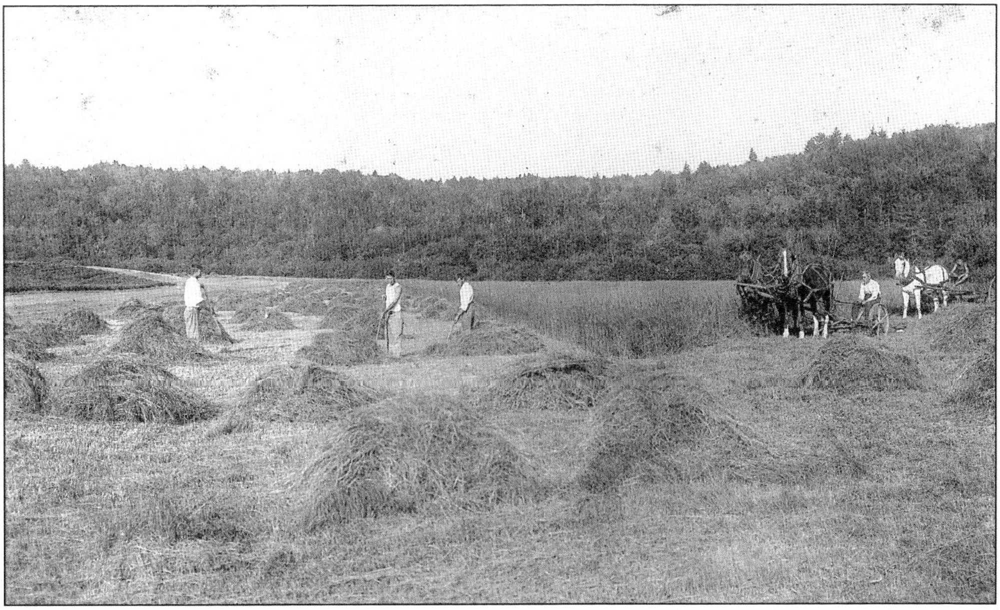

"Make hay while the sun shines." Yes, Mother Nature often called the shots that determined farmers' tasks for the day. In this *c.* 1900 photograph, unidentified farmhands use pitchforks to gather the hay in Carr's Meadow (later Woodruff's Meadow) off Fairview Road. Note the horses and rudimentary equipment in the background.

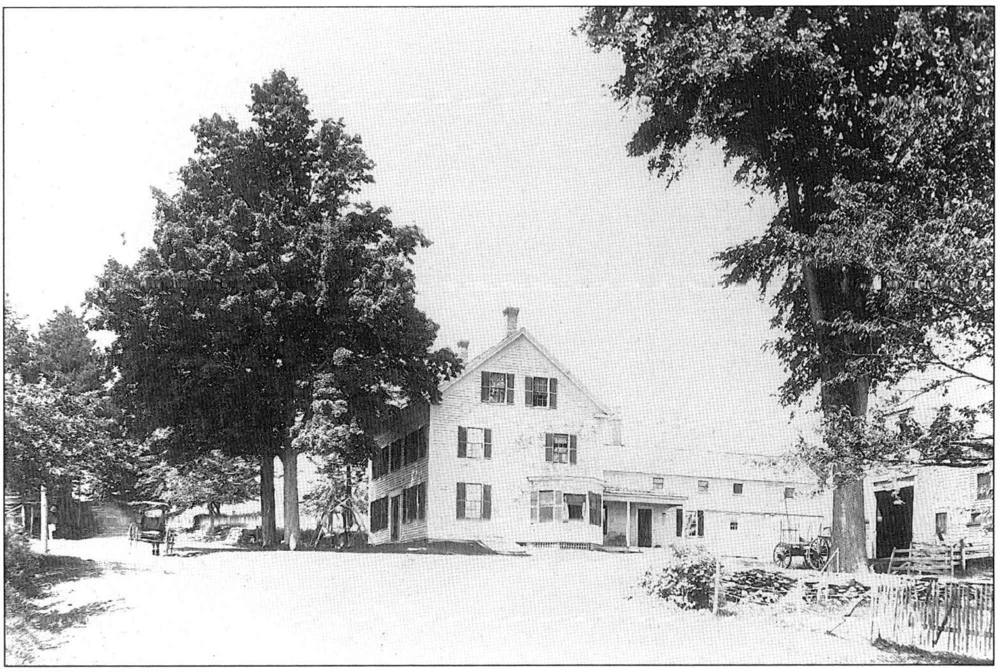

This classic, durable farmhouse is still impressive at 264 West Street. Built before 1805, with its surrounding 57 acres extending over the hilltop, the property was owned by Houghton and Proctor before Al Pierce purchased it in 1934. He and his family resided in the house and farmed the land, maintaining a small peach orchard on the hillside until 1986, when Miller purchased the property.

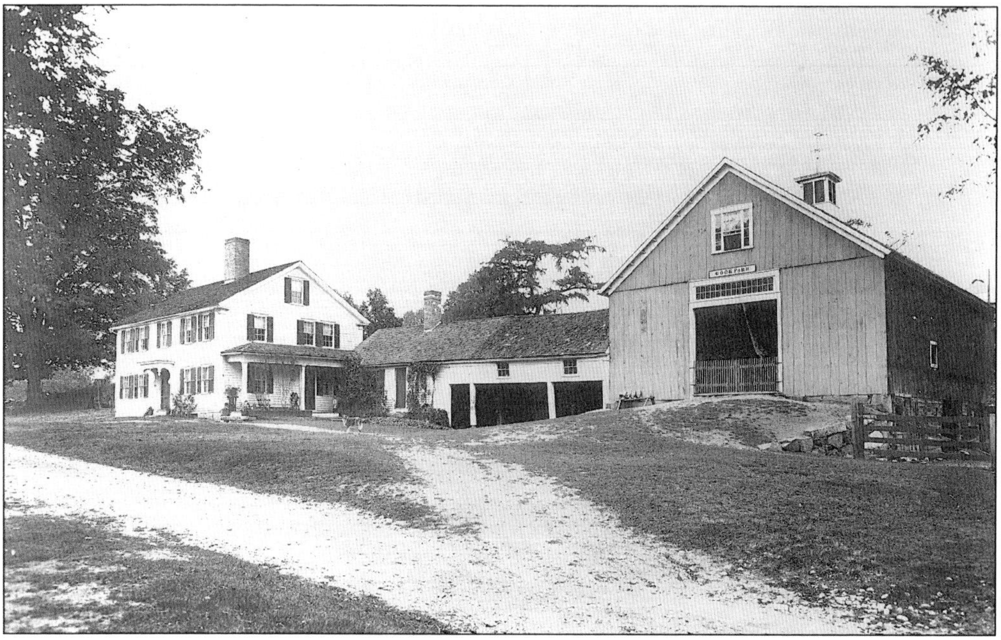

The Cook Farm House and adjacent buildings were a fine example of Lunenburg's picturesque farms. They occupied a small corner of the extensive property owned by the Cook family since 1808. The farm was surrounded by open fields on both sides of Mulpus Road, extending as far as Hunting Hill and into what the natives called Goshen. The majestic barn still stands. The adjacent buildings were destroyed by fire in 1921.

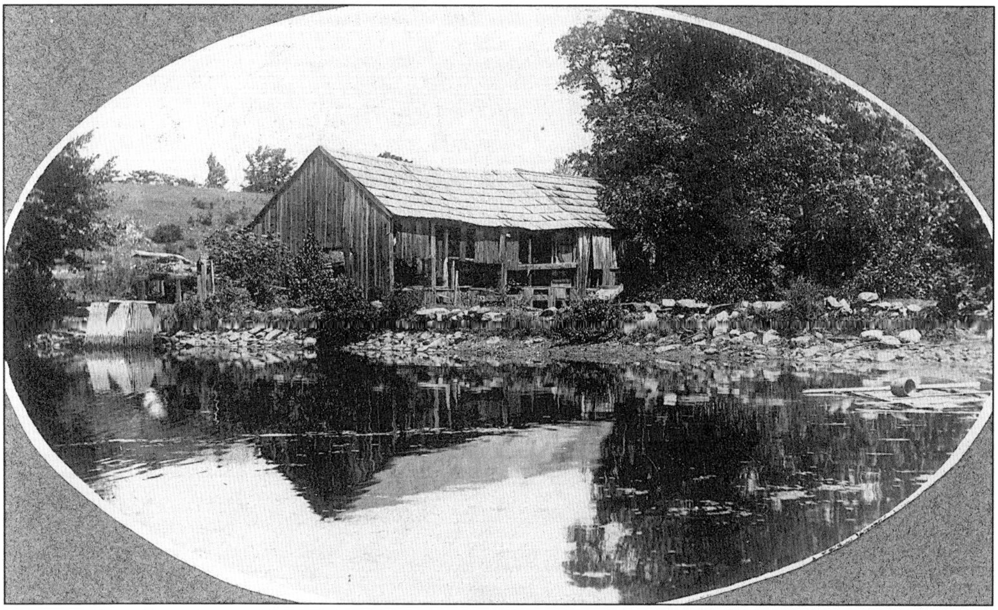

In 1870, brothers Marcellus and Willard Perrin bought this sawmill on Mulpus Brook, where they conducted an extensive lumbering business for 20 years. During busy seasons, this mill operated both night and day. The mill was located on the Town Farm Pond, also called Perrin's Pond. Part of its original foundation is still visible today on the Cross Street property of H. and R. Brockelman.

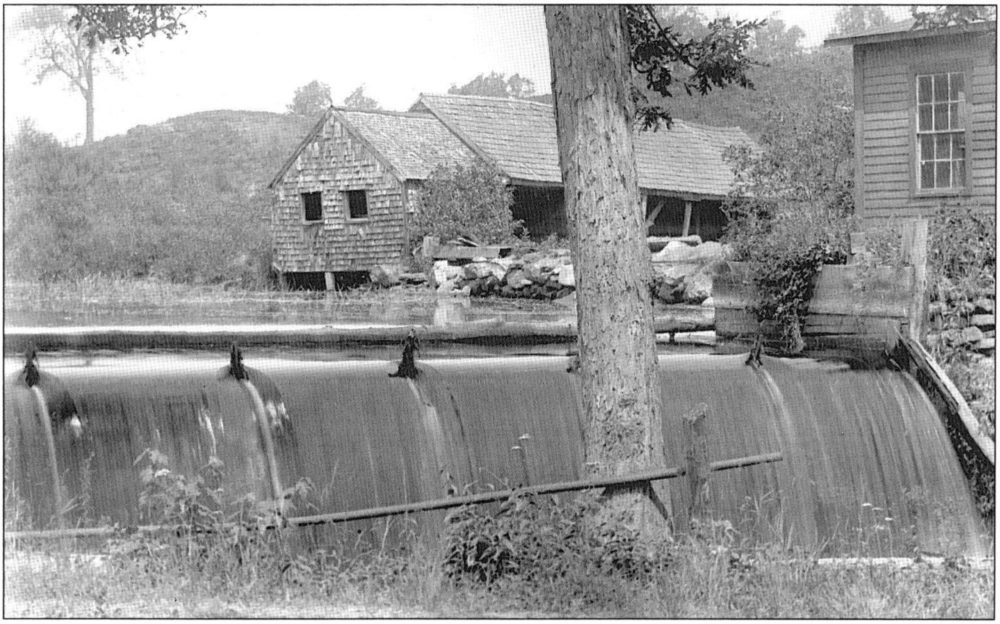

This photograph, taken in 1915, shows the Agustus Cook Mill on Mulpus Brook. The original mill on this site was destroyed by fire. Through subscription, it was rebuilt. It was the only Lunenburg mill able to operate with either steam or water, depending on the availability of water. It was known for box making and custom sawing. In 1921, it became unprofitable and was the last mill to operate on the Mulpus.

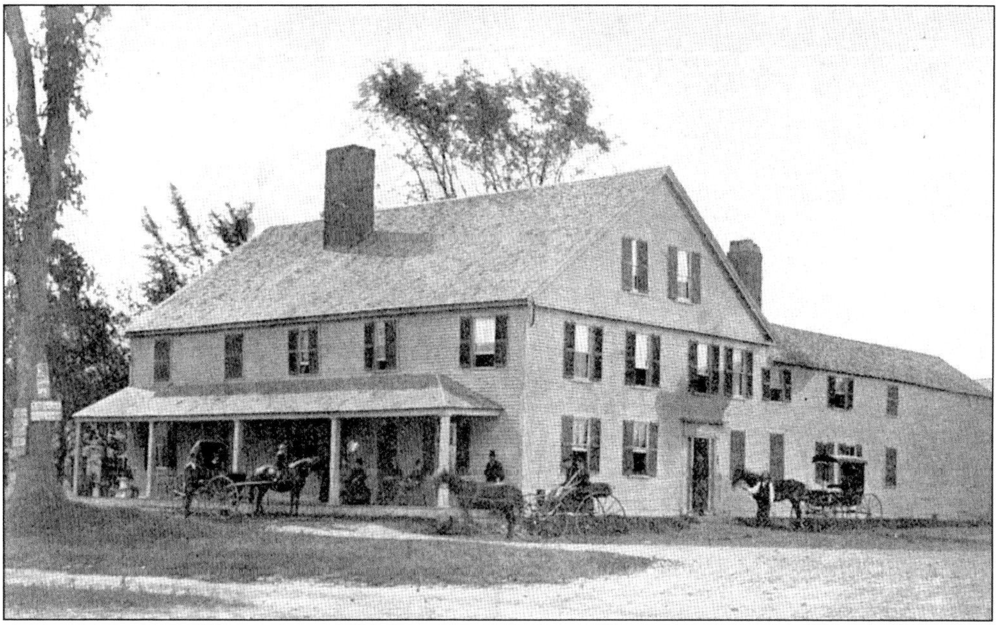

The land now occupied by the Ritter Memorial Library was, for many years, the location of this building. It was built *c.* 1780 by Joseph Bellows and operated as a tavern with a succession of proprietors. In 1872, the building became an inn, briefly called the Central House. Three years later, a new owner named it the Revere House. The land was purchased by the town after the building was demolished in 1900.

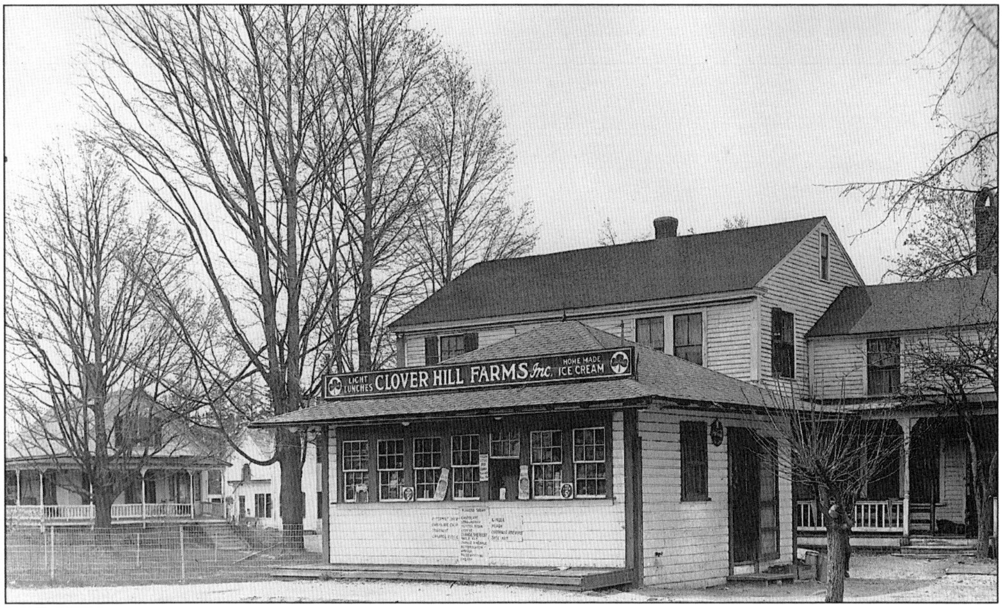

One of Lunenburg's early gas stations stood on the land now occupied by the post office. Lizzie Francis Proctor was the owner of this building and the house behind it. In 1933, the station was replaced by a building moved to the site from Clover Hill Farm and bought by Proctor in 1939. Later owned and operated by her son-in-law Harold "Hare" Harley, it was familiarly known as "the Stand."

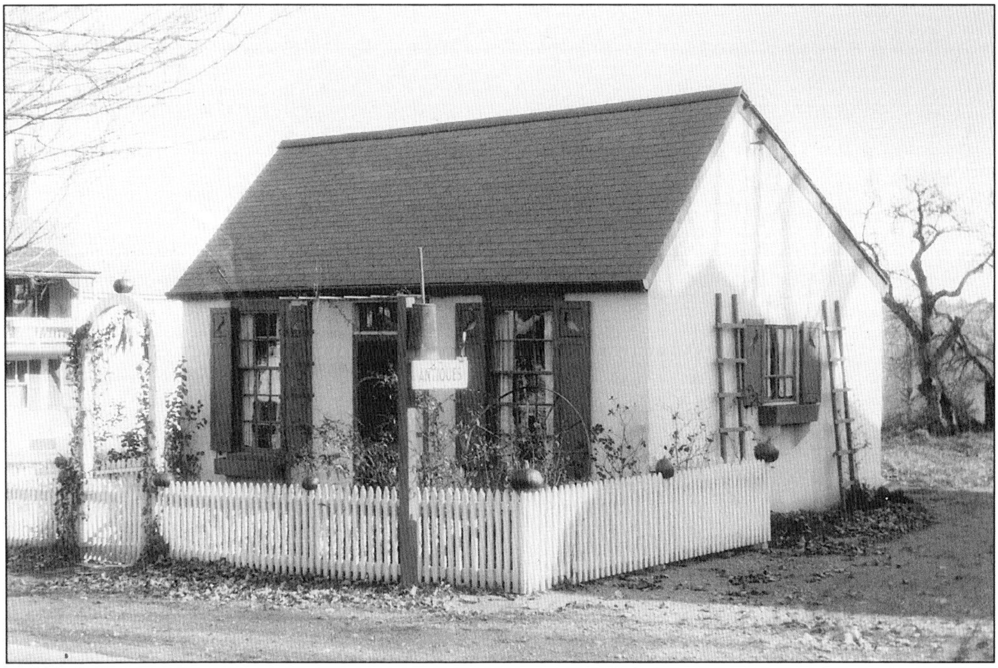

The Turkey Hills Antique Shop, owned by Electra (Eddy) Francis, wife of Sidney Francis, occupied this small building built in 1924. It was located a little east of 3 Lancaster Avenue in space now filled by the parking lot for the A.K. Francis House (the Corner House). It later became a real estate and insurance office operated by Ralph Foster and Ralph Whitcomb.

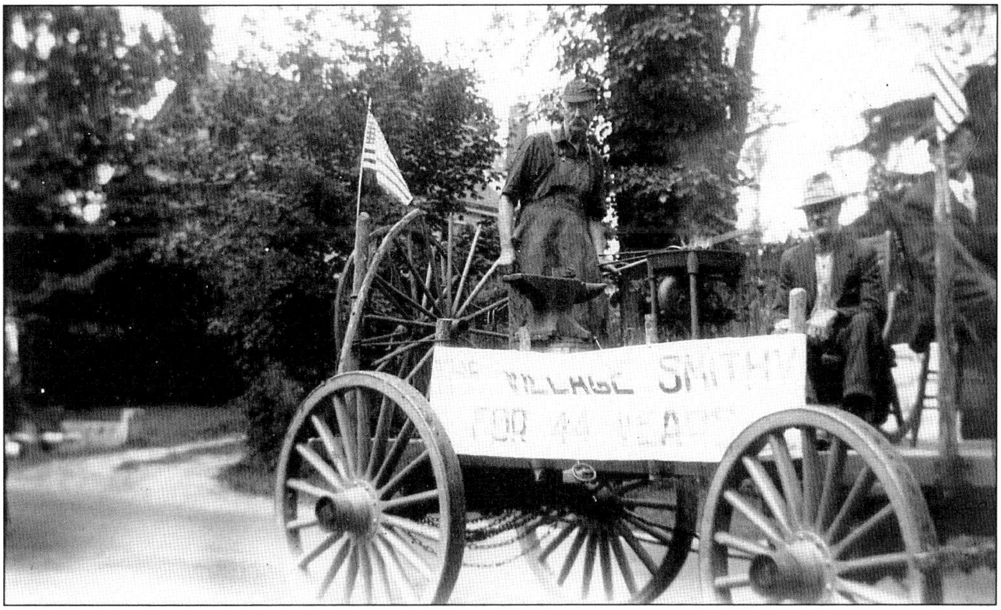

Thomas Archibald (above, left) was a blacksmith who operated his business in Lunenburg for 44 years. His first shop was on the site of 925 Massachusetts Avenue from 1884 to 1918. He is pictured in one of the earlier parades for Old Home Day with the tools of his trade—apron, anvil, and hammer. His banner and flags decorate his wagon, proclaiming his trade together with the spare wagon wheels at the back. He sold his shop on Massachusetts Avenue and moved into a building at the rear of his house at 20 Stevens Street, shown in the lower photograph. Here, he continued his business until 1932. Thomas Archibald is best known for creating the metal band that Franklin Francis placed around Fitchburg's famous boulder in 1889 before it was moved.

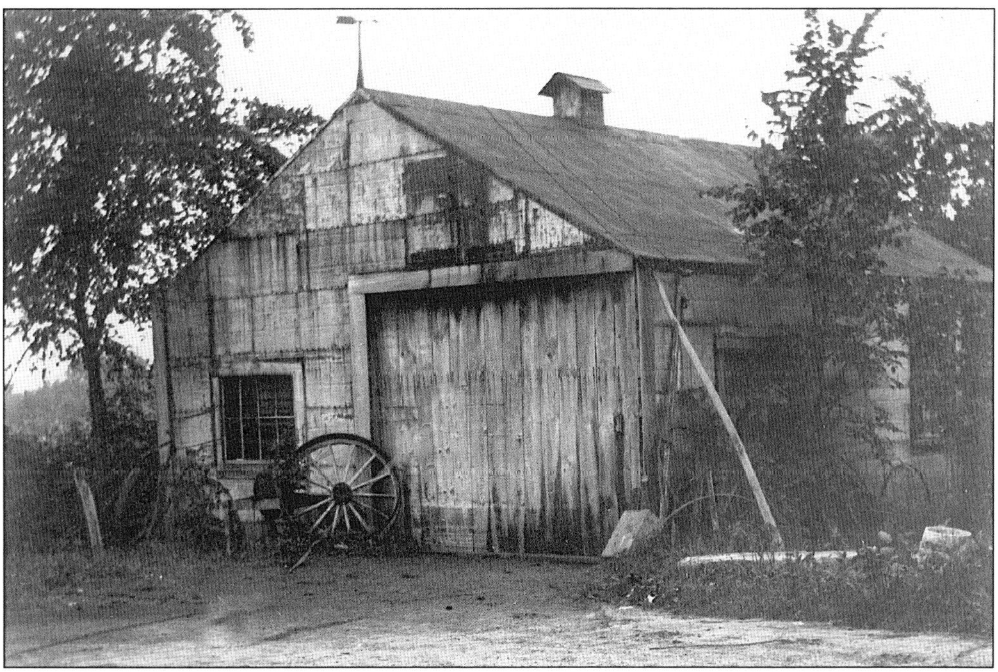

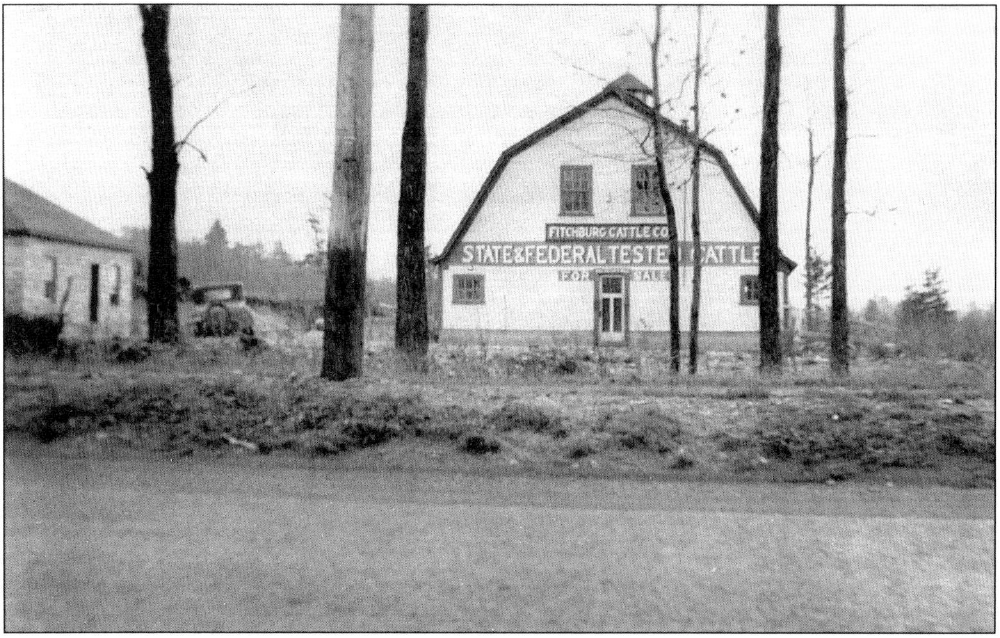

At the time this picture was taken, c. 1935, this building housed the business of a cattle dealer named Chitoff. It was later owned by "Red" St. Germaine, who operated Acme Country Store until it was destroyed by fire in 1961. Acme Rugs now occupies this lot. The building partly visible on the left was Tony's Donut Shop.

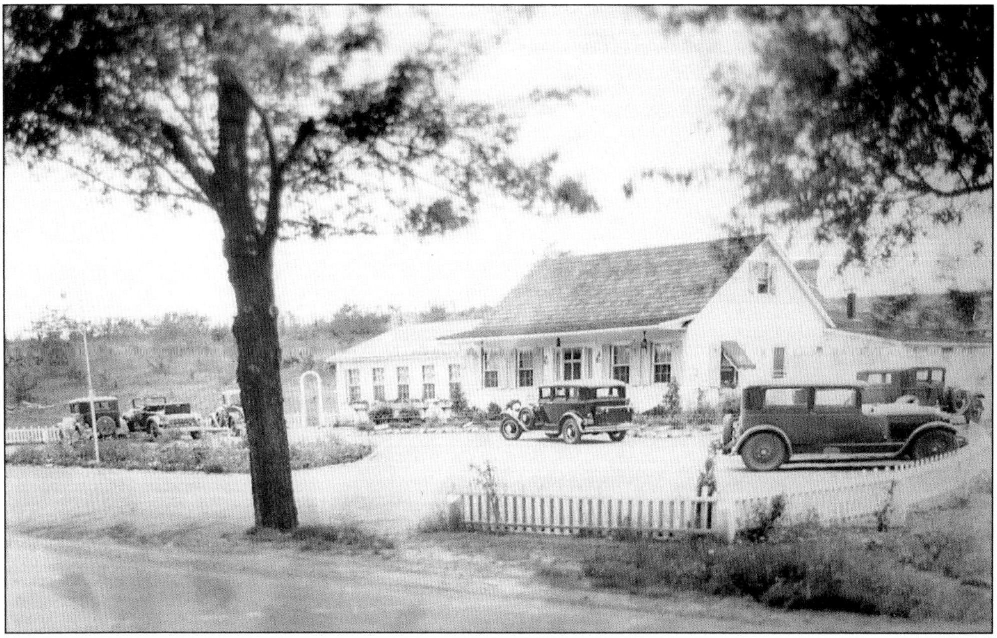

Buttercup Hill Tea Room on Massachusetts Avenue was, from 1928 to the late 1930s, a prestigious restaurant in the heart of this small town. It offered gourmet dining in an elegant atmosphere. Alcoholic beverages were also available during Prohibition. The Xarris family purchased the establishment in the 1940s and operated a fine restaurant and dance hall called "the Buttercup." Workers' Credit Union now occupies this site.

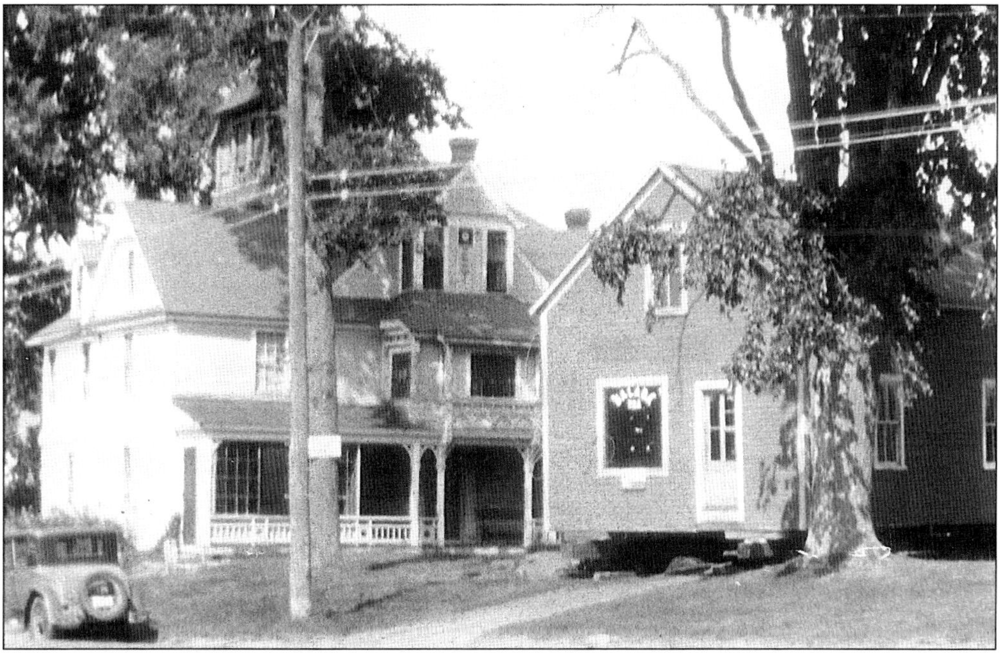

The small and unpretentious building to the right in this picture has had a surprisingly varied history. It was located between the Eagle House and the United Parish Church in the 1920s and 1930s, approximately at the beginning of Memorial Drive on Main Street. The front was a barbershop, with a poolroom behind. Later, the building was briefly occupied by a meat market. Arnold Dickinson donated this building to the town. In 1937, it was moved to Holman Street, shown in the bottom photograph. Here, it was fixed up and is now used as the Lunenburg Cemetery Department office.

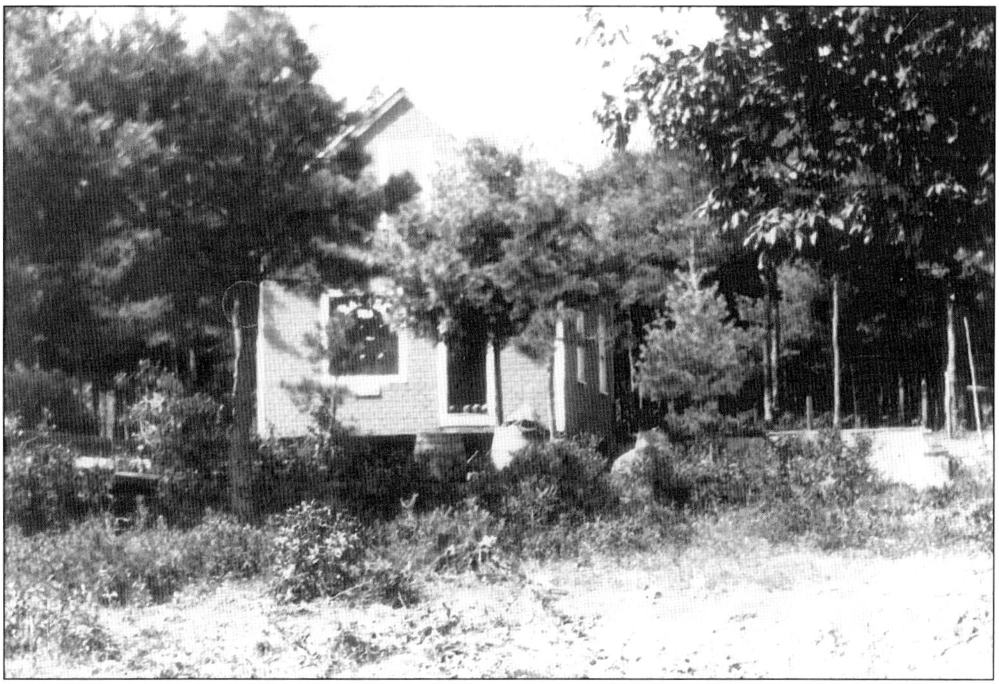

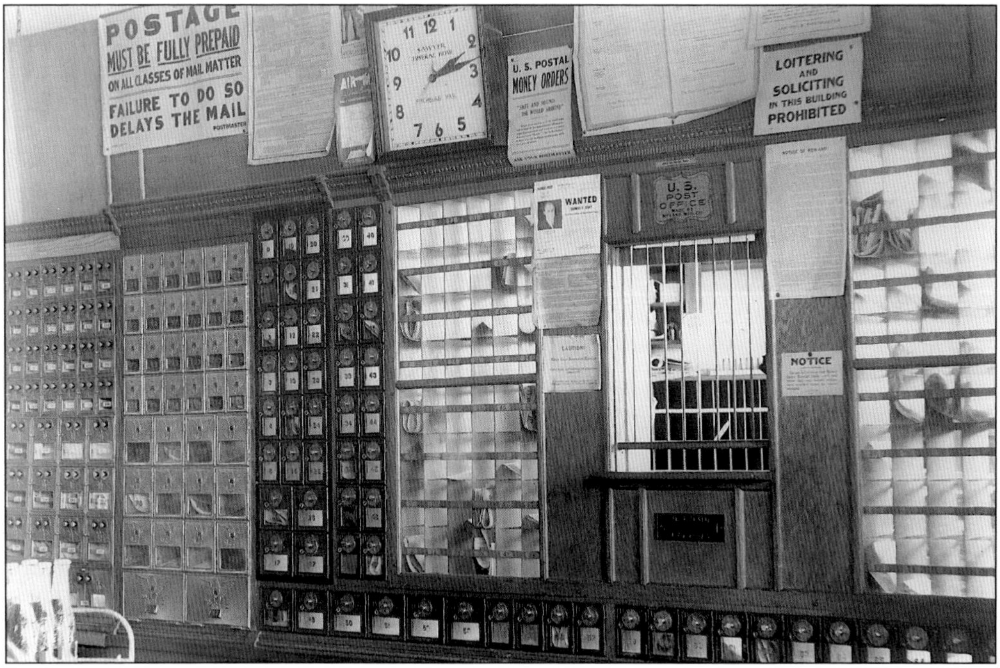

Around the middle of the 19th century, the Lunenburg Post Office was located in Daniel Putnam's store and remained here for about a century. The store evolved into Warren Lewis & Company and then Carl E. Brown & Sons; it is now called Honey Farms. Carl Brown served as postmaster for 32 years. This was the appearance of the general delivery window and the lockboxes in the 1940s.

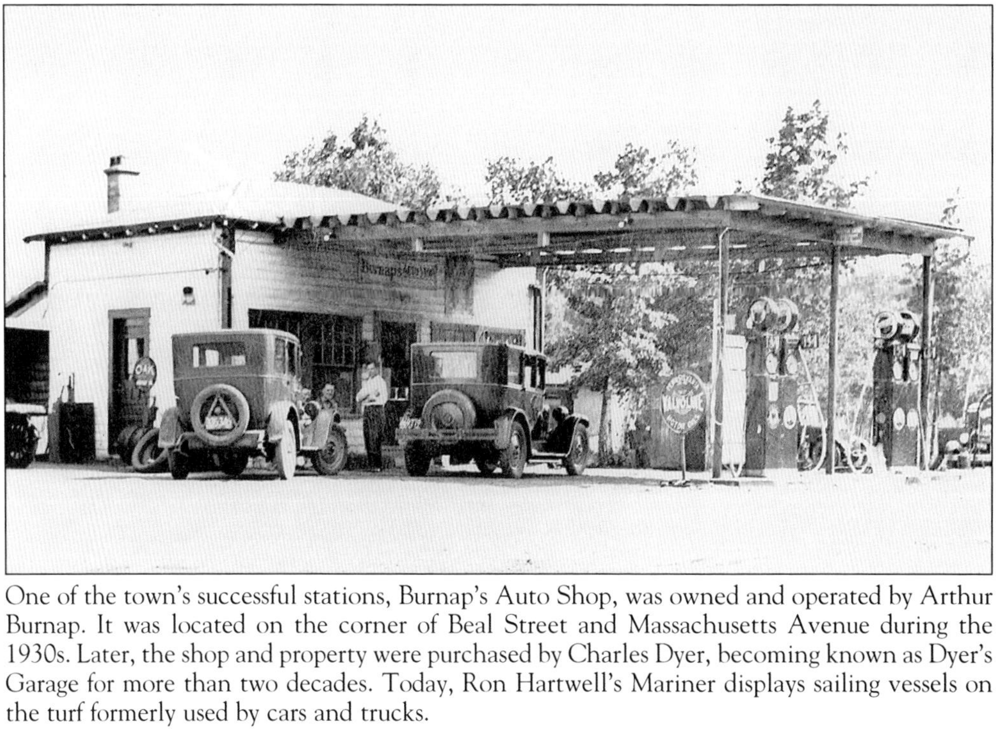

One of the town's successful stations, Burnap's Auto Shop, was owned and operated by Arthur Burnap. It was located on the corner of Beal Street and Massachusetts Avenue during the 1930s. Later, the shop and property were purchased by Charles Dyer, becoming known as Dyer's Garage for more than two decades. Today, Ron Hartwell's Mariner displays sailing vessels on the turf formerly used by cars and trucks.

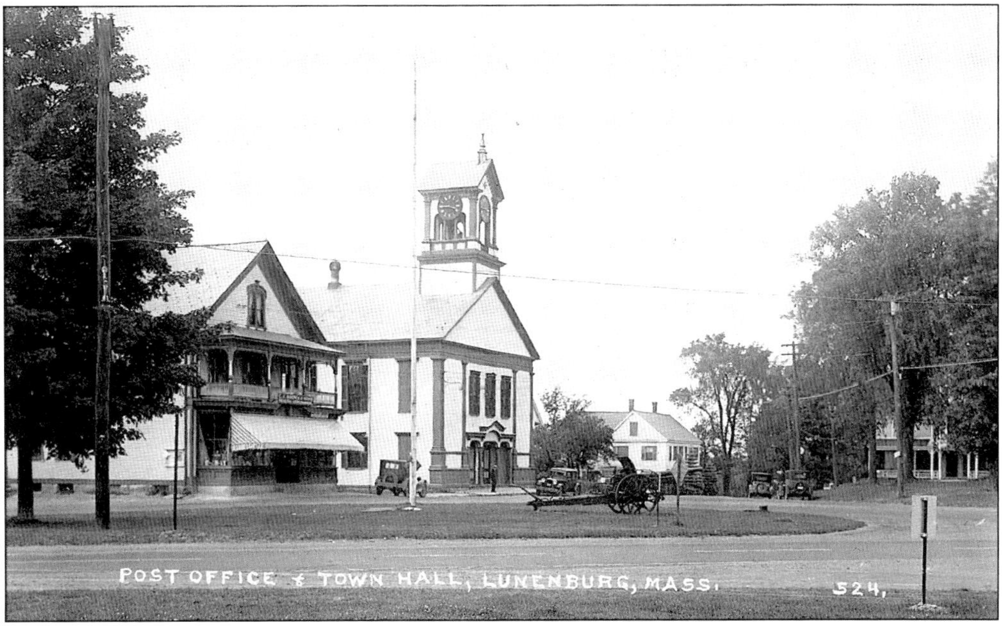

In the 1930s, the Lunenburg Town Hall sported green trim, later restored to the original white. The building on the left, now Honey Farms, was at that time C.E. Brown & Sons, housing their grocery business and post office. On the upper common, to the right of the flagpole, is an Austrian cannon. The bottom photograph gives a better view of the cannon.

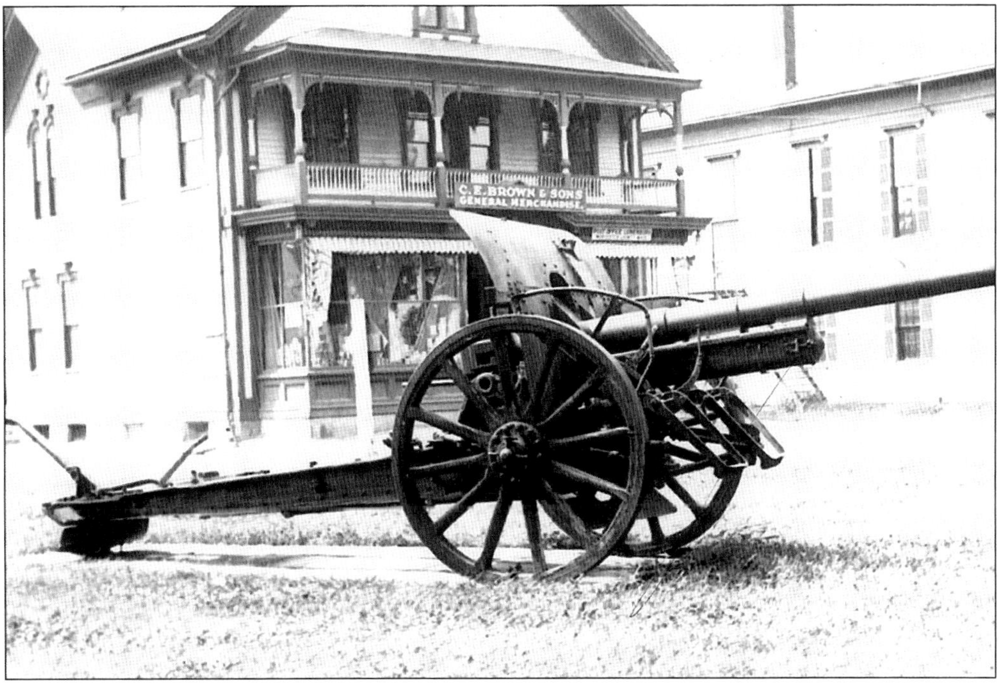

After World War I was over, the American Legion presented the town with an Austrian cannon 88, which was placed on the upper common facing east. Despite being bolted to cement, on October 1, 1942, the cannon was removed, smashed, and put on the town's salvage heap by vandals. A sign was placed with it reading, "This gun came from Germany, send it back."

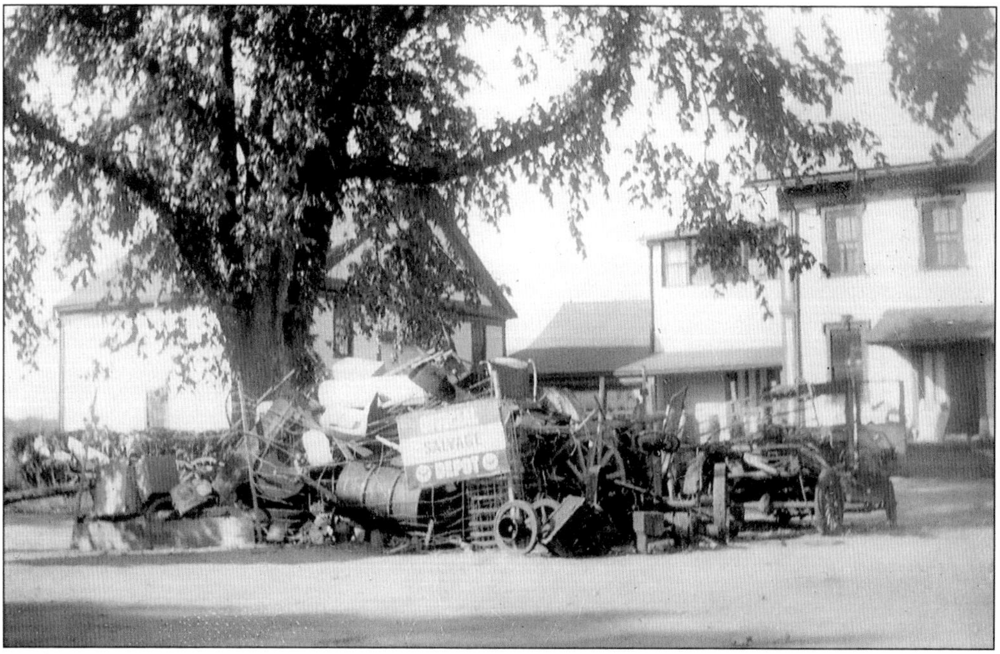

In the World War II years, it became the patriotic duty of every civilian to turn in scrap metal to be used in the war effort. The town put up a wire enclosure for collection under a large tree that stood on the left of the present Honey Farms store. The building behind the tree was the barn attached to the store at that time.

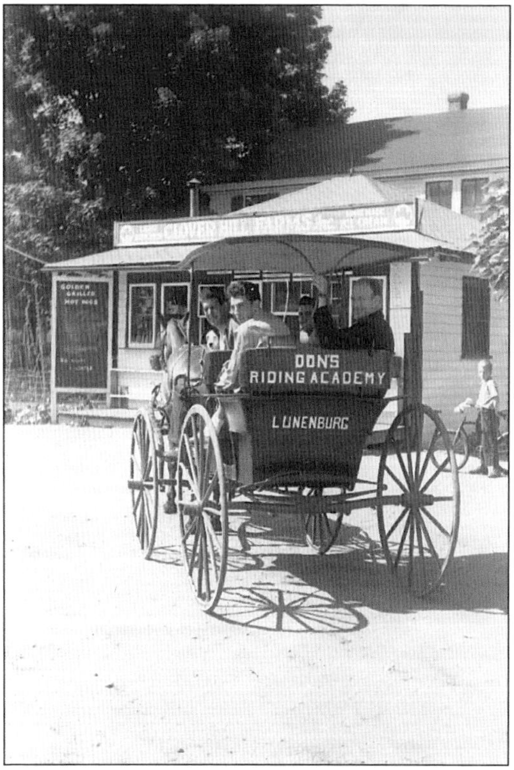

This unique 1940s photograph features Dominic Imprescia advertising his riding academy, located on Lancaster Avenue. Harley's Clover Hill Farm Stand is in the background. Imprescia's love of horses was evident throughout his life. He later became a famous horse trainer. Clover Hill Farm Stand was a popular business in the center of town.

Six

WHALOM PARK

Whalom, originally called Uncacchewalunk, has had at least 29 different spellings of its name over the centuries, most of which were Native American names. The Native Americans thought its beauty so great that surely a magician had created it. Today, it is known as Whalom Lake, on whose shores is the widely advertised amusement park, or Whalom Park.

This area was part of the earlier 2,000-acre Woburn farm grant in 1664. In 1719, when Turkey Hills (Lunenburg) was surveyed and granted a six-mile square portion of land, it included the lake and the Woburn Farm. The original Woburn Farm was sold to Isreal Reed for the handsome price of $3,666.67.

In 1790, the Wilder family bought additional acreage on the lake. A dike and dam were built in 1831, which raised the level of the water by approximately 10 feet and increased the size of the lake. The following year, a three-floor, 54-by-35-foot Wilder Cotton Thread Mill was established containing 500 spindles, on which cotton thread was manufactured. This mill burned in 1836 and was never rebuilt.

Jeremiah Stiles leased 11 acres to Daniel Lowe in 1805. In 1881, Stiles secured a 10-year lease from Lowe, cleared the land, and built a platform with a canvas cover, where he held weekly dances for the next five years. Stiles also provided boats to rent and served the best clam dinners. This was the beginning of Whalom Park, which was to have several owners and many additions over the years and become famous.

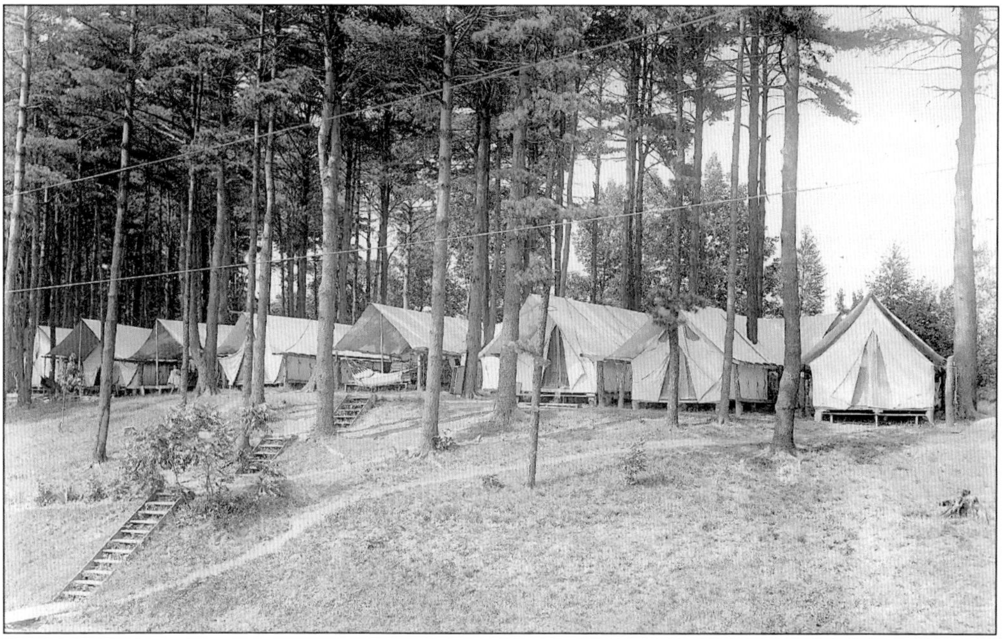

As early as 1881, Jeremiah Stiles "discovered the beautiful lake with majestic pines surrounding it" and decided it had a great future as a recreational area. He cleared a path to the lake, purchased a few boats, and built a platform with a canvas top. Weekly dances were held here for five years. This 1907 scene shows a YMCA tent camp with a view of the lake and the shelter of the tall pines.

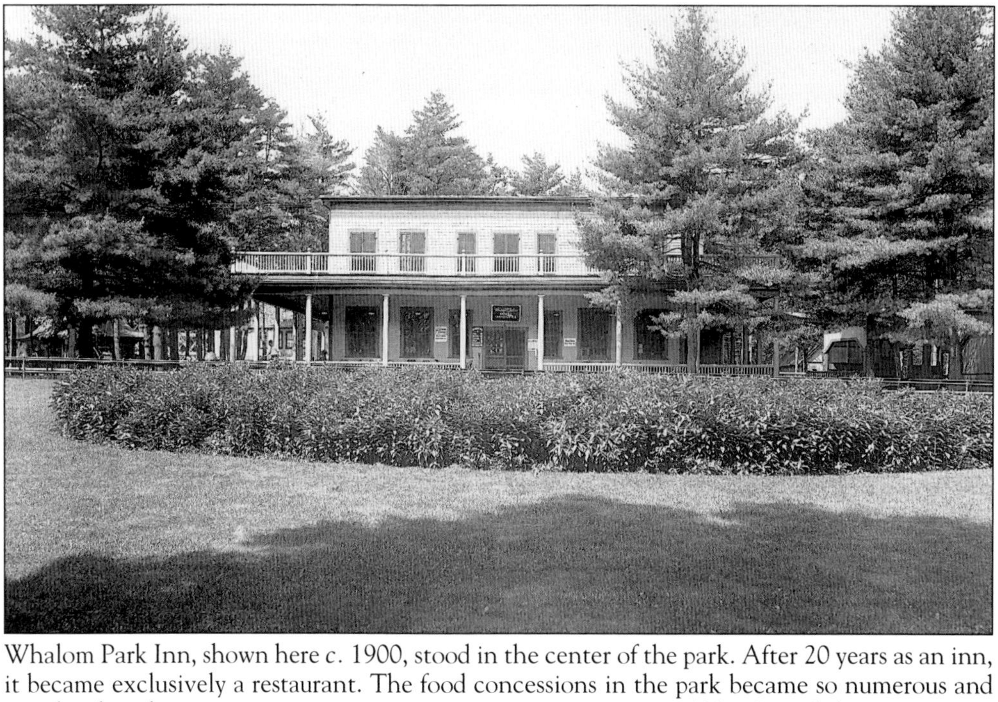

Whalom Park Inn, shown here *c.* 1900, stood in the center of the park. After 20 years as an inn, it became exclusively a restaurant. The food concessions in the park became so numerous and popular that the restaurant gave way to an amusement center *c.* 1934. It ended its career as a place to play Beano, a game subsequently banned. Shortly after, the inn was torn down.

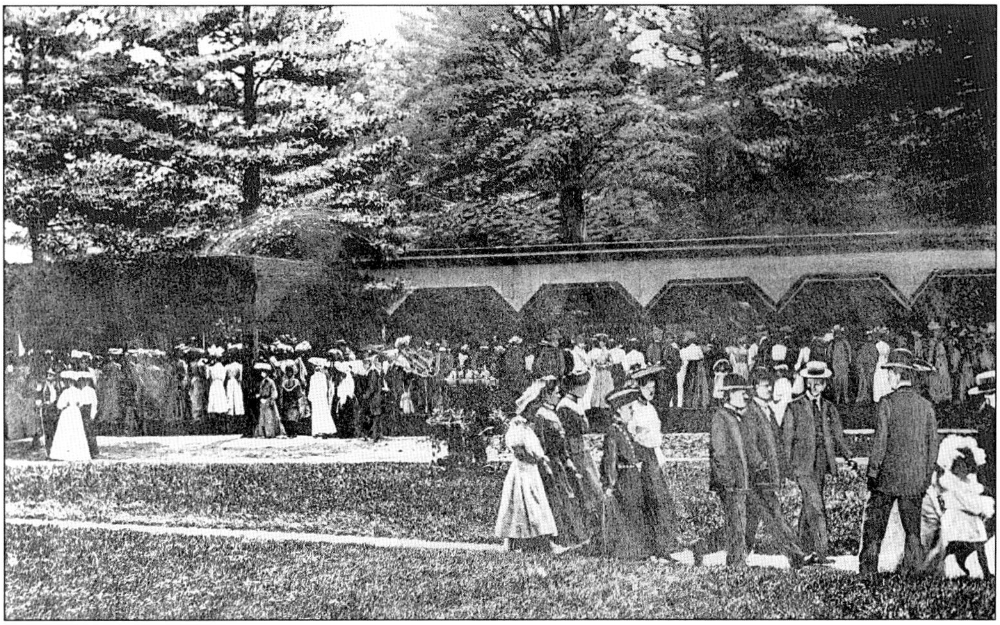

Visitors to Whalom are seen strolling along one of the paths inside the park. The building to the left is a refreshment stand known for its delicious clam chowder. Other refreshments and beverages were available. To the right of the refreshment stand is the Whalom Ballroom. Jazz was popular during the 1920s through the 1940s. Mondays featured all-time great bands. Wednesdays and Saturdays were devoted to various local bands.

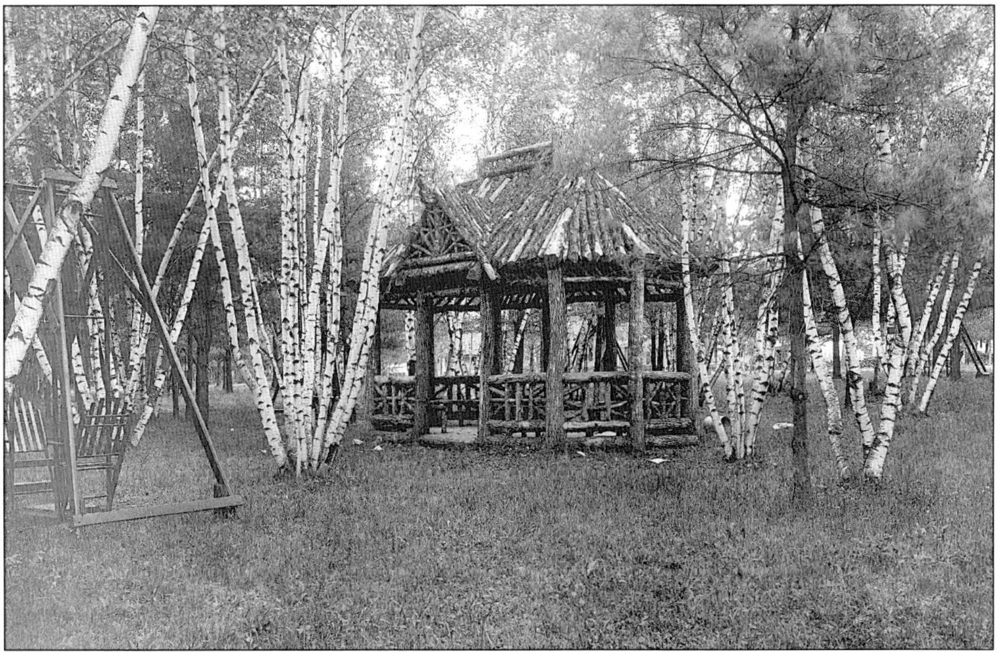

When Whalom Park first opened in the late 1800s, it was just that—a park. It was situated in a beautiful pine grove with clumps of birches placed here and there, and the scenic lake provided a beautiful backdrop. There were several rustic shelters (one is shown here) for picnicking or simply enjoying the scenery.

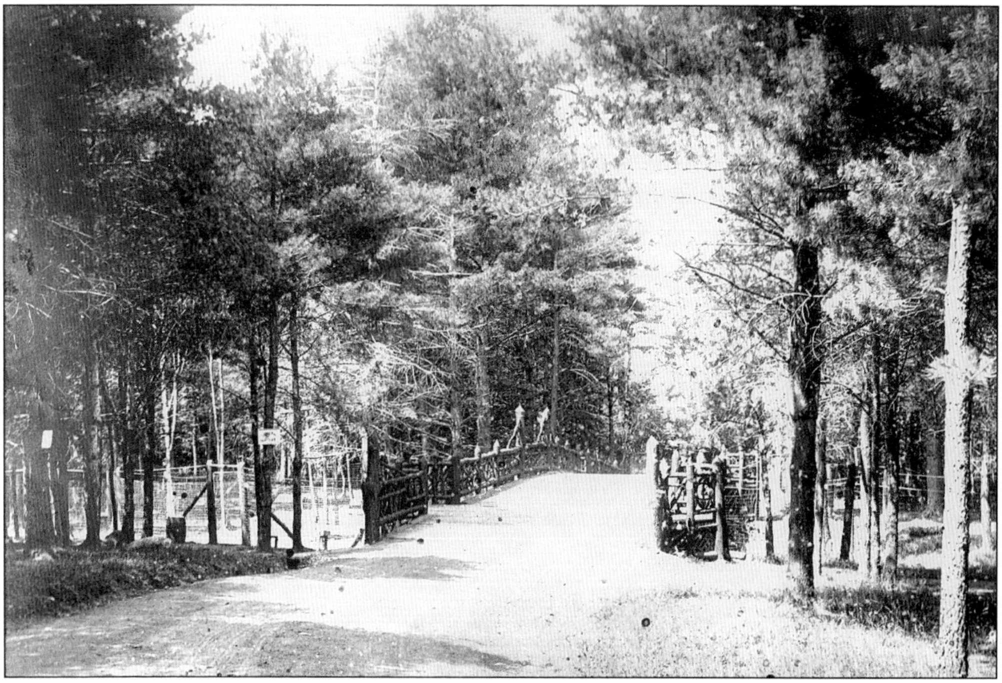

This beautiful rustic bridge in Whalom Park spans Deer Park. Visitors could walk across the bridge and see many animals in the park's collection. As well as providing a scenic structure, the bridge provided an excellent view of the enclosed animals. The lower photograph shows the rustic bridge from beneath this solid structure. The entire Deer Park is strongly fenced in for both the animals' and visitors' protection. In addition to deer, moose, elk, and sheep, many other interesting animals were included. This exhibit was more like a local zoo, enabling folk to view sights not normally seen in Lunenburg.

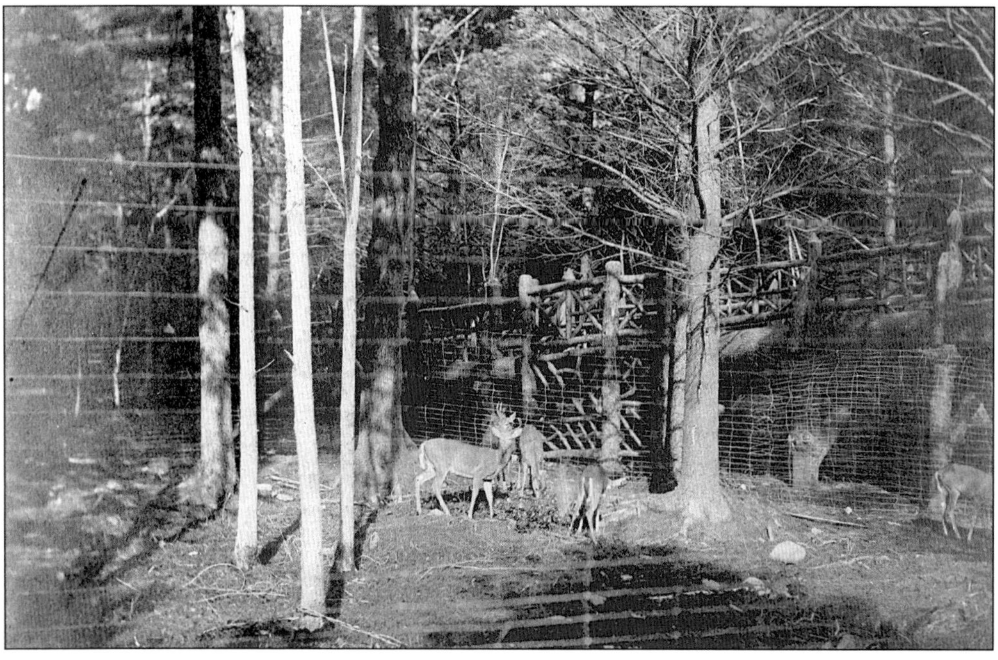

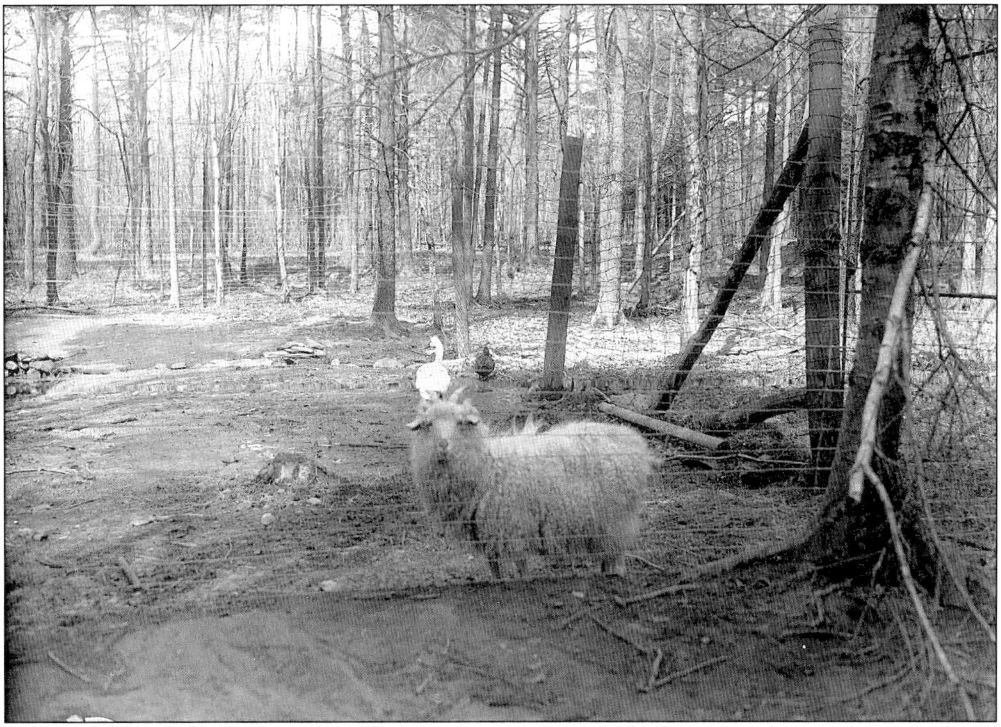

Here are two additional views of the enclosed Deer Park. The top photograph shows a goat, a goose, and fowl in a different section of the park. Below, the adequate fencing surrounds a few of the deer herd with a substantial building to the left used by the groundkeepers to contain adequate supplies needed by the animals.

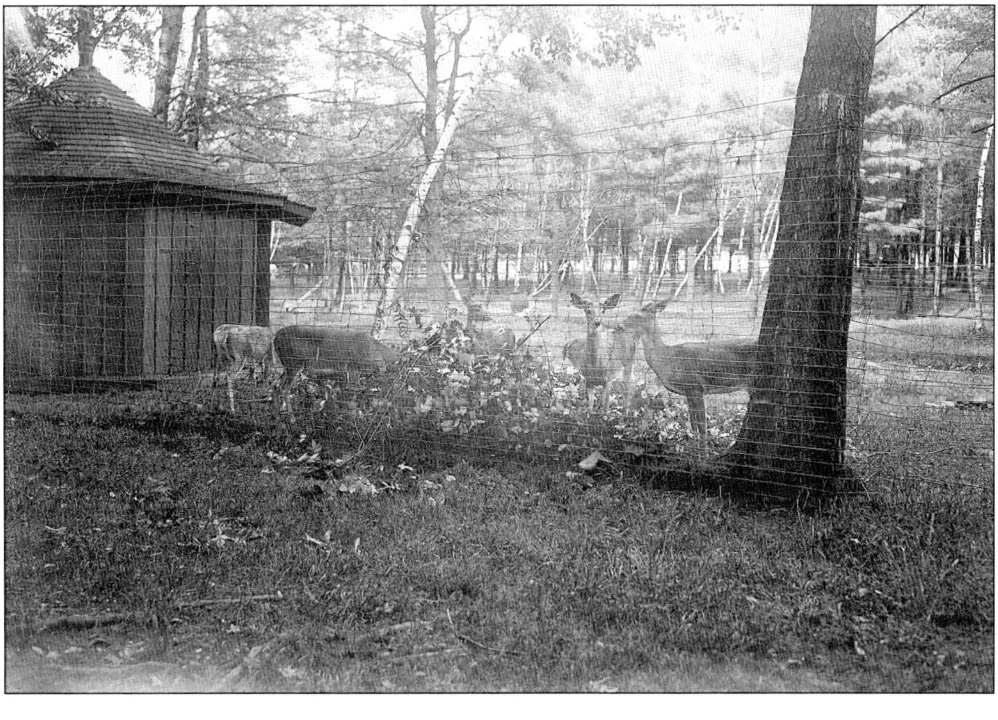

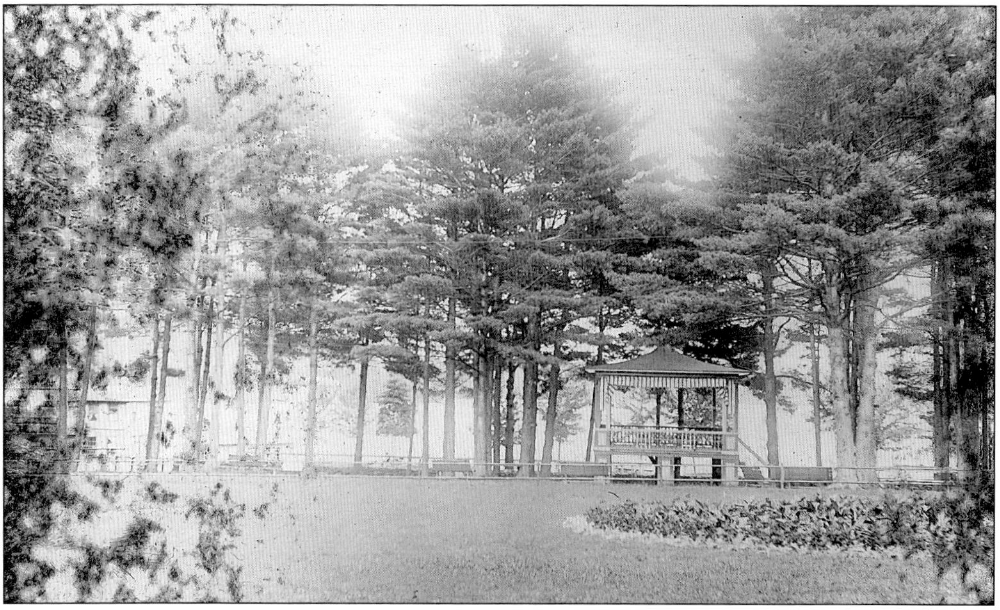

This bandstand was built in 1902 in Whalom Park overlooking the lake. Many pine trees originally stood throughout the park. A tornado struck the park on July 17, 1924, and numerous pine trees were damaged or destroyed. In 1938, another tornado struck the park, followed by a hurricane a month later. All the rest of the trees were destroyed. That fall, 300 new trees were planted.

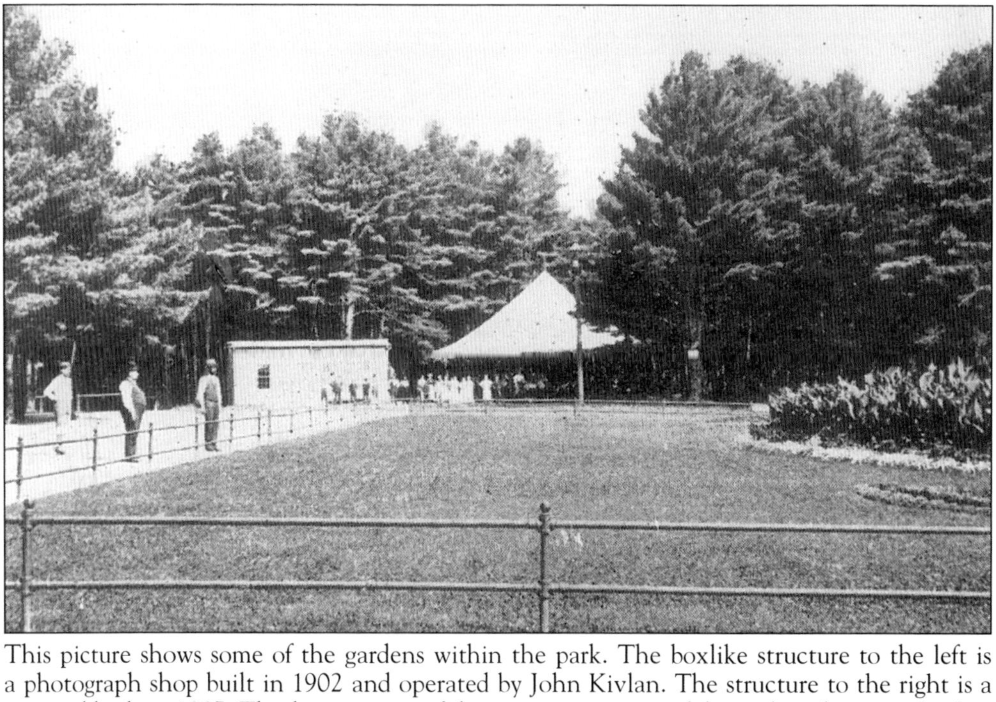

This picture shows some of the gardens within the park. The boxlike structure to the left is a photograph shop built in 1902 and operated by John Kivlan. The structure to the right is a carousel built in 1907. This became one of the main attractions of the park and among the first rides offered to the public. Other main attractions added in this year were a Ferris wheel and a penny arcade.

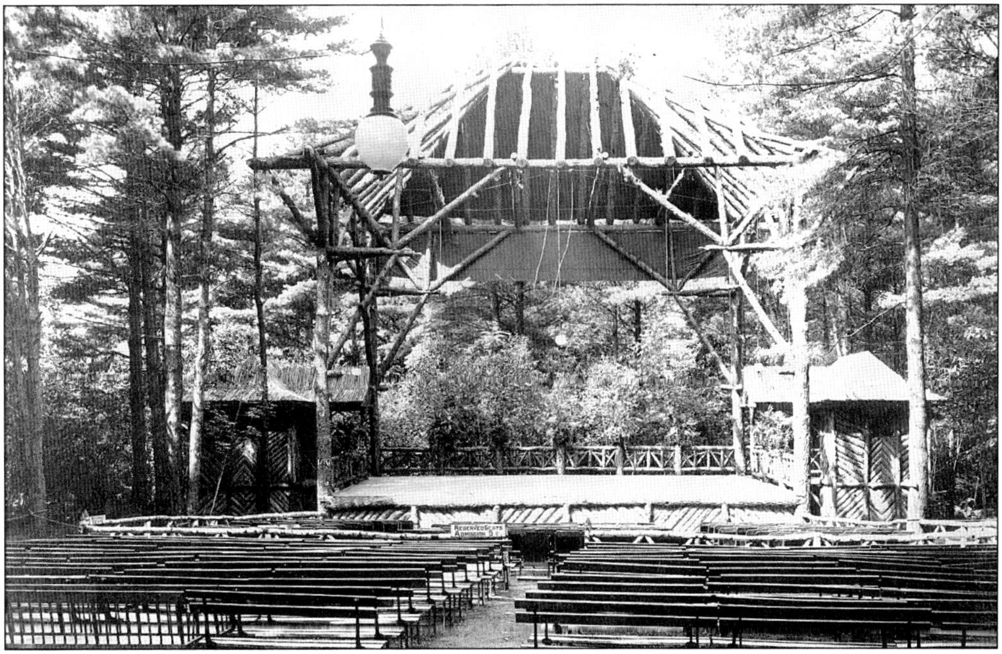

The original Whalom Theater was built in 1893. It consisted of a wooden platform with no roof and no seats. It was then enclosed by birch rails, with a canvas covering overhead and some benches. The light opera *The Mikado* was performed in 1898 to an enthusiastic audience. A new circular theater with a roof replaced the old one in 1901.

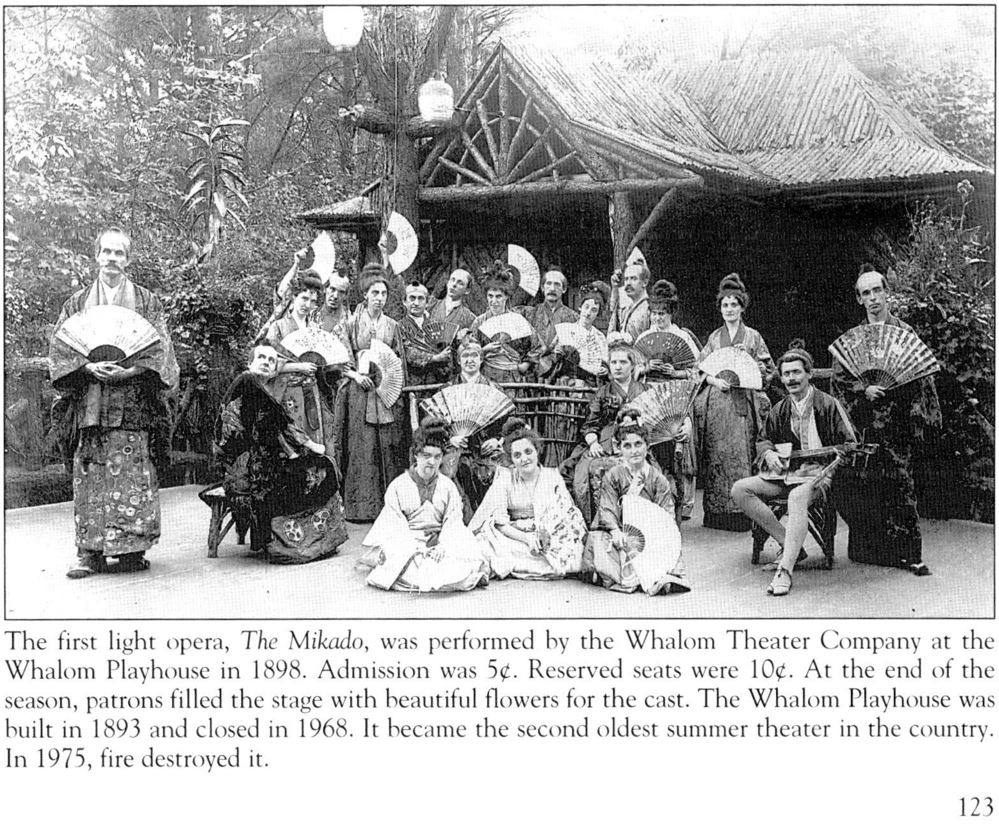

The first light opera, *The Mikado*, was performed by the Whalom Theater Company at the Whalom Playhouse in 1898. Admission was 5¢. Reserved seats were 10¢. At the end of the season, patrons filled the stage with beautiful flowers for the cast. The Whalom Playhouse was built in 1893 and closed in 1968. It became the second oldest summer theater in the country. In 1975, fire destroyed it.

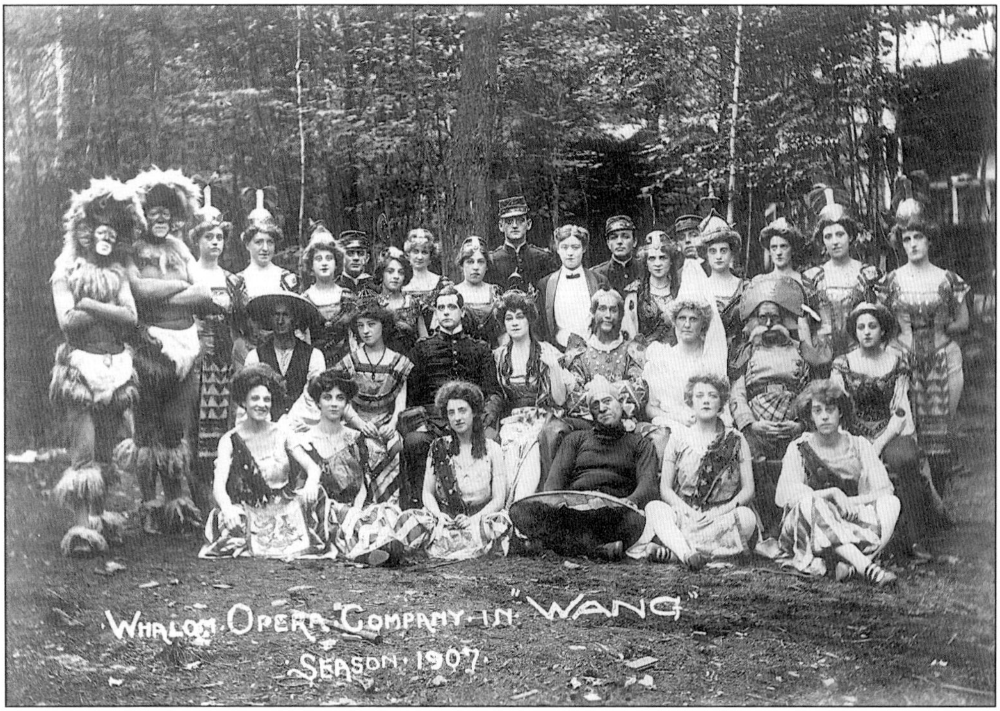

During the 1907 season, the Whalom Opera Company staged a production of *Wang*, much to the delight of its audiences. This photograph captures the entire cast of that opera. Later, opera gave way to other types of performances offered to Whalom patrons, including musicals, dramas, melodramas, and even animal acts, to the delight of its younger clientele.

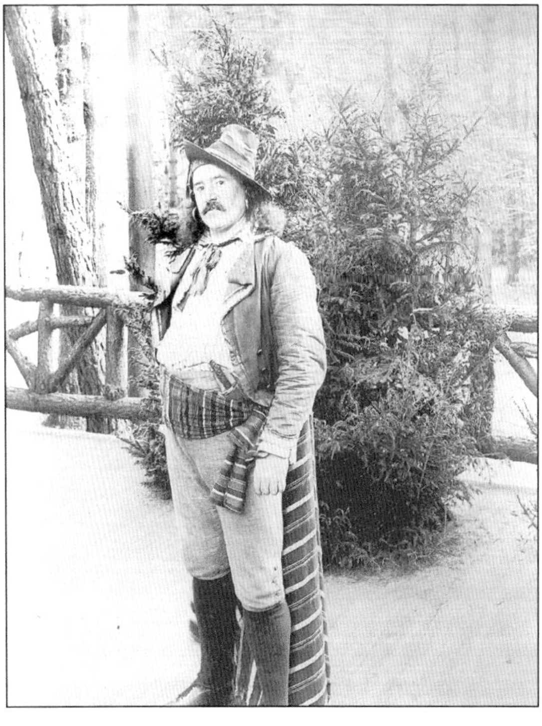

His name is no longer remembered and fans have ceased their applause, but this actor performed in *The Pirates of Penzance* at Whalom's very popular open-air theater in 1898. His haughty, costumed appearance generates smiles, and one can almost hear the applause rewarding his performance more than a century ago. Whalom's summer theater attracted many talented actors from all over the country.

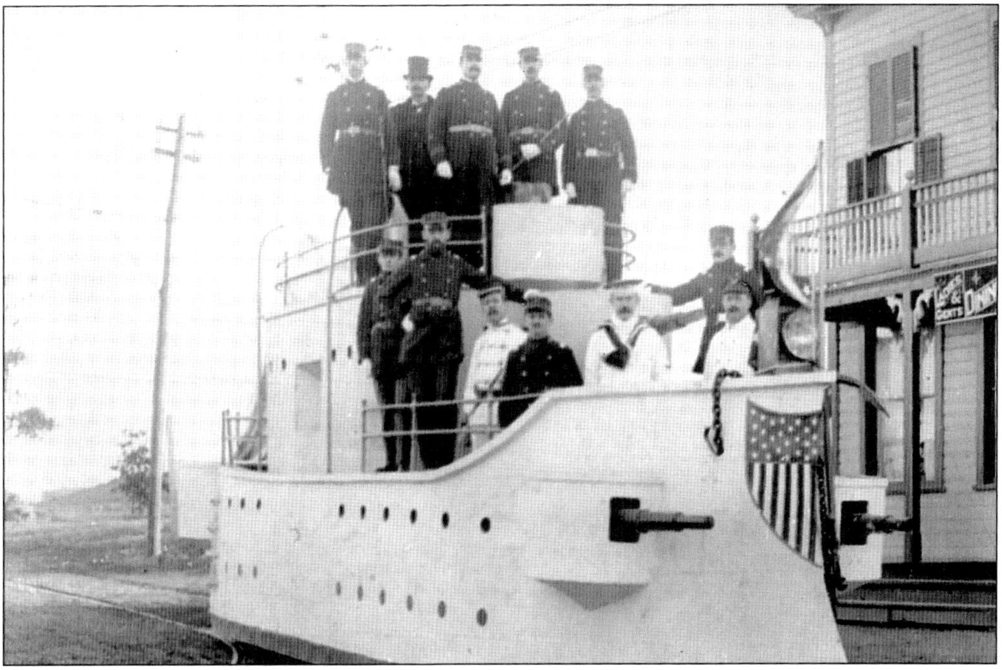

The McKinley Cruiser, dreamed up by Maj. Charles K. Darling in 1896, was a float gimmick for the Republican Party during the campaign of the McKinley presidency. In the above photograph, it is shown on the trolley tracks manned by a crew of Republicans. After the election, the Fitchburg and Leominster Street Railway purchased it and placed it on pilings in the waters of Lake Whalom. This cruiser burned in July 1908 between 2:30 a.m. and 3:00 a.m. and was replaced with another, identical to the first, on July 27, 1908. It remained on the lake for several years and became a colorful tourist attraction for Whalom Park. Lights were added and fireworks were displayed from its deck for every Fourth of July celebration.

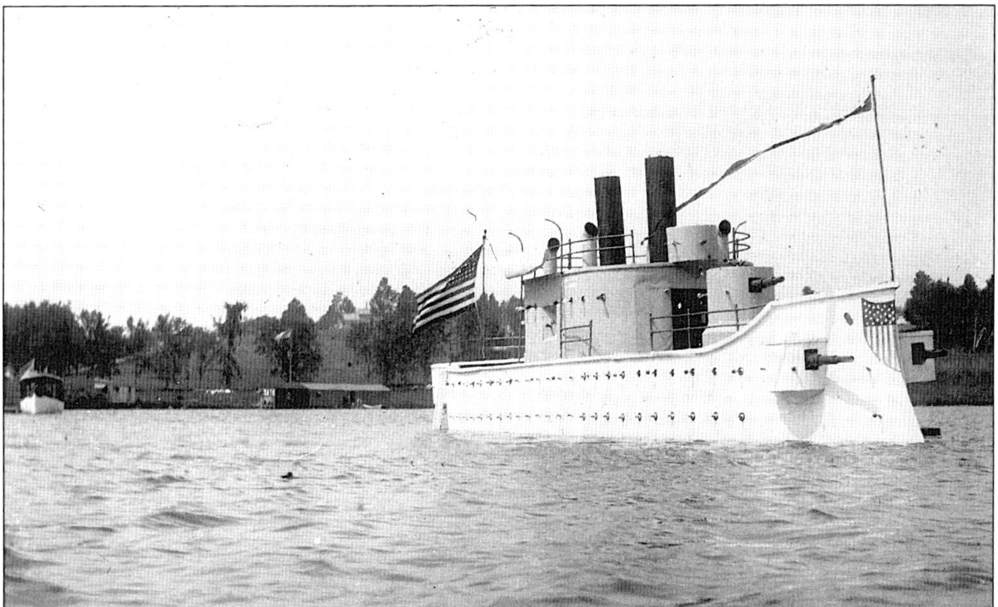

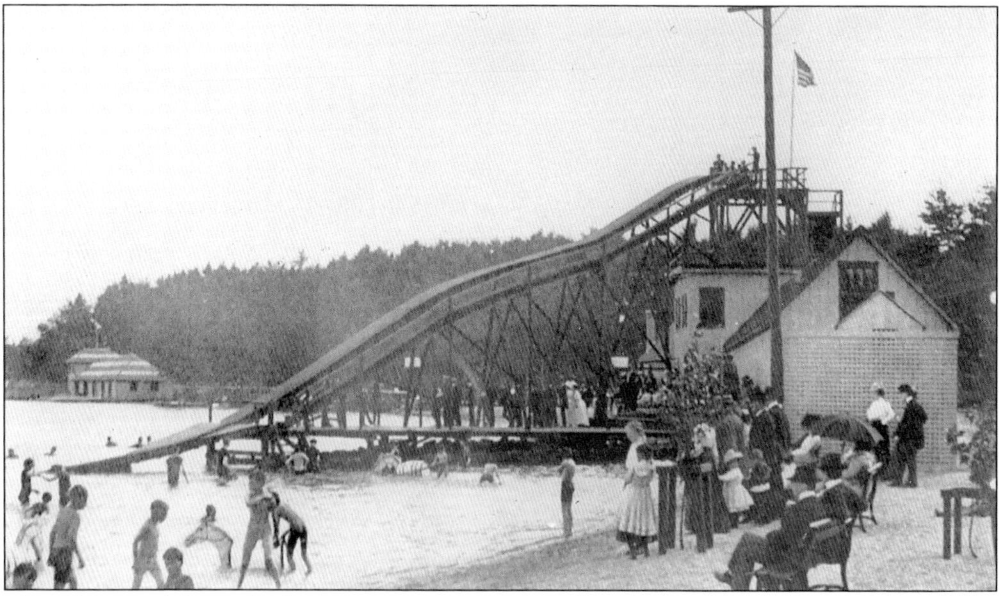

The toboggan slide was built in 1901. It started from a tower 40 feet above the water and proved to be a thrilling ride, as shown by the crowd. Note also the horse head barrels in the water, which were called "Sargent's Ponies" and were "harder to ride than a bucking bronco."

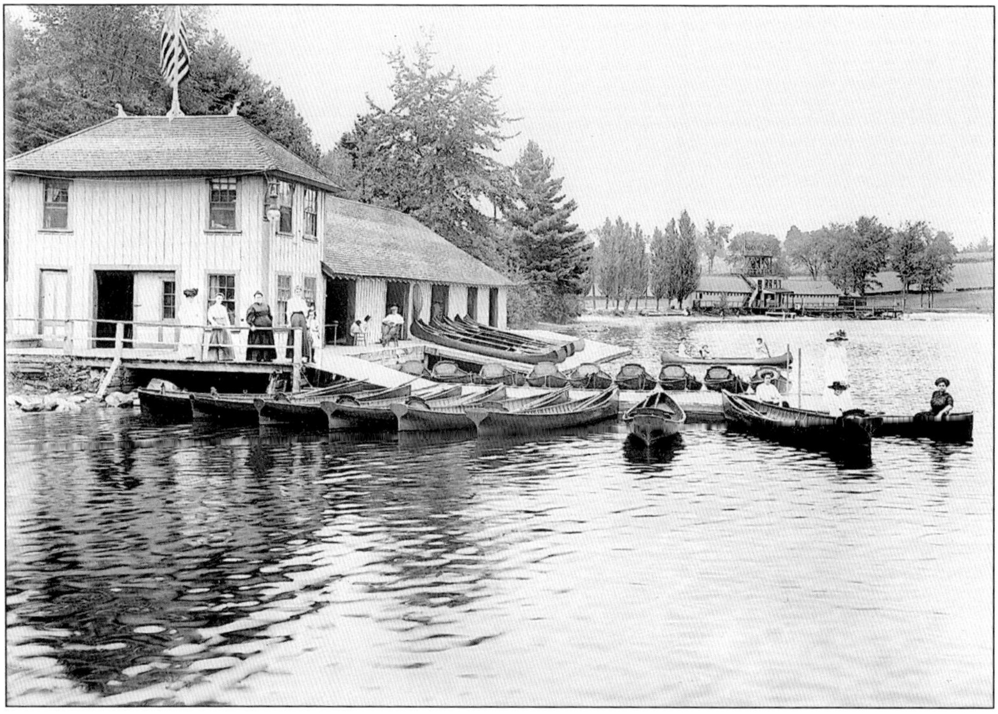

The Whalom Lake Canoe Club was a major attraction on the lakefront during the 1930s. The club provided beautiful Old Town canoes, made in Maine of birch and mahogany panels. This photograph, taken from the other side of the lake, also shows the F. and L. Bathing House, with the popular toboggan slide in the background. The Canoe Club house was destroyed by the Hurricane of 1938 and never rebuilt.

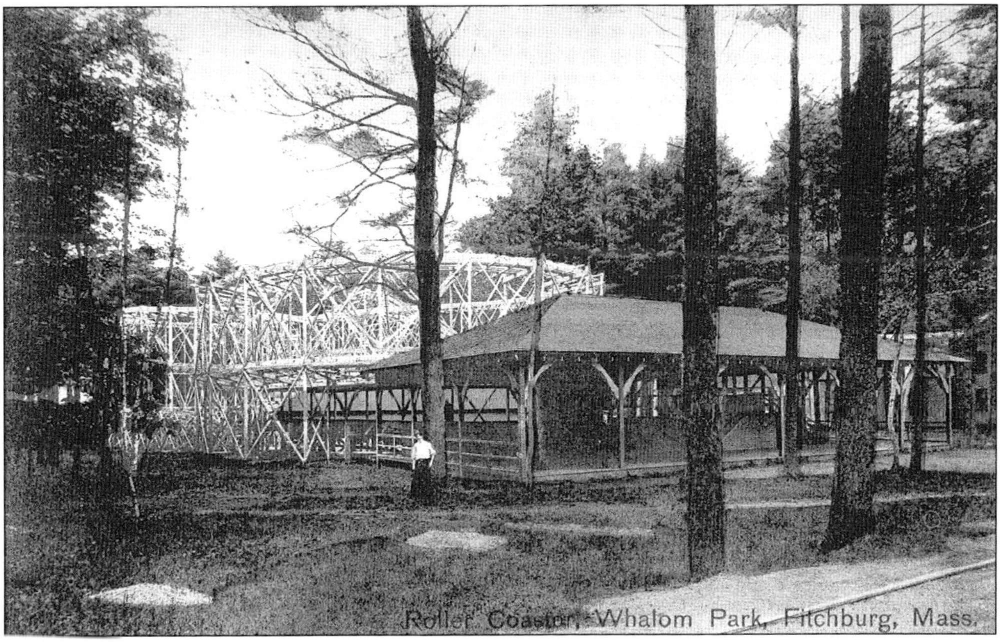

The above photograph shows the old wooden figure eight roller coaster (built in 1905 for $16,000) in Whalom Park. In the lower photograph, we see the same roller coaster after a visit from a tornado in August 1938. The well-known Hurricane of 1938 came along in September and finished the job. A second roller coaster was finished in 1940, replacing the original.

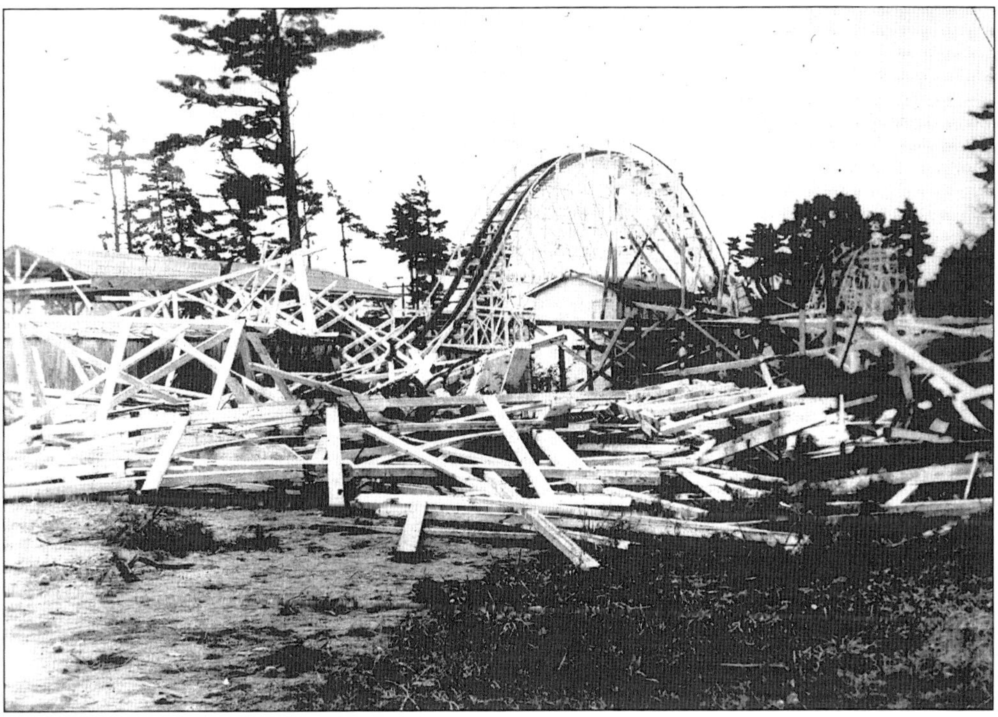

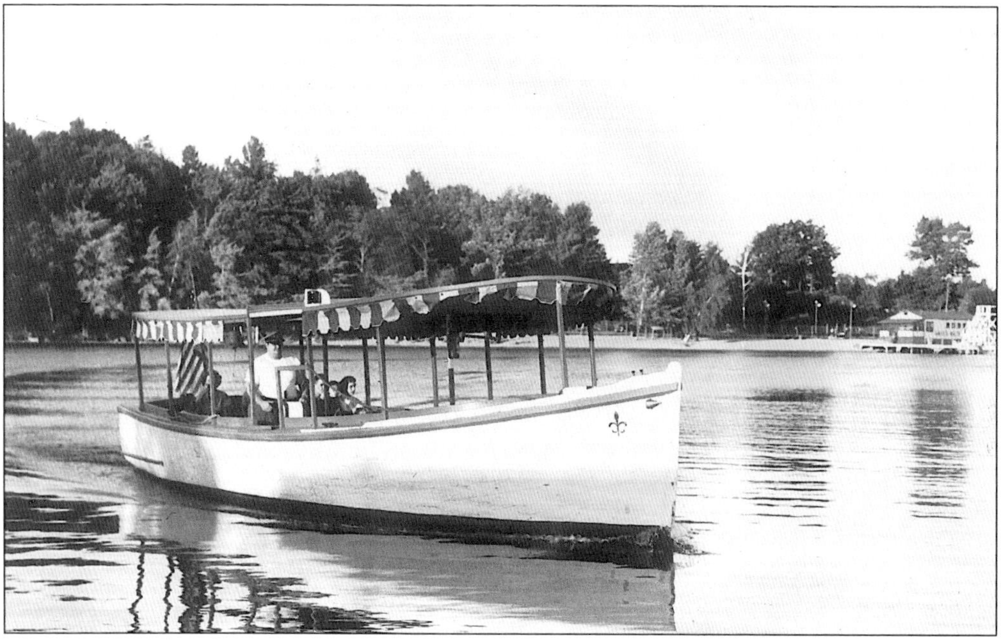

This is one of the closer views of a tour boat on Whalom Lake. Its name is the *Alfretta*. This 40-passenger boat chugged around the lake at the speed of 16 miles per hour. It was a thrill for its passengers, enabling them to see the entire shoreline of the lake. Barges brought people from both Fitchburg and Leominster to the park.

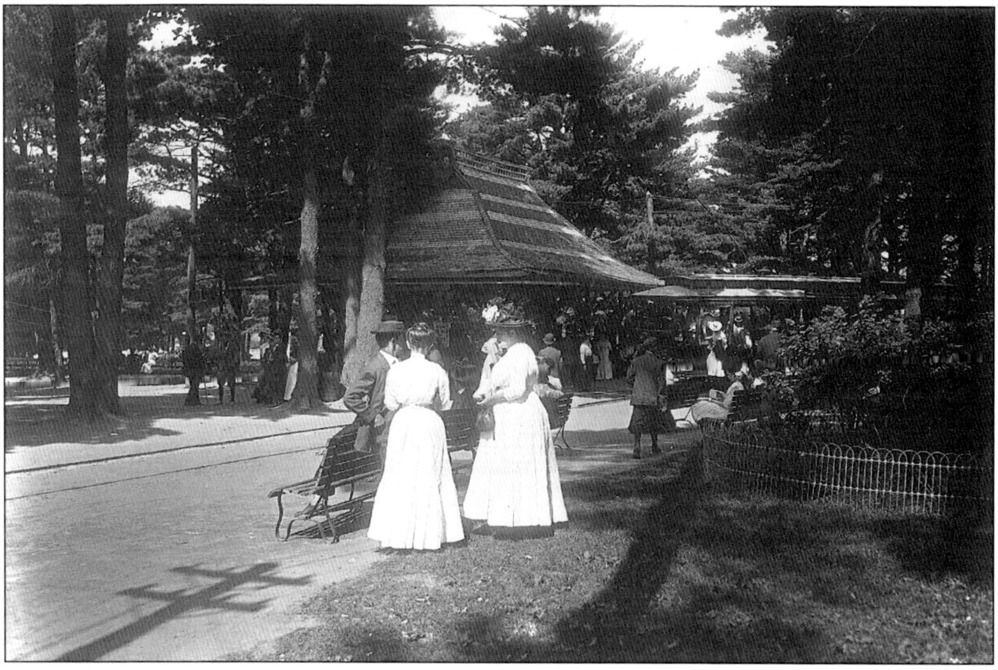

After a long day at Whalom, some of the visitors are ready to return to their homes for the day. Customers are waiting at the depot for the trolley. With this photograph, we end our stay at Whalom and our visit to *Images of America: Lunenburg*. We hope you enjoyed "the best town in the country."